Beyond the Politics of the Closet

BEYOND THE POLITICS OF THE CLOSET

Gay Rights and the American State
Since the 1970s

EDITED BY
Jonathan Bell

PENN

UNIVERSITY OF PENNSYLVANIA PRESS

PHILADELPHIA

Published by
University of Pennsylvania Press
Philadelphia, Pennsylvania 19104-4112
www.upenn.edu/pennpress

Printed in the United States of America on acid-free paper
10 9 8 7 6 5 4 3 2 1

A catalogue record for this book is available from the Library of Congress.
ISBN 978-0-8122-5185-2

CONTENTS

Part III
Beyond Liberalism and Conservatism

Beyond the Politics of the Closet

Privilege, Power, and Activism in Gay Rights Politics Since the 1970s

Jonathan Bell

"The organized gay movement has become sorely unrepresentative of its own constituency," argued the leaders of the New York City Union of Lesbians and Gay Men, one of many grassroots activist organizations to spring up during the height of the AIDS epidemic of the 1980s. "In trying to pass as legitimate, we compromised those of us who are the most illegitimate—dykes, queens, poor lesbians and gay men, gays of Third World nationality. For many of us, the struggle for survival goes beyond that of democratic rights and is inseparable from the hardships faced in a worsening economy."[1] At a time of the Ronald Reagan administration's attacks on the nation's ramshackle and inadequate welfare system, when thousands of Americans were dying of AIDS-related illnesses without access to adequate medical care, it should hardly have been a surprise that many activists returned to a gay liberationist politics linking sexual dissidence to wider struggles for social justice. And even before the AIDS crisis made plain the inseparable bond connecting sexuality politics with social and health policy, one of the most important ways in which gradually emerging legal rights for sexual minorities translated into actual lived experience in the 1970s lay in the extent to which they could receive medical care and social services. LGBT rights self-evidently required more than the elimination of sodomy laws and of the intrusive policing and regulation of individuals' private lives. Both private and public bodies and agencies provided services that would prove vital to the well-being and security of gay and trans* people, including sexual health procedures and access to housing and welfare. That the sexual rights revolution took shape at the very point when both state and private providers began withdrawing from any commitment to care for citizens as part of a political trend to delegitimize the nation's social safety net and to embrace a global neoliberal turn has proven to be a major tragedy. Yet the need for a politics of solidarity connecting sexual dissidence with questions of economic and social inequality has been an important leitmotif of the history of sexuality over the last forty years.

This collection of essays emerged from an oft-recognized but still not fully understood question framing the New York Union's call to arms that opened this book: given that sexual minorities encompassed all classes and races in American society and that all of them had need of state and private social policy patronage at some time in their lives, made explicit with the advent of AIDS, why has gay rights politics had such a difficult relationship with broader questions of inequality? The quotation above suggests a straightforward answer: gay rights advocates were "trying to pass as legitimate" in the eyes of gatekeepers of political power in the United States. Given that cisgender white men of privilege continued to dominate the political landscape throughout the post-rights revolutions era, many self-appointed leaders of the gay rights movement tailored their advocacy to that reality. Queer historians have sometimes highlighted these strategies of legitimation, as in Allan Bérubé's account of the Campaign for Military Service (CMS), a group lobbying Congress to allow gay men and women to serve in the U.S. military in 1993. He shows how "the CMS tried to project an idealized image of the openly gay service member that mirrored the senators' racial makeup and their publicly espoused social values and sexual mores," erasing the complex interplay of class, racial, and gender disparities embedded in sexual dissidence.[2] Sociologist Elizabeth A. Armstrong also illustrates how mainstream gay activist appeals to universal rights for all sexual minorities in the 1970s "emerged from the particular experiences of a cohort of American middle-class urban white men" and did not speak very effectively for the specific experiences of people of color, lesbians, or trans* people, all of whom established their own networks and communities.[3] These narratives of appeals for political legitimacy on the basis of white privilege are stories of racial identity one the one hand and strategy (what approach, based on expediency rather than ideology, is needed to gain political traction) on the other.

The essays presented here speak to these themes but also consider the very blurred lines separating expediency from ideology when constructing paths to political acceptance and access to social goods. The decision of any political group to tie itself to a broader movement of civil rights and social justice (or not) can be an active process, not simply a response to external forces or innate hierarchies of privilege. In the 1970s, as some of the case studies in this book show, gay rights politics was intimately connected to wider struggles for social justice and access to health care. The AIDS crisis also highlighted the desperate need for coalition building to tackle the appalling inequities in health service delivery. Yet several essays in these pages point to the obstacles to meaningful social policy advocacy across racial and class boundaries, often a product of activist strategies as well as inbuilt economic and societal inequalities. Homophobic and conservative forces could be quick to exploit gay rights activists' choice to highlight class and racial status in their battle for political recognition. And gay rights advocates could themselves be conservative and committed to the fortunes and ideology of the Republican Party and manifestly inattentive to issues of inequality and marginality, as one of the essays here explores.

This collection of essays seeks to explore the impact that gay rights politics and activism have had on the wider American political landscape since the rights revolutions of the 1960s. The essays are particularly concerned with the changing relationship between sexual minorities and the state in a period when their legal status became much more contested than previously. Historians have long been attuned to the ways in which sexual minority populations formed their own communities and political affiliations in a hostile social environment, creating social spaces, sites of solidarity, and a shared sense of belonging through which to negotiate the legal and societal discrimination they faced throughout the twentieth century.[4] These processes of community formation prior to the 1970s took place in the context of relentless political and legal oppression and often required those involved to hide their identities from governments, the police, and employers. It was therefore inevitable that a more recent turn in historical scholarship toward the intersection of sexuality and the state would also highlight the repressive and hostile nature of state power when faced with challenges to heteronormative social structures. Historians such as Margot Canaday and Marc Stein have shown how politicians and the courts utilized their powers to exclude sexual minorities from the benefits of social and economic citizenship, including access to social welfare benefits and to the right to immigrate to the United States.[5] All of these rich and important works focus on the period between World War II and the 1970s, a time before the various and multifaceted LGBT rights movements of today fully gained traction in U.S. political life, ensuring that they have all had either a state-centered focus or a "history from below" framing, with little scope for an analysis of the intersections between them.

This book showcases historians whose work on the political history of gay rights delves into the decades between the mid-1970s and the millennium, a period in which the relationship between activist networks, the state, private capitalism, and political parties became infinitely more complicated. In the 1970s, queer Americans began seeking access to mainstream Democratic and Republican Party politics and attempting to gain recognition in party policy formation.[6] Gay rights activists made common cause with other political movements especially on the Left, including the Latin American solidarity movement.[7] One important legacy of the explosion in the number of people coming out in the 1970s was a huge demand for health and social services for LGBT populations, a development that encouraged new relationships between grassroots clinics and organizations on one side and state and local governments on the other. The coming of the AIDS crisis in the 1980s made the battles for access to welfare, health care, and social services for HIV-positive Americans, many of them gay men, a critically important story in the changing relationship involving sexual minorities, government, and health capitalism. Although the work of historians and political scientists such as Jennifer Brier and Patricia Siplon has highlighted the complex and often discordant responses of political elites to the epidemic, belying simplistic narratives of total indifference and inaction in the Reagan era, we still know less than we should about state and private-sector policy making on HIV/AIDS in the first decade of the epidemic.[8] The 1980s and 1990s also marked a period in which Religious Right attacks on the civil rights of minorities, including LGBT people, offered opportunities for activists to mobilize and fight back, campaigns that could galvanize a wider support base and contribute to the gradual legitimization of sexual minorities in American society. While the increasing "normalization" of the nonheteronormative in political terms has received some sharp criticism on the part of certain activists and theorists, there can be little doubt that we can no longer talk about either the state or private capitalism as exclusively "straight" in the way we perhaps could before the 1980s.[9]

The book is therefore centrally concerned with power at a time of massive political flux and changes in the capacity of sexual dissidence to achieve traction in local, state, and national politics. The essays all consider how political influence and access to social capital take shape and how sexual dissidents form and reform their strategies and political outlooks as a result of their involvement with state forces. One consequence of our focus is a strong emphasis on histories of organizations and groups that engaged with dominant political bodies and authorities, which inevitably means that the book does not function as a comprehensive history of LGBT communities. Many of the protagonists in these pages are cisgender men, and racial and gender hierarchies embedded in LGBT politics are evident in the essays. I did not set out to assemble essays that privilege the experiences of white men, and at many points the essays range much more widely, but it became clear when thinking about the work that the historians in this book are doing and the stories they tell that gendered power dynamics have been central to the historical relationship between gay rights and mainstream politics. The essays also all center on a specific time period between the early 1970s and the millennium when activist politics was forced to contend with a mainstream political culture increasingly unresponsive to issues of inequality, raising questions of how far a fully liberationist queer politics could function without a fundamental reordering of the nation's political economy.

In making this argument, I am not downplaying the importance of scholarship on, for example, lesbian or trans* communities, which has dramatically expanded our understanding of the diversity and complexity of movements for social change contained within the LGBT umbrella. Historians and activists including among others Susan Stryker, Joanne Meyerowitz, and Lillian Faderman have provided richly textured portraits of the emergence of organizations and movements dedicated to broadening the parameters of the rights revolutions to represent the full spectrum of sexual dissidence.[10] It is also important to highlight the body of scholarship documenting the lived experiences of queer communities of color, reinforcing Allan Bérubé's exhortation to consider race when constructing histories of sexuality in the United States. Many of these works probe the complex and problematic relationship between sexual labeling and racial and ethnic identity outside the boundaries of whiteness and encourage us to resist easy generalizations that occur when we rely on handy shorthand such as "LGBT" or "sexual minorities."[11] The connections that these scholars have made between the history of sexuality, legal history, and histories of immigration, race, and racism also make plain the ways in which state authorities have categorized and regulated minorities and suggest that historians of the state must consider race and gender when they consider sexuality. Yet much of this work, in cases where the state comes into play at all, highlights the repressive and discriminatory nature of government power that, while hugely important, does not center the role of activists privileged enough to push back against homophobia in ways that reveal specific sites of contestation within sexual minority politics at the end of the twentieth century. How and why privilege functioned in U.S. sexual politics in a period when sexual dissidence itself became less uniformly suppressed but minority status in general became even more a badge of marginality is the central focus of this book.

The essays in the pages that follow form arguments that place the politics of sexuality at the center of the wider political history of the United States. Many of the essays are snapshots of bigger projects that seek to understand the possibilities of post-gay liberation sexual dissidence for shaking up American politics and institutions. Before turning to a discussion of the essays themselves, it is worth setting out here some of the conceptual interventions that the volume will make to understanding and periodizing modern U.S. political history through the lens of sexuality.

Strategies of Legitimacy in a Post-New Deal World

Tim Stewart-Winter, one of the contributors to this volume, used the term "queer clout" as helpful shorthand for the complex ways in which gay rights activists, given new legitimacy and visibility in the wake of gay liberation, managed to gain access to the corridors of power in Chicago city politics.[12] As several essays in this collection demonstrate, the process of coming-out in the 1970s and beyond was not simply an individual experience but rather a collective political project to harness economic as well as political power. Increased visibility for sexual minorities in society provided opportunities to develop specialist social services, such as health clinics and community organizations. Many of these collective projects were rooted firmly in the tradition of civil rights organizing and grassroots politics and were suspicious of traditional modes of power brokering in city halls, state legislatures, and political parties. Nevertheless, the period after 1970 saw the gradual erosion of the heteronormative certainties of state power as gay rights activists sought funding for social services and access to welfare and health benefits and mobilized against conservative ballot initiatives and legislation designed to block their legal rights. These battles took place in the context of the collapse of the New Deal political order and the advance of a neoliberal economic and political agenda in the Reagan years, developments that have worked to obscure the place of sexual minorities in wider U.S. politics.[13] Indeed, the whole New Deal order analytical landscape of twentieth-century American history needs to consider the resolutely heteronormative ideological fundamentals of New Deal statecraft. An apparent golden age of strong labor unions, high wages, robust private health and social benefits, and impressive levels of economic growth provides only one narrative among many for an understanding of modern political history.[14] Gay rights organizations pushing for greater access to the fruits of economic and social citizenship may have faced a world in which the New Deal social safety net was increasingly precarious and under attack, but this does not mean that their efforts to extend their civil rights beyond the purely legal were insignificant. State governments in particular expanded their policy-making reach in the 1970s and 1980s to include LGBT peoples in terms of not simply civil rights laws but also laws relating to health care access, among other things.

A foregrounding of LGBT issues in the wider public sphere in terms of clout has often examined queer Americans as consumers or as economic actors under capitalism. Spending power was an important tool in the arsenal of campaigns for equality, and businesses specifically catering for an LGBT clientele form an important part of the story of civil rights for sexual minorities in the late twentieth century as well as a lens onto the socioeconomic and racial divisions bisecting queer communities.[15] In the 1980s, a decade of heightened vilification of poor and minority populations and of a wholesale political assault on those dependent upon government for welfare and health services, privileged access to private capital for economic security became a central concern of many LGBT activists during the AIDS crisis, evidence of the maturation of sexual nonconformity as a political category within capitalism. HIV/AIDS rendered gay men in particular as visible economic subjects, with the capacity to place strain on employer health insurance policies as well as the nation's ramshackle welfare state. Thus in this context, gaining and maintaining clout has involved accessing the trappings of previously heteronormative capitalism, including the economic benefits of marriage, employment rights, and the private health system, and avoiding the stigmatizing and pauperizing travails of state programs. Placing sexual minorities at the center of debates over neoliberalism, the harsh instabilities of modern capitalism, and the fragmentation of New Deal coalition politics is a central concern of these essays.

Queering White Privilege

Watching *How to Survive a Plague*, David France's moving documentary about AIDS activism in the 1980s to accompany his recent book of the same title, it is hard not to be struck by the whiteness of the key protagonists.[16] Early activist accounts, in particular that of Randy Shilts in 1987, ardent

in their desire to search for meaning in the crisis, had a problematic relationship with race, buying into origin narratives about HIV that reinforced
racial stereotypes and ethnocentric narratives of activist politics.[17] Much
scholarship since that time has highlighted the intersectional nature of the
public health crisis of the 1980s and 1990s that affected a variety of populations, including in particular people of color.[18] Seeing the AIDS crisis as
a convergence of multiple epidemics, prompting varying responses by government, health care systems, and activists, highlights a much wider issue
of the complex relationship between sexuality and race in post-civil rights
U.S. history and politics. Whereas much work centering race in our understanding of the history of sexuality does so from the vantage point of a specific ethnic population, the essays in this volume interrogate race explicitly
through the lens of white privilege as a theme underpinning many of the
issues discussed. The mainstreaming of sexual dissidence after the 1970s
exposed to queer activists the power of whiteness as an organizing force in
American society, one they had to contend with. For those demanding a seat
at the table of a mainstream political party, their whiteness was precisely the
marker of their right to be there. For middle-class health care activists working to maintain private health insurance and combat employment discrimination in the 1980s, they were confronting the reality of an underfunded,
ramshackle public welfare system that they associated with an underclass,
often racialized in their political imagination. Those pushing back against
equality for sexual minorities in law attempted to construct barriers between
civil rights movements by casting gay rights advocates as white and not a
"real" minority deserving of protection. The use of whiteness as a political
tool or framing device for sexual rights politics runs through this collection
in ways that speak to broader questions of the dynamics of minority activism
in an era of multiple rights movements.

Alongside the political trope of whiteness ran constructions of the racial
other in many of the cases examined here. Opportunities for genuine coalition
building to challenge homophobia and the politics of exclusion and marginalization existed but in tension with long-standing reluctance of some white
gay activists to see themselves in common cause with other stigmatized populations. The decline of welfare liberalism during and after the Reagan era only
exacerbated tensions, as the increasingly besieged social safety net became
ever more undesirable in public discourse. In addition, the gross underresourcing of the public health system virtually invited competition between
activists battling to access services during a major public health crisis. By the

twenty-first century, moreover, conservatives traditionally deeply hostile to gay rights felt able to appeal to racial stereotypes of black violence to recruit white gay people to their own agenda of legalized private policing of minority populations. A growing, if still limited, acceptance of LGBT populations in American life has occurred in the context of racialized neoliberal economics and the recalibration of institutional racism in modern America.

What Happened to the "Straight State"?

A final theme that runs through these essays concerns the role of government in framing the politics of sexuality since the 1970s. As I have already mentioned, groundbreaking work by historians such as Margot Canaday has served to center the state in understanding the politics of sexuality but during a period prior to the emergence of LGBT activism as a potent organizing force.[19] Starting in the 1970s, we have witnessed the erosion of the New Deal welfare state at the very moment LGBT populations have been in a position to demand access to it. Scholarship on the relationship between sexual minorities and the state at all levels since the 1970s has often focused on grassroots activism in opposition to the state, especially in terms of accessing treatment for HIV/AIDS.[20] Yet the state, in its various forms, has played a critical role in shaping LGBT politics in recent decades in a variety of ways beyond political repression. State, local, and federal governments have funded sexual health clinics in some cities while not in others. Cities at the epicenter of the AIDS crisis had to tackle a massive public health crisis that threatened to tip an already precarious county hospital system over the edge. Congress in 1985 passed a bill allowing people no longer able to work or recently unemployed to keep their group health insurance for a certain period, and many state governments extended and expanded that law in the 1980s. More and more local communities were passing antidiscrimination laws in favor of LGBT people, prompting in some cases a furious backlash. The U.S. Department of Justice in 1990 finally acknowledged that same-sex sexuality was no longer considered a psychiatric disorder and ordered the Immigration and Naturalization Service not to exclude sexual minorities from entering the United States. All of these examples ask us to dismiss easy notions of a universally hostile, repressive American state during and after the Reagan era and think instead of the complex interactions among government, private interests, and minority communities.

The Structure of This Book

Given the dozens of possible ways of thinking about the themes discussed here, too many to consider in a single volume, I decided to prioritize depth over breadth and allow authors space to showcase their ideas on as wide a canvas as possible. The book is composed of three parts so as to conceptualize the period between the early 1970s and now both chronologically and thematically. Part I highlights ways in which the immediate post-rights revolution period created new demands on the part of sexual minorities for social services, especially in health and housing, but also encouraged activists keen for a seat at the political table to frame their demands in ways that excluded or marginalized many of those most in need of protection. Part II contains three essays examining the impact of the AIDS crisis on different populations and cities, revealing the extent to which it promoted racial divisions within sexual minority activism. Part III asks readers to consider ways in which an examination of gay rights politics in an apparent era of neoliberal capitalism complicates our understanding of American political categories. Sexuality as a political issue has not fitted very easily into ideological boxes largely constructed before LGBT issues gained traction in mainstream politics, resulting in huge challenges for those seeking to integrate questions of sexual rights into broader political narratives, whether of the Left or the Right.

In chapter 1, Katie Batza considers the creation of local health services for sexual minorities in the 1970s. Initially not established explicitly as a clinic for LGBT people, the Fenway Community Health Center gradually became associated with queer health issues over time, in part as a result of increased government regulations and bureaucratic control that required the clinic to clarify its mission and professionalize its management. New clinic directors moved the clinic further from its origins as a neighborhood antipoverty organization and saw the opportunity to access a wider range of government funds. "Ultimately," she writes, "the board's commitment to the clinic's growth and sustainability, rather than to gay liberation, drove its decision to focus on gay health services." That decision did not come lightly or easily for many working at the clinic, committed to its egalitarian, countercultural founding, and their relationship to government was complex and contradictory throughout the 1970s. The clinic's interaction with the state did much to advance LGBT health activism in Boston, even if that came at the expense of the much wider political mission of the clinic in its early days.

Ian Baldwin also examines public policy and the state in the 1970s but using the example of housing policy in Los Angeles. He charts how lesbians and gays expanded the parameters of the War on Poverty and accessed state resources, eroding the heteronormative assumptions of the Great Society welfare regime. Gay liberation activism's development in tandem with anti-poverty politics made an association between the two inevitable. In addition, the California Democratic Party's strong association with multiple civil rights movements in the Golden State rendered it a useful vehicle for advancing a social policy agenda in the 1970s inclusive of sexual minorities. The U.S. Department of Housing and Urban Development under President Jimmy Carter rewrote its definition of what constituted a family for public housing purposes, demonstrating the impact that nonheteronormative welfare activism had made. "Through housing, social service, and political activism, lesbian and gay activists in Los Angeles helped destabilize heteronormative welfare policies that were foundational to breadwinner liberalism," Baldwin argues. His essay, together with that of Katie Batza, is suggestive of the vitally important yet still not fully understood role that economic and welfare issues played in forging LGBT politics in advance of the AIDS crisis of the 1980s, one that would bring issues of economic inequality into sharp focus.

Jonathan Bell explores the limited capacity of gay rights politics of the 1970s to develop a truly inclusive and radical approach to the health and social welfare needs of different LGBT populations by contrasting local grass-roots efforts to provide services to their communities with a national gay rights movement consciously downplaying socioeconomic inequality in its engagement with the Carter administration. Bell examines campaigns for an accessible sexual health infrastructure for lesbians, transgender people, and gay men that highlighted questions of poverty, inequality, and race and gender privilege as central features of the American social contract in the 1970s. He then turns to national gay organizing politics from the mid to late 1970s, arguing that activists emphasized policy demands that downplayed or even erased these questions in favor of issues of individual rights that would play well with a post-Great Society liberal political worldview. White cisgender males dominated the top echelons of the National Gay Task Force and the Gay Activists Alliance, and they found it easy to adopt a political strategy that seemed most likely to resonate with a political mainstream increasingly hostile to redistributive antipoverty policies. Activists gained access to national politics in the mid-1970s, a time when a liberal political class was increasingly keen to turn its back on antipoverty politics of the 1960s and break the association of Democratic Party politics with welfare dependency. Local-level health activism in the 1970s made plain the varied health needs of the different sexual minority communities, whereas national gay rights politics tried to subsume sexual identity behind a respectable face of normative citizenship in which sexuality, a concept made real in part through questions of access to services, was essentially irrelevant.

The public health emergency that has cast a long shadow over queer politics ever since the first cases of HIV were discovered in 1981 is the subject of the next three chapters. Tim Stewart-Winter places the state front and center in his examination of urban responses to the AIDS crisis in the context of massive federal cuts to public services. Major U.S. cities were faced with a spiraling health crisis at the very moment that their public hospitals and social services were at their weakest in a generation. In San Francisco, an urban model made possible by strong LGBT activism, a compact geography, and a sympathetic city government offered a highly developed system of home-based care and dedicated AIDS treatment centers. But in major cities such as Chicago and New York, huge urban spaces in which many people with AIDS were impoverished minorities, options for accessing quality care were woefully limited. Stewart-Winter's study of AIDS politics in Chicago forces us to consider multiple levels of discrimination and exclusion in social policy in which race and poverty interacted with sexuality in shaping responses to the epidemic. In cities such as Chicago, "AIDS drove a wedge between black and white gay and lesbian people" and "made the gulf between African American neighborhoods and the mostly white gay enclaves on the city's north side—with respect to organizational infrastructure, political economy, sexual cultures, and customary networks of care—more consequential than they had been." The crisis also exposed the serious shortcomings of a divided health care system in which state and local governments struggled to manage a ramshackle public health system into which only the marginalized, lacking significant political clout, were consigned.

The role of race in America's cities in shaping responses to AIDS is also the subject of Dan Royles's essay on Philadelphia in the 1980s. While Tim Stewart-Winter's contribution focuses on the interaction between activists and city government, Royles centers his attention on divisions within AIDS health advocacy groups. Early AIDS activism largely sprang from existing LGBT networks in the city in which white Philadelphians dominated. Yet as was the case in many cities across the United States, the AIDS epidemic was no respecter of racial divides, holding a mirror to the damaging levels of distrust and in some cases blatant racism of some at the forefront of the health emergency. In the fall of 1986, for example, the city's first AIDS walk and vigil served as a lightning rod for bitter divisions over the intersections of race, class, and sexuality. Angry at the decision to route the march away from the city's main Gayborhood as a way of highlighting the diversity of those affected by AIDS, one white gay activist lamented that "we couldn't even do this thing right and remember our own," a phrase that served to emphasize the whiteness of his sense of community in Philadelphia.

In his essay "Black Gay Lives Matter," Kevin Mumford examines the role of the AIDS crisis and the rise of conservative politics in spurring a radical African American activism, one that made alliances across the racial divide but also highlighted the need for racial minorities to set their own terms of engagement with the politics of the 1980s. Mumford charts the multiple ways in which activists and cultural leaders of color gained a new purchase on political representation at a time of backlash against the legacy of the civil rights movements of the 1960s. Mumford also considers the periodization of the Reagan era and its relationship to race as well as sexual dissidence by comparing minority activism in the United States with that in the United Kingdom, a country viewed as similar to the United States in terms of its perceived neoliberal turn and also home to a black radical tradition. He argues that "despite powerful conservative pressure on several fronts—indicated by the rightward turn toward family values and against civil rights in the Ronald Reagan era as well as the struggle over gay age of consent laws and racial immigration restriction leading up to the Margaret Thatcher era in Britain— neither of these rightward mobilizations produced a total backlash." Rather, a variety of factions, organizations, and collectives joined together to fashion alternative positions or definitions of black and queer identity. In so doing, Mumford also points to the difficulties inherent in building a genuinely multiracial, nonhierarchical attack on inequality and discrimination in these years when the political languages and cultural reference points of sexual dissidence movements were so racialized.

The final three chapters chart interactions between the politics of sexuality and wider political movements since the 1980s. Given the context of the Reagan era and the rise of the New Right, the relationship between sexual minorities and American conservatism is an important site of historical inquiry. Clayton Howard provides the first in-depth treatment of the Log Cabin Republicans, a network of primarily white gay men who yoked their sexual identity to a doctrine of individual rights and antistatism that took them into the arms of the GOP. Not all gay rights politics sprang from the Left; a significant minority of gay men in particular saw their political lineage as coming from the Right, especially in the context of a New Deal and Great Society liberalism that served to police sexual dissidents as much as pull them into the mainstream. Still, the New Right, in its close association with evangelicals after the 1970s, proved to be an inhospitable home for gay people, especially as the AIDS crisis furnished homophobes with a new weapon with which to delegitimize sexual nonconformists. We need to understand those who saw their home in the Republican Party as well as the gay rights movement, as the seeming paradox of the Log Cabin Republicans points to a wider tension in American politics between identity politics and programmatic parties that have to pull together diverse coalitions.

Rachel Guberman extends this analysis of the complex relationship between the New Right and the politics of sexuality in her essay charting the limited success that the Right had in rolling back a gay rights ordinance in Colorado in the early 1990s. The successful passage of Amendment 2 in 1992 is often seen as a success story of the Religious Right at the height of the so-called culture wars, as it banned any government in the state from offering protection from discrimination to LGBT people. It took the U.S. Supreme Court to overturn the amendment in the 1996 *Romer v. Evans* case. Yet the dominant arguments during the referendum campaign revolved around questions of affirmative action and special protections, not religious "family values," which fell flat. "Only when they jettisoned religious and moral arguments against homosexuality and adopted instead a racially coded language of fairness and economic access did Religious Right operatives gain traction with voters," argues Guberman. At the same time, the alliance of gay rights groups with corporate interests in opposing discriminatory legislation pointed to the evident integration of sexual politics and neoliberal capitalism in a post-Reagan era America, an ongoing trend highlighted recently with the corporate boycott of states such as Indiana and North Carolina that have enacted antigay legislation.[21] Guberman's story suggests the limited utility of the political categories "liberal" and "conservative" when considering sexual politics at the turn of the twenty-first century.

Julio Capó's provocative essay pulls together the strands of race, class, sexuality, and state power running through this book and applies them to the contemporary political scene. His focus is the prosecution in a Florida state court of George Zimmerman, a white resident of a gated community in Sanford, Florida, who shot and killed Trayvon Martin, an African American, after a confrontation in February 2012. Zimmerman claimed that he had been pursuing Martin, suspecting him of criminal intent, and was defending himself in the face of a violent attack after Martin noticed that he was being followed. Zimmerman's acquittal in July 2013 has widely been viewed as yet another case exposing the ongoing racial oppression of minorities in the United States in spite of the election of Barack Obama as president. For Capó, the case serves as a study of how narratives of white privilege and racial hierarchies have been deployed to decouple gay rights issues from broader civil rights movements. Elements of the U.S. Right attempted to portray Martin as a homophobe who feared that Zimmerman was a sexual predator, tempting gay activists into an alliance with those defending Zimmerman and promoting state-sanctioned private violence against racial minorities. A growing political acceptance of gay rights in the context of twenty-first-century neoliberalism has not developed in tandem with a decline in racist paradigms but has in fact served to reinforce them, as antihomophobic politics has become ever more distinct from a wider civil rights agenda. A number of LGBT organizations recognized the Zimmerman case as a wake-up call for a rights politics that needed to rediscover its intersectional passion and stand up against all forms of discrimination and prejudice, and some queer activists have played formative roles in the Black Lives Matter movement. The death of Trayvon Martin has at least served to energize a genuinely queer politics sensitive to multiple sites of discrimination and state repression and dedicated to challenging them.

This collection of essays started as an effort to showcase exciting current scholarship on the politics of sexuality in the United States between 1960s gay liberation and the early twenty-first century. But reading the essays together, it becomes clear that they all speak to wider questions of state power, racism, identity politics, and party politics in a supposed era of conservative political dominance. The essays do not cover every aspect of sexual identity or minority politics in these decades, but they all seek to show how the political trajectory of the country looks very different if we explore the apparent rise of neoliberalism and of the Right using studies of sexual dissidence.

PART I

Public Policy Comes Out

The 1970s

CHAPTER 1

A Clinic Comes Out

Idealism, Pragmatism, and Gay Health Services in Boston, 1971–1985

Katie Batza

Today Boston's Fenway Community Health Center is closely associated with the city's LGBTQ communities, as it presides as one of the largest and most influential gay health institutions in the United States, offering a wide array of services, conducting trailblazing research, and consulting the larger medical profession on how to best serve members of the LGBTQ communities. However, even as the first decade of the clinic's existence coincided with the 1970s and gay liberation, gay and to a lesser extent lesbian health, politics, and identities factored only tangentially in the origins and initial growth of the clinic. The clinic began in 1971, serving and unifying the diverse population in the emerging Fenway neighborhood as part of the neighborhood's response to destructive state and municipal urban renewal campaigns. However, by the early 1980s, the enforcement of new government regulations focused on efficiency and professionalism posed a challenge to the Fenway clinic community and opposed the clinic's philosophy and organizational structure. As it struggled to adapt to the new political and economic environment, the clinic reluctantly shifted its focus to the gay (and lesbian, though initially less so) community of larger Boston. Responding to both the AIDS crisis and the lesbian baby boom within months of its new emphasis on gay and lesbian health, the Fenway clinic quickly solidified its reputation as an important gay medical institution. Thus, while consistently centered on "community," the community at the heart of the Fenway clinic shifted over time from the racially and economical diverse residents immediately surrounding the clinic to a constantly expanding community of sexual and gender minorities in the larger city and region.

The clinic's unexpected and protracted coming-out story makes meaningful additions to historical understanding of this time period. First, the federal, state, and local governments played a critical role in creating what became an important and long-lasting gay institution, illustrating that the state's relationship to sexual minorities in this period needs much more nuance and complexity than current scholarship offers. The Fenway clinic's history also decenters the role of gay liberation in 1970s gay institution building. Rather, the "straight" origins of Fenway locate gay health activism within the reverberations of Lyndon Johnson's Great Society domestic policies and a national conversation about health and poverty rather than emanating from gay liberation. Centered in Boston, the Fenway neighborhood's history continues to expand the map of LGBTQ history beyond just New York City, San Francisco, and Los Angeles but does so in a way that highlights the important role of a racially diverse low-income neighborhood rather than a predominantly white middle-class gay enclave. In these ways, the Fenway clinic illuminates the politics of the closet in the age of gay liberation, Ronald Reagan, and AIDS.

The clinic threw out nearly all of its historical records as part of a move in the early 1980s, so the bulk of this history results from oral histories, secondary sources, and tangentially related archives. This approach proved quite challenging at times, as oral history subjects often proved difficult to locate and/or had difficulty remembering specifics. Additionally, the calamity and trauma of the AIDS epidemic of the 1980s often overshadowed or minimized the work of the clinic in the 1970s in many oral history retellings. However, with use of a snowball method for identifying interview subjects as well as a timeline of historical events compiled through newspaper reporting and a menagerie of similar sources ranging from medical journals to personal correspondence found in collections across the country, this history took shape as though a very complex jigsaw puzzle.

The Beginning

The idea of opening a health clinic in the Fenway neighborhood came to two resident activists after they visited a newly opened Black Panther-operated health clinic that earned notoriety in the local press and fame among Boston activists.[1] That clinic not only provided health services to the surrounding community but also politically mobilized area residents. It also stood directly in the path of bulldozers slated to raze the neighborhood in preparation for the Inner Belt Road, or what would have been called I-695, that would demolish the community.[2] The Black Panther's free clinic, consisting of just a trailer, embodied the struggles of neighborhood residents who had limited access to health care and whose poverty had placed them in the sights of redevelopers. David Scondras, the director of community services at the Boston Center for Older Americans in Fenway, remembered how he saw the Black Panther Clinic as "an organizing tool to get everyday people who otherwise were not very political involved in the Black Panther Party. . . . It gave all of us an idea, which was that we should go out to the neighborhood and start organizing our community."[3]

The political strategy behind the Black Panther Clinic resonated with the Fenway activists, as developers and bulldozers from the Boston Redevelopment Authority (BRA) also threatened their financially struggling neighborhood. The duties of the BRA, which was funded by the federal, state, and local governments, were numerous, stretching across the spectrum of urban planning and development and giving the BRA overwhelming and omnipotent political power in every step of the process.[4] One community activist recalled that the BRA urban renewal projects, "also known as urban demolition," were massive, sweeping, and often corrupt.[5] In 1965, the BRA formally set its sights on the Fenway neighborhood. Building upon an expansion plan submitted by the First Church of Christ, Scientist, in the Fenway neighborhood, the BRA created the expansive Fenway Urban Renewal Plan that outlined the demolition and redevelopment of much of the Fenway neighborhood. The approval of the plan by the Boston City Council on November 1, 1965, set the plan in motion. Within two years, the BRA had acquired federal funding. Soon, wrecking balls and bulldozers demolished over three hundred low-income housing units on the eastern border of the Fenway neighborhood as part of the first phase of the Fenway Urban Renewal Plan.[6] Discussing one portion of this first phase of construction, one longtime Fenway activist and resident remembered that "where the new Christian Science Church is, used to be I think eighty apartments and twenty stores and nice little . . . brick buildings. All that was torn down and people were displaced."[7] Initially, the BRA met disorganization among residents of Fenway. In fact, the concept of Fenway as a neighborhood emerged out of the BRA's plan and the residents' response. Aware of both the political power of the Black Panther Clinic and the unmet medical needs of their own racially diverse and economically struggling residents, David Scondras and a Northeastern University graduate nursing student, Linda Beane, teamed up, using their complementary interests to open the renegade Fenway clinic in the Boston Center for Older Americans.[8] The clinic was one of many community-based organizations, including a food co-op, a newspaper, and child care, designed to make residents more politically engaged, unified, and organized to combat the state-approved developers attacking their neighborhood. In short, the clinic served as a larger effort by residents to create a neighborhood and invoke a sense of community in Fenway designed to thwart the BRA and gentrification efforts.[9]

On a summer evening in 1971, the first in a long line of Fenway residents in need of medical care arrived at the Boston Center for Older Americans, a senior drop-in center located on the neighborhood's eastern edge and operated by the First Church of Christ, Scientist. Scondras had decided to use the center's space for an after-hours neighborhood clinic despite the Christian Science Church's teachings that members should maintain their physical and mental health through the use of prayer rather than medicine. Unbeknownst to the center's management or church officials, Scondras with the help of a "Hippie doctor" and Beane began offering health services to Fenway residents, including gay-friendly venereal disease (VD) testing to the resident gay community.[10] Scondras, a recent Harvard graduate, antiwar activist, and computer programmer, had become a resident of the neighborhood while working as an economics instructor at Northeastern University on the neighborhood's eastern border. In Fenway, he continued his work in the antiwar movement that had begun at Harvard and took the job at the Center for Older Americans as a way to get to know neighborhood residents. At Northeastern, the young instructor/political activist with a bushy black beard also befriended Beane, a graduate nursing student at Northeastern who led a student group dedicated to the community health movement and providing free medical care. Beane, a fellow Fenway resident, was also a veteran of the antiwar movement who brought her political acumen to neighborhood issues through organizing Fenway residents at the area's Westland Avenue Community Center.[11]

The teachings of the church, Scondras's decision not to ask if he could use the space, and the quickly increasing number of patients made it impossible for the Fenway clinic to operate out of the Boston Center for Older Americans for long. As a result, in early 1973 the group found and rented the basement of a small building, "a defunct antique shop," on Haviland Street in the heart of the Fenway neighborhood to house a new community clinic.[12] The basement on Haviland Street was a far cry from a clinic at the time Scondras rented it. As one activist reminisced in an interview, "They got my brother-in-law to be their pro bono lawyer who got them their lease for a dollar a year."[13] Community members cleaned the abandoned basement and painted it and constructed makeshift exam rooms, a filing area, a waiting room, and a lab. One remembered, "I helped with some of the physical stuff when they were building, putting some of the flooring down and things like that which was all done by probably some people who knew what they were doing and most people who didn't and were just helping."[14] They furnished the clinic with a hodgepodge of secondhand and donated furniture, including movie seats from a defunct movie theater on Boylston Street that served as waiting room chairs and medical equipment from a retired Back Bay doctor, and opened their doors to the surrounding community in August 1973.[15] Medical supplies were often "acquired" by volunteers who were also physician's assistants, nurses, doctors, or medical students dedicated to providing free health care. A longtime volunteer physician at the Fenway clinic remembered, "I'd filch stuff from the hospital and bring it over."[16] Nearly everything in the clinic was borrowed, used, or homemade, but from its opening it was busy serving the Fenway residents who oftentimes had limited or no access to other health care.

The Fenway Community Health Center, both in its nascent stage at the Boston Center for Older Americans and in its first official home in the basement on Haviland, reflected and served, according to its patient demographics, the diverse neighborhood residents. A third of the Fenway neighborhood lived below the poverty level, scraping by with a median annual income of $2,027.[17] One reporter writing in 1977 described the area as a "low-income, low-rent neighborhood, its population of 4,000 is somewhat transient, consisting mainly of students, welfare families, young working people, and elderly people. It has long had a reputation for street crime, drugs, and prostitution and was once one of Boston's more notorious red-light districts."[18] In a city infamous for its racial segregation and tension during the 1970s, Fenway was a rare example of integration not only of blacks and whites but also a considerable immigrant, mostly Latino, population. Responding to the neighborhood's needs, the clinic treated almost all nonemergency medical needs ranging from child immunizations, blood pressure tests, and cases of strep throat and the flu to testing and treating VD, pre- and postoperative care for most surgeries, and gynecological care.[19] A longtime volunteer physician described the clinic services as a "basically primary care model. If you had high blood pressure, you'd come in. If you had diabetes, you'd come in. If you needed an annual physical, you'd come in."[20] While at the Boston Center for Older Americans, the clinic served a small but diverse population that included the elderly, women, children, and gays.[21] After the move to the Haviland basement in 1973 there was more physical space, and there were also more volunteers to reach out to each of these groups specifically. In addition to its regular daytime operating hours during which anyone could schedule an appointment or drop by, the clinic opened its doors to specific populations in the evening and on the weekends. Among these evening programs was a gay health clinic on Wednesday nights.[22] While these evening programs took a few months to formalize, the services and outreach to these specific populations existed at the Fenway clinic from its opening on Haviland Street, reflected the diversity of the neighborhood, and illuminated the deficiencies in the existing health care system of the early 1970s.

In an attempt to include and galvanize as many residents as possible, the clinic often opened its doors after hours to socials and weekend film screenings for kids, and board meetings looked more like town hall meetings. Board meetings easily lasted a number of hours, a fact that undoubtedly made them inaccessible for some in the community with limited time.[23] One described how meetings would last "anywhere from three to five hours; yeah, they were long. Most of us on the board with some exceptions didn't have experience in health care or the management of clinics or human resources—we were the blind leading the blind."[24] In the early years, anyone who was at all associated with the clinic (founders, volunteers, patients, or even just neighbors) was welcome to attend these meetings, create agenda items on the spot, engage in debate, and vote on any and all decisions.[25] This democratic structure reflected the political approach of many young New Left-affiliated organizations of the period and, like the clinic itself, was meant to foster personal investment and enthusiasm in the clinic and the larger Fenway community in the face of the encroaching redevelopment. Both the board meetings' structure and the use of the space for social off-hours events successfully nurtured investment in the notion of Fenway as a neighborhood and strengthened resistance to gentrification efforts.

With the clinic's open organizational structure and its dedication to serving the entire Fenway community (of which gay men were a small part), creating and maintaining a gay health collective to formalize the clinic's already established treatment of gay men was relatively easy. A doctor at Boston's Homophile Community Health Center, which provided gay-friendly counseling to gays from around the city, asked clinic cofounder, David Scondras, if the Fenway clinic could provide medical backup to his patients. Taking advantage of the open town hall-style board meetings, Scondras pitched the idea in April 1974 and received a warm reception. The Gay Health Collective of the Fenway Community Health Center began offering Wednesday night sessions on May 22, 1974.

Neither the inclusion of gay services from the start at the Fenway clinic nor their formalization in the Gay Health Collective's weekly sessions should be mistaken for gay liberation activism. While a handful of the Fenway activists were gay, Scondras among them, few were explicitly out or active in gay liberation organizations, focusing instead on the antiwar movement or the struggle with the BRA, but they "wanted supportive health care for ourselves and others, so we decided that the health center should provide it."[26] In fact, those who had insisted on the inclusion of gay health services at the clinic's founding were often not out to one another or the Fenway clinic community: "it was sort of an unspoken thing. No one ever got up and said 'hey, I'm gay.'"[27] Shedding more light on the political affiliations of the Fenway clinic during this period, one activist recalled, "It never really became a gay anything; it was just a place where gay people came. . . . You advocated for anybody who needed help—we never thought of ourselves as gay, straight, white, black."[28] From this vantage point, Fenway residents never thought that the Fenway Community Health Clinic directly related to gay liberation, and neither did the clinic itself. Rather, the clinic was an embodiment of New Left politics that challenged oppression in all forms, including homophobia. The clinic and many of its activists appear as more strong gay allies rather than actually gay. However, the existence and success of gay health services at the clinic from its inception did make it unique.

While Scondras, who could not remember ever specifically disclosing his own gay identity to the Fenway clinic community, was central in creating the Gay Health Collective, Ron Vachon perhaps more than anyone was the "gay face" of the Fenway clinic.[29] Vachon was "the backbone of the thing—big, tall, strong, French Canadian, very gentle but six foot three, bearded, probably could have been a professional wrestler if he didn't go into medicine. He was working full-time at the Fenway clinic as a physician's assistant and was gay."[30] While finishing up his degree as a physician's assistant at Northeastern University in 1975, Vachon "wandered into the Wednesday night clinic for the first time because the man he was dating came in to pick up some files. There, he met then-medical director Sandy Reder, who on learning that Vachon was a physician's assistant, put him to work on the spot. Vachon stayed to become part of the collective, and ultimately, the center's first paid staff person."[31] He quickly became a leader at the clinic, even being considered for the executive director's position in the late 1970s and always making sure that the clinic considered and met the medical needs of the gay community.[32] In short, because they "were already part of the we," already part of the Fenway community, a few activists who were gay were able to use the clinic's organizational structure and mission to shape the services of the clinic and meet the medical needs of the gay community specifically without appearing to be outspoken gay activists.[33] Gay health services emerged at the Fenway clinic because they were needed in the community, not because of any specific gay organizing. In this way, both the activists and the clinic itself have a very different relationship with the closet—they were more in the closet or at least downplaying their gay affiliations—than appears typical in the existing history of out and proudly vocal gay institutions of this period.

Boston's gay population, including those beyond the bounds of the Fenway neighborhood, welcomed the opening of the Gay Health Collective at the Fenway Community Health Clinic for a number of reasons. Fenway offered the only local, free, gay-friendly health services, allowing gay men to avoid the ridicule faced in many public clinics, the price gouging in private doctor's offices, and the inherent risks of using medical insurance.[34] Furthermore, the clinic was within less than a five-minute walk from the eastern border of the Fens Park cruising grounds, making it an ideal location for gay men to stop in and get tested on their way either to or from the park. A volunteer doctor of the Gay Health Collective, himself a gay man, described his patients as "college kids, young adults, the bartenders—just the panoply of gay people as gay people were defined in the '70s. There definitely would be a mix of a stock broker or lawyer, but not so many."[35] Another volunteer remembered, "I think we were caught off guard by the deluge of students and young folks that came for sexually transmitted diseases."[36] Word of the Fenway clinic's gay-friendly services quickly spread throughout the city's gay community via word of mouth, flyers in bars, and ads in *Gay Community News*. Shortly after its opening, the Fenway Community Health Clinic's Wednesday night Gay Health Collective saw gay patients from all across the city and the region. The clinic and its staff viewed and presented its gay services as an incidental subsidiary to the larger mission of serving the neighborhood and providing low-cost, high-quality care, allowing it to remain a strong gay ally but not actually gay. Regardless, they secured the Fenway clinic's position as a new Boston gay institution among the city's gay community.

Shifting Politics

During the battle with the BRA, the Fenway Community Health Center's relationship with the state was fairly simple. At the municipal level, the state proved largely antagonistic through redevelopment plans as well as licensure requirements and limited funding opportunities. Access to federal funds through direct grants and match grants with area hospitals counteracted many of these municipal hindrances and allowed the clinic to open and survive its early years. However, after the battle with the BRA ended victoriously for neighborhood activists in 1973 with a legal ruling that demanded a neighborhood-elected board approve and aid in designing all development projects, the Fenway clinic's relationship with the state grew increasingly complex. On one hand, the Fenway clinic was dependent on the state, both federal and municipal, for funding, licensure, and inspection approvals to provide health services to its quickly growing number of patients. Both the federal and municipal governments began to more regularly and strictly enforce compliance with existing and newly created regulations before granting more funding and licensure. On the other hand, the policies and culture of the Fenway Community Health Clinic, which emanated from a distrust and dislike of the government's instigating and antagonizing role in the neighborhood's battle against redevelopment, focused more on providing services and creating community than on complying with government regulations. The defeat of the BRA gave Fenway activists greater certainty that the political backlash of attacking a community health clinic insulated the clinic from any real governmental threat. David Scondras described their rationale: "they didn't want to kick us out, they didn't want to look like bad guys."[37] However, new regulations under Richard Nixon's second administration requiring that clinics receiving federal funding meet building and licensure codes, use only trained and certified medical professionals, and comply with standard bookkeeping practices for billing and payroll called for massive changes in culture and protocol in some volunteer-run community clinics such as the Fenway Community Health Center.[38] In short, the politics of the Fenway clinic grew progressively out of sync with the government's increasingly regulatory policies for community health clinics as the decade progressed.

While offensive to the culture of the clinic and its volunteers, Nixon's new approach to federal health programs and regulation enforcement initially had little impact on the quotidian activities in the busy Fenway clinic. The everyday work of the clinic overshadowed the threat of increased enforcement of local, state, and federal regulations for the clinic's volunteers. Within months of its opening on Haviland Street, the clinic saw a steady flow of people displaying both the diversity and energy of the neighborhood residents. The clinic was open five days a week, seeing everything from cases of the flu and child immunizations to blood pressure checks and postoperative care.[39] Within two years of the opening of the Haviland Street space, the Fenway clinic logged over 5,000 patient visits.[40] To care for the ever-growing number of patients, the Fenway clinic drew from the ranks of nearby Harvard Medical School, the New England Deaconess Hospital, and the Brigham Women's Hospital. The clinic became a hot spot for medical students and residents. Excited to hone their medical skills while also serving the surrounding community, "they were getting really good experience."[41] This constantly changing cast of characters gave the space a vibrancy that illustrated the clinic's central role in shaping the Fenway neighborhood, but it also made complying with government regulations both difficult and seemingly unimportant.

The volunteers at the Fenway Community Health Clinic were there because they were passionate about the neighborhood or about providing free health care to those who needed it. Just as community members literally built the clinic, despite their ignorance of building construction, they also ran it, despite limited community health know-how. In both instances, the enthusiasm of the Fenway volunteers did not always make up for lack of experience. As one volunteer recalled, the clinic flooded with sewage "whenever it rained. . . . There was no central heat, ventilation or air conditioning. Privacy for patients was limited to three unsound-proofed exam rooms and one unisex bathroom."[42] The Fenway clinic volunteers focused on providing care and building community among Fenway residents, caring less if a volunteer met outside standards for professional qualification, which were often set by the state or medical profession, that the clinic critiqued. Placing greater value on volunteers' passion than on their qualifications translated into having "some physicians on staff . . . who had not completed their training, . . . nurses who had backgrounds that were not relevant, . . . laboratory personnel who were chemistry majors in college but never had taken any chemical laboratory training."[43] The volunteers responsible for billing often had some bookkeeping experience but often "didn't know the first thing about really setting up medical billing and grant writing and the like."[44] Compounding these issues was a situation whereby numerous volunteers were responsible for single tasks within the clinic because most volunteers only worked a handful of hours per week. Scondras remembered that "we had no particular group of people running the place; it was just a collective—if you showed up, you ran it."[45] Consequently, the more detailed and ongoing tasks such as billing and building management fell between the cracks.

When not lost amid the bustle of the clinic, the Fenway clinic met the state's increased enforcement of regulations with resistance. In the eyes of Fenway residents, government policies at the federal, state, and municipal levels had contributed to the neighborhood's decline into poverty and eventually encouraged an army of wrecking balls. The resulting cynicism among Fenway residents was deep and lasting, so much so that the government's plan to better enforce regulations and impose professional standards at the community clinic engendered both frustration and renewed hostility toward the state. Scondras recalled getting a notice from the state regarding the clinic's noncompliance with licensure and inspection codes: "The state tried to clamp down on us because we didn't have a license to operate as a clinic. . . . I remember getting the letter and ripping it up. . . . They told us to stop and we said, no. . . . It was politically impossible to touch us."[46] Many believed that the neighborhood's engagement and successful defeat of the BRA in court meant that the clinic was above reproach or consequence from the state. During the BRA struggle, the clinic had played a central role in successful political and publicity strategies to gain sympathy and support for the Fenway residents. Certainly, few local politicians publicly criticized the thriving clinic, just as few took issue with the Black Panther Clinic blocking another major city redevelopment project that had inspired Scondras and Beane to open the Fenway clinic. In fact, the clinic welcomed Boston mayor Kevin White and many other local government officials to its official opening in 1973, even as the clinic was a clear and intentional threat to the city's redevelopment plans.[47] As a result of their perceived unassailable political position, the Fenway activists who knew of the regulations and requirements often chose to ignore them or work around them. The clinic operated for seven years without obtaining its full licensure from the Massachusetts Department of Public Health; full licensure was granted in 1978.[48]

While the "thankfully slow-moving state bureaucracy" edged the Fenway clinic to its inevitable day of reckoning with regulators, inspectors, and state licensing boards, a more immediate problem challenged the culture of the clinic: money.[49] Before moving into the Haviland Street basement, Scondras and Beane had secured federal funding in the form of a seed grant for the Fenway clinic, most of which had been spent on transforming the space from an abandoned antique shop into a suitable clinic space.[50] Additionally,

Deaconess Hospital provided the Fenway clinic with a small medical staff and grants for medical supplies as part of a federal fund-matching program.[51] Beyond these limited funds, "something like $30,000," the clinic had no other immediate sources of income, and by refusing to make any significant changes to comply with government regulations for licensure, it faced a shrinking pool of possible grants for which to apply.[52] Scondras remarked that "we would steal equipment and medicines for the health center because we didn't have a way to buy them, and that couldn't go on forever."[53] Though existing in legal incompliance and financial precariousness was not unprecedented among similar community clinics of the era, Fenway clinic's commitment to do so as an act of protest was unique and clearly not sustainable.

In 1973, just a few months after opening the clinic, some volunteers broached the topic of charging for services in one of the town hall-style board meetings. While charging for services seemed a likely and obvious source of badly needed revenue for the struggling clinic, the idea was in direct opposition to the founding ideals of the clinic, and the resulting debate was both long and contentious. Providing free health care, a political goal reignited by the missed opportunity during President Johnson's push for Medicare and Medicaid in 1965, had been as much an organizing principle for the clinic as preserving the Fenway neighborhood had been.[54] To be sure, no one liked the thought of charging for services, and those who brought it up only did so due to a lack of other options. However, factions quickly developed between those who felt it a necessity to sustain the clinic and those who felt that it so clashed with the founding ideals that it was tantamount to destroying the clinic. Scondras described the debate: "There were the people who felt, like myself, like if you charged anything that it would violate a principle that health care should be free for everyone. Then there were the people who said, yeah, but in real life nothing is free and we have to find a way to get money to pay for it."[55] Another volunteer remembered, "In our minds, the 50 cent fee would lead to corruption and bureaucracy!"[56] However, after more than twenty-four hours of debate spread over several board meetings, idealism bent under the weight of the harsh fiscal reality that the clinic faced.[57] The Fenway volunteers and community members settled on a compromise agreement whereby the clinic would charge fifty cents per visit, with the caveat that patients who either could not or did not want to pay the fee could either volunteer in return for services or pay whatever they could afford.[58] This deal preserved the clinic's identity as a free clinic while also placing it on a slightly better financial footing.

Just as the clinic community crafted an acceptable compromise for one financially rooted ideological challenge, another surfaced. Toward the end of 1973, a fight over whether to hire its first paid staff dominated the board meetings. The battle with the BRA had hinged on the political belief that all Fenway residents should have the same rights and political value to the state as the wealthy residents whom the redevelopment plan hoped to attract. This sentiment filtered into the ethos of the clinic. Volunteers were uncomfortable paying some for work that others did for free, as this could easily be interpreted as the Fenway community placing greater value on one volunteer over another or valuing one form of qualifications or training above another. Paying staff seemed to many at the board meetings to be a slippery slope where judgments over who to hire and for how much pay could easily clash with the ideals of the clinic.[59] Again, after numerous hours of debate the board settled on a compromise in which staff could be paid, but "everyone made the same hourly wage, no matter what you did."[60] The first paid Fenway clinic staff member was physician's assistant Ron Vachon, who also helped coordinate volunteers.[61] Within a year, the clinic had ten paid staff members: some doctors, some physician's assistants, and other former volunteers who assisted with clerical work. Longtime volunteer physician Lenny Alberts recalled, "It was a big deal when we started getting $10 a session, though, of course, we were encouraged to donate it all back into the pot."[62] Board members endorsed this unconventional pay scale as an attempt to preserve the ideal that every person regardless of education, job, or experience had the same worth and value to the greater community.

The compromises struck in the debates over charging for services and paying staff show Fenway volunteers' struggle to remain true to their founding ideals in the face of a changing fiscal and political reality. One activist and board member recalled that "there was just a lot of figuring it out as we were becoming more of an institution and less of a group of people that came together to do something."[63] Despite these changes in its policies, the clinic thrived, seeing its patient numbers rise exponentially throughout the decade. The Gay Health Collective, by far the fastest growing of the clinic's services, expanded to two nights a week.[64] The clinic developed more services and new relationships, teaming in 1976 with the Department of Public Health to educate various communities, including gay men, about VD prevention and treatment.[65] These and similar relatively small and low-cost projects allowed the clinic access to more grants, but none were of the size or magnitude that the clinic needed to avoid deficits. Government grants that did not require major changes at the clinic became scarcer and less lucrative as regulations became more common and more strictly enforced over the decade. Instead, the clinic focused on programs and grants for which it could easily qualify without licensure as a clinic, such as family planning grants through Title IX programming, rat-prevention grants through the city, and university-funded health research and outreach programs.[66] In 1978, a Tufts-based researcher offered to pay for Giardia testing for gay clients at the Fenway clinic who were willing to answer a medical questionnaire, thus allowing the clinic to offer the test to its clients.[67] These smaller grants, in addition to Deaconess Hospital's match grant that paid for some medical supplies and provided staffing, permitted the Fenway clinic to continue operating without significantly changing its political or organizational culture but did little to relieve its growing financial instability or put it more in step with the larger social and political trends of the decade.

In late 1979, facing patient numbers far outpacing revenue, the board hired a new executive director for the struggling Fenway clinic with the hope that the leadership change would bring about greater financial stability. With a history of health care management and community projects, Sally Deane started her tenure as the executive director in January 1980, only to realize that the organization was on the brink of collapse. In addition to "no written standards for employment, personnel policies, quality assurance standards, or management reports," the clinic required significant renovations before its inspection for licensure renewal, which was due to take place just three months after her arrival.[68] However, the clinic's financial situation quickly became her greatest concern, especially after "finding . . . signed checks made out to the . . . government for withholding taxes that had never been mailed because the checks would have bounced. . . . Even though they alleged that they were operating on a $200,000 budget with 7,000 patient visits, maybe 2,000 patients, they were technically in bankruptcy."[69] On her tenth day as the executive director, Deane learned that the clinic had not paid payroll taxes for quite some time and that the Internal Revenue Service (IRS) was on the verge of closing it down. The clinic's avoidance of professionalization and regulatory compliance had left it in great danger of losing its license and its funding and shutting down completely.

Seeing no other option, Deane looked to Deaconess Hospital to give Fenway clinic a loan to pay for the back taxes. The decision marked the moment when clinic's trajectory changed. Before lending the needed money, Deaconess Hospital required assurances of better business practices on the part of the clinic. For Deane, promises to reform the more slapdash aspects of the clinic were easy, as she already had plans to put into practice new professional standards, implement billing practices, and streamline the decision-making process. One longtime volunteer remembered how she felt when the Fenway board agreed to accept the loan from Deaconess Hospital: "I thought it was a necessary thing to do, but I thought it was a sad necessary thing to do."[70] For many of the Fenway clinic community at large, the loan from Deaconess Hospital, along with the professionalization it demanded, was bittersweet, allowing the clinic to remain open but also demanding an end of the political culture and structure that defined the clinic.

In a vote that formally marked the end of the consensus and democratic days of the Fenway clinic, the board granted Deane much more oversight and control of policies and procedures at the clinic in an effort to expedite all the necessary changes demanded by the loan and required for the upcoming licensure inspection. With this new power, the immediate threat of closure behind her, and the IRS paid, Deane focused her attention on transforming the clinic into a more professional organization. First, she "took a stand that the medical staff had to be qualified to do the work that they were doing."[71] Under these new policies, physicians had to be eligible for board certification in order to volunteer or work at the clinic, which meant "no more med students."[72] Nurses and laboratory technicians also had to have proper training and licensure. However, personnel were not the only issue as Deane struggled to bring the clinic up to code. She faced an inspection by the Massachusetts Department of Public Health in order to renew the clinic's license. While the previous generation of Fenway clinic staff had avoided licensure for many years, Deane saw maintaining the clinic's license as crucial to its future. After numerous renovations, paid for with money from Deaconess Hospital, the clinic passed government inspection and renewed its license in 1981. Going beyond the physical structure and the personnel within it, Deane, along with newly hired staff, instituted a new accounting system that "allowed for third party billing, including Medicaid and private insurers, making the financial base ... more solid."[73] As a result of these major institutional changes, the Fenway Community Health Clinic went from evading and circumnavigating any form of organizational hierarchy and professionalization to embracing and epitomizing both—all within a year of Deane's hiring.

While internecine battles had not caused the Fenway clinic's change, internal schisms certainly resulted from it. When the clinic finally succumbed to the pressure to professionalize in the interest of becoming a financially and medically strong institution, Fenway neighborhood activists and the free health care movement that had been at the clinic's core parted ways. Many neighborhood activists left the Fenway clinic shortly after the acceptance of the loan, falling victim to Deane's insistence on standards for employment. Volunteering and community involvement had been at the very core of the clinic and were crucial ingredients in making the clinic so interwoven with the Fenway neighborhood as it battled against the BRA. However, as a result of many of Deane's new policies, many staff and longtime volunteers were suddenly "unqualified" to do the jobs they had been doing, in some cases for years. One community member recalled how the transition influenced her decision to leave the board: "I quit the board because I didn't think I could make a contribution. . . . There was nothing left for an ordinary citizen to do. I wasn't the right match for that board anymore."[74] Many volunteers and community members no longer felt welcome in the clinic that many had come to think of as a community center, a home away from home. While the neighborhood had proven itself to be a sustainable political entity with the victory over the BRA, the Fenway clinic, on the other hand, was on the brink of collapse. With its survival taking precedence, the clinic's definition of community and its role in building that community began to shift.

By the end of 1980, Deane's changes at the Fenway clinic filtered into its every aspect. Its new structures and policies made for faster decision making, although more hierarchical and excluding of community members. Billing Medicare, Medicaid, and insurance companies was more consistent and reliable than ever before, and the clinic's financial situation slowly became more stable, shoring up its sliding fee scale. With its new professionalization, the clinic saw the number of grants for which it was eligible increase and had trained volunteers and staff applying for them.

Becoming Gay

In agreeing to work with the Fenway clinic, both the IRS and local funding partners insisted that the clinic plot a clear financial path forward. Thus, with an eye for building a long-lasting institution, the clinic also underwent a strategic planning process in the early 1980s that focused on how the clinic could have the largest and most stabilizing and sustained impact as a clinic while cutting unused or underused services that other area clinics made redundant. As part of the four-month strategic planning, the clinic collected information on the services of other clinics, surveyed their patients, and assessed each of their programs. The final strategic planning report was over one hundred pages long and included multiple appendices detailing the redundancies with other nearby clinics and the willingness of the Fenway clinic's clients to visit other clinics when more convenient and charting the strengths and weaknesses of each program down to the hours of operation and the number of patients seen. The main recommendation of the strategic planning process was clear: the Fenway Community Health Clinic needed to become a clinic focused predominantly on serving Boston's gay and lesbian community. The strategic plan's recommendation grew as much out of supply-and-demand market forces as it did the insistence of the clinic's funders and the state to ensure future solvency and longevity. Thus, while the recommendation appears market-driven, the state's professionalizing hand was merely one small step removed.

The Fenway clinic's indifference to gay liberation politics made the recommendation of the strategic planning process unexpected. With few other providers of quality health services for gays and lesbians available throughout the 1970s, little doubt existed among the gay community that the Fenway clinic was the clinic for them, "a gay institution" as one 1978 article in the *Gay Community News* described.[75] However, there was no confusion among clinic founders, volunteers, and staff that the clinic was a neighborhood clinic, not a gay one. This distinction informed not only the diverse services of the clinic but also the experiences of the gays and lesbians who worked there, giving insight into a closeted or gay ally organization rather than a fully out gay organization of the period. Sally Deane remembered that in preparation for her interview for the executive director position at the clinic in late 1979, "friends had advised me not to share with the search committee of the board that I was gay, even though several members of the board were gay. . . . These people were on the board because they cared about the services but not because they were gay political activists."[76] Those volunteers who maintained the Gay Health Collective were more likely to be out and politically active in the gay community, as in the case of Ron Vachon, yet their work within the clinic focused on the politics of health care rather than gay liberation.[77] Clearly, their work in providing gay health services was at some level an outgrowth of gay liberation in that gay liberation allowed for the clinic to publicize its services in gay newspapers, attract out gay doctors and medical professionals to volunteer their time, and, of course, serve patients who benefited from, if not identified with, gay liberation. However, few of the staff and volunteers at the Fenway clinic saw themselves as gay liberation activists even as the larger gay community saw the clinic as providing vital services for the burgeoning gay community.[78]

Though the strategic plan's recommendation for the Fenway clinic to focus on gay and lesbian health care surprised both the gay community and the clinic, the advice made sense when framed within the larger community health and political context of the city. As the 1970s progressed, coalitions between movements and diverse groups gave way to identity-based services.[79] Just as Boston's gay community flourished and became more insular and concentrated in the area around Boston Common over the decade, other groups began to separate themselves both physically and politically, with feminists rallying in Cambridge and blacks in Roxbury. As these groups created their own health organizations, community clinics such as the Fenway clinic saw their services become increasingly redundant.[80] In short, the abundance of identity-based services forced the Fenway clinic to specialize its services as well. This speaks to a shift in the Fenway neighborhood community as well as to a change in the way that the Fenway clinic defined community. The clinic's moment as a political rallying point or community organizing entity for a struggling neighborhood had passed. Initially, the clinic services were both useful and convenient health care as well as part of a larger struggle to save residents' homes. In this new era the battle for the neighborhood's survival had ended, and residents simply needed the services and did not mind getting them elsewhere if more convenient. Both the clinic and the neighborhood residents seemed to be altering their definitions of community. This shift in political context along with the clinic's structural changes that alienated some of the more committed volunteers and clients made the clinic's neighborhood patient base unreliable. As the Fenway clinic's strategic planning process sought ways to ensure the clinic's sustainability, its services to the gay community emerged as its strongest option for growth for three reasons. First, the gay community was growing quickly and steadily in this identity-based political atmosphere. Second, the Fenway clinic was the only area clinic to offer gay-friendly physical health services. Third, the number of clients at Gay Health Nights grew consistently throughout the second half of the 1970s.[81] In this way, the expansion of identity-based politics and identity-based services forced the clinic to abandon its broad service offerings and simultaneously created a community with little access to identity-specific services.

Even as this reasoning was convincing, the recommendation to become a predominantly gay and lesbian clinic raised concerns for the board. Some,

Deane among them, saw the proposed change as necessary not because of an allegiance to the gay community or to gay liberation politics but rather in the hope of ensuring the clinic's survival.[82] Yet before accepting the decision, other board members raised a number of questions, again revealing some of the divisions within the Fenway clinic community that resulted from the recent changes. While the changes at the Fenway clinic in the wake of the IRS back taxes and the loan from Deaconess Hospital had upended many of the founding ideals, policies, and structures of the clinic, it still remained a community health clinic that served the diverse Fenway neighborhood residents. Many of the board members feared that becoming a gay and lesbian-focused clinic would mean abandoning this last remaining aspect of the original clinic and potentially alienating existing heterosexual clients.

There was also great concern about creating tension with the neighborhood that the clinic had been so influential in building, especially as the gay clientele of the Fenway clinic were much more white and middle class than many of the neighborhood residents. One *Gay Community News* piece highlighted the whiteness of the clinic's gay clients when it asked, "the gay night at Fenway Health Center . . . where are the black faggots and lesbians, the Hispanics and other minorities?"[83] While the clinic at large offered its services to everyone and had a racially and economically diverse clientele generally, white and middle-class men made up an increasing percentage of the patients seen specifically by the Gay Health Collective in the late 1970s. This homogenization of gay health consumers reflects two compounding problems: the social and political conflation of gay identity as a white (and male) identity in the 1970s and the Fenway clinic's failure to specifically target gay communities of color with its outreach and services, making it complicit in the construction of gay as inherently white.

Beyond concern for the neighbors, critical board members were also concerned for the clinic and for themselves. Over the 1970s, many of Boston's gay organizations had been targets of violence and vandalism ranging from a fire at the Other Side bar to repeated break-ins at the *Gay Community News* offices.[84] Combined with the regular acts of violence against gays in the nearby Fens Park, the fears of violence and vandalism against a gay-identified clinic were legitimate.[85] Some individual board members also had worries over being personally affiliated with an explicitly gay organization: "a lot of people on the board had corporate jobs and things and were just not fully out."[86]

Ultimately, the board's commitment to the clinic's growth and sustainability, rather than to gay liberation, drove its decision to focus on gay health services. The board adopted the recommendation to focus its services on the gay and lesbian communities in the summer of 1980.[87] In an effort to avoid tension with existing clients or the larger Fenway neighborhood, the board insisted that services be given to anyone who came to the clinic, regardless of their sexuality, and that the clinic attempt to reach out to gay minorities.[88]

While business and the clinic's survival prompted the decision to focus on gay and lesbian health, the Fenway clinic and its board proved fully committed to serving gays and lesbians even as their health needs expanded exponentially in the early 1980s. AIDS emerged on the Boston landscape in late 1981, with Fenway clinic's Dr. Lenny Alberts diagnosing the first case of the disease in New England.[89] Dr. Kenneth Mayer, who joined the staff and immediately initiated research and community education programs in 1980, quickly became a researcher and clinician on the forefront of the disease. Within a year of the first Boston AIDS case, the basement clinic hosted experts from the Centers for Disease Control, the National Institutes of Health, and Harvard Medical School hoping to learn from the clinic's response to the epidemic.[90] The Fenway clinic became a national leader in terms of community-based research, experimental treatments, hospice care, and support groups for patients, community members, and the staff who faced death and trauma to an extent previously unseen in American community health clinics.

At the same time, the Fenway clinic blazed a trail for lesbians seeking to become mothers through alternative insemination (AI). Though initially hesitant to divert any attention and resources away from the AIDS crisis or draw more critique from the public at a time when AIDS-inspired homophobia peaked, in 1983 the Fenway board approved a proposal, two years in the making, from the Fenway AI Task Force to offer education and insemination services for lesbians wanting to conceive.[91] Among the first in the nation, the AI program at the clinic became a model for similar services across the country that granted lesbians easier access to fertility services than ever before.[92] While the clinic downplayed its affiliation with the gay and lesbian community in the 1970s, it emerged as a gay and lesbian health gladiator after coming out in 1980.

Conclusion

Over a dozen gay and lesbian-focused health clinics emerged over the course of the 1970s in the United States, with the majority closing within two years.[93] Local politics shaped each clinic's structure and relationship to the state

more so than any universal notion of gay liberation during the 1970s. Consequently, each clinic, even the clinics that failed to thrive, offers a window into
the politics of the closet in the age of gay liberation, Reagan, and AIDS. The
Fenway clinic was unique in many ways, most notably in its adversarial posi-
tioning to the state for nearly a decade that inspired its creation, impacted
its funding, and informed its structure. Of those clinics that remained open
for many years, the Fenway clinic's resistance to state involvement proved
to be the most sustained and permeating. In fact, most other long-lasting
gay and lesbian-focused clinics linked their survival and success to the support and approval of the state through licensure, funding, and tax status from
the outset. The clinic's battle with the state makes it an ideal case to examine the driving role of the state in shaping and nurturing a gay institution in
the 1970s and 1980s, first by galvanizing residents through encouraging the
redevelopment of the neighborhood and then by demanding professionalization and regulation of community health clinics. Similarly, the Fenway clinic's tangential relationship to gay liberation at its inception sets it apart from
other organizations offering services explicitly for gay and lesbian patients,
providing a glimpse into an institutional coming-out process during the gay
liberation and early AIDS periods. The clinic's initial reluctance to embrace
its new identity as a gay clinic and its emergence as a national leader in the
early AIDS response speak to the limits of gay liberation and the realities
of the early epidemic that have scholarly implications far beyond the small
basement clinic.

CHAPTER 2

"A Ray of Sunshine"

Housing, Family, and Gay Political Power in 1970s Los Angeles

Ian M. Baldwin

One morning in 1970, Don Kilhefner traveled to the Los Angeles County Hall of Administration in downtown Los Angeles. An organizer with the Los Angeles Gay Liberation Front (LAGLF), he arrived "looking like Allen Ginsburg" and insisted that he speak to a county supervisor about gay community needs. The main clerk asked him to wait in the lobby. Then she called security. Kilhefner was swiftly escorted out and told not to come back. He later admitted that he had been "naïve as hell" when it came to local politicking. A few years later, however, he returned to the Los Angeles County Hall of Administration under very different circumstances. Now an employee of the Gay Community Services Center (GCSC), Kilhefner came by invitation of Los Angeles County supervisor Ed Edelman to discuss a recent GCSC grant application that had been rejected by the Los Angeles County Health Department. Gathering GCSC and health department officials together in his conference room, the usually soft-spoken supervisor grilled the county employees. After only a few minutes of debate, he put an end to the conversation with five simple words: "Just give them the money." At this point, Kilhefner remembered, "it was all over; they caved; they gave us the money."[1] These divergent encounters reveal the remarkable degree by which lesbians and gays gained political power in Los Angeles in relatively short order. What had changed?

Connecting gay rights with economic rights, activists utilized the cause of affordable housing to access liberal political coalitions, expand the definition of family, and achieve unprecedented public financing at the county level throughout the 1970s. Their success encourages us to complicate the nature of both liberalism and gay political power in the decade. By emphasizing the needs of housing, gay activists were able to speak a common language with local liberal officials, who defined their liberalism primarily in economic and antipoverty terms. As Robert Self, Marisa Chappell, and Margot Canaday have all illustrated, this version of liberalism was built on patriarchal breadwinning and heteronormative family planning.[2] Yet, like scores of racial justice activists, lesbians and gays learned to speak the language of midcentury liberalism in order to secure needed resources for their communities and subvert the meanings of liberalism from within.[3] As they gained political influence and attacked heteronormative housing policies, lesbians and gays asked liberal policy makers to rethink what a family looked like in America, helping them to unmoor economic policy from breadwinner ideology. They proved surprisingly successful in doing so. Ironically, however, this evolution in liberal thinking occurred at the precise moment when many began to embrace punitive law and order initiatives that disproportionately targeted racial minorities and built a mass incarceration crisis in the United States. In other words, as liberalism widened to incorporate queers, it began to punish others with more severity, which fundamentally limited the inroads of lesbian and gay activists along racial lines. The scale of gay activism in Los Angeles is equally important, for it was exceptional. Scholars have mostly focused at the city level to document the rise of gay political power. Cities such as Chicago, Timothy Stewart-Winter has suggested, proved to be a model of the slow process by which lesbians and gays achieved political clout through city halls.[4] That would have been the case in Los Angeles too had activists placed their energies in the overly bureaucratic art of city politics. But they did not. Instead, they bypassed the city, achieving unprecedented breakthroughs at the county level. Less cumbersome and better funded, the county was the source of real power in Los Angeles, and its support of gay rights allows us to better assess the vital role of the welfare state in the construction of gay politics in modern America.

From Sex Parties to Liberation Houses: Housing Activism in the 1960s and 1970s

Housing was a constant concern for lesbian and gay Angelenos in the 1960s and 1970s. Like others, they struggled amid shortages and rising costs but faced additional burdens because of their sexualities. Discrimination was a two-armed beast: while state "family" requirements barred individuals from public subsidies, harassment and evictions awaited others in the private market. Moreover, as Martin Meeker has argued, California cities were magnets for lesbian and gay migrants, which escalated demand.[5] Throughout the 1960s and 1970s, activists fought against discrimination and built safe and affordable housing solutions of their own. In doing so, they rejected heteronormative assumptions about family and constructed a discourse of gay rights rooted firmly in the urban political economy.

As scholars have shown, housing policies were designed with heteronormative nuclear families in mind. When it came to the nation's first public housing projects, Gail Radford explained, "It was taken for granted that applicants should live in what was then regarded as an optimal family unit consisting of mother, father, and children—no more and no less."[6] During the postwar housing boom, this goal remained important. Clayton Howard's exploration of suburban development in California's Bay Area revealed how housing projects encouraged married couples to migrate to the South Bay, while "large numbers of unmarried people, including many gay men and lesbians, [came to be] concentrated in places like San Francisco."[7] By sanctioning a restrictive definition of marital and biological family, housing policies excluded lesbians and gays from vital subsidies. In the 1960s, homophiles began to push back against these restrictions and laid important foundations for activism in the 1970s.

Founded by W. Dorr Legg and his partner Merton Bird, the Knights of the Clock emerged alongside other homophile groups in Los Angeles, such as Mattachine and ONE.[8] Moving to Los Angeles from Michigan in 1949, Legg and Bird face two obstacles to securing housing: their sexuality denied them a mortgage backed by the Federal Housing Administration (FHA), and they were barred from many parts of the city because Bird was black. Heteronormative and racially restrictive housing policies dealt them a combined blow.[9] Although the lack of detailed records prevents us from fully grasping the scope of the organization, it is clear that the Knights of the Clock helped same-sex couples, especially interracial couples, secure housing through referrals.[10] Known also for adventurous sex parties, the group fused the erotic with the economic. Similarly, the homophile organization ONE created a "social service division" to offer housing referrals and economic counseling. The inspiration seems to have emerged from readers who wrote of troubles finding housing.[11] Both the Knights of the Clock and ONE prioritized middle-class struggles, focusing mainly on home ownership. Such was not the case with the United States Mission (USM), which targeted low-income and homeless needs. Founded in the early 1960s, the USM advertised itself as both a physical and emotional shelter. "At some deep and central level of our emotional lives," one pamphlet explained, "we all carry a sense of dread that we will someday be abandoned. The existence of a 'home,' an address, a place where someone we know can be found, where we belong, is the only solace for that universal fear." Located on Western Avenue in eastern Hollywood, the USM shelter offered free lodging and meals to those in need, be they gay or straight. Yet fliers were mostly distributed at gay bars, social functions, and social service agencies. Many were also printed in Spanish and distributed in Los Feliz and Echo Park. By the mid-1970s, founder Bob Humphries admitted that it was a "gay organization." Indeed, he believed it to be "the largest shelter program for homeless gay men and lesbians in the world."[12] The emphasis on housing to Los Angeles homophiles helps us to paint a richer portrait of the movement pre-1969. Amid the backdrop of the War on Poverty and the Great Society, homophiles broadened their message to emphasize the economic needs of queers.[13] This made them useful bridges between the movements of the 1960s and 1970s.

For those seeking private rental housing, no law existed to protect lesbian and gay tenants from discrimination. Moreover, since many settled in the unincorporated area of West Hollywood, they remained outside city jurisdiction (thus, even when a gay rights ordinance was approved in 1979, these renters remained unprotected). One woman living near MacArthur Park reported that she was "being evicted from her apartment for no reason except that she was a lesbian." Similarly, a man reported that his landlord was "evicting him because he [was] GAY." His county supervisor suggested that he "call the Housing Authority," an unhelpful suggestion since no law existed to protect him. Homophobic landlords could be especially bold. Writing to a county official, one owner complained of the "public nuisance created by gay persons" and wanted to verify her right to "evict all gay tenants" from her property. Others were vindictive. In response to the "gay takeover" of the neighborhood, one apartment owner promised to "evict all trash." When "two gay night clubs" opened near the complex of another landlord, he barred lesbians and gays from renting. Another decried "special favoritism towards gays," which resulted in the loss of "*good* tenants" in exchange for "*moral perverts*." When a handful of gay men rented a house together, the owner of a nearby apartment building asked, "Isn't there a law against this?" To safeguard the neighborhood, he urged a "ban [against] gays from renting" in Los

Angeles County.[14] Thus, for lesbians and gays, the housing market could be a hostile one that framed them as threats to families and neighborhoods. Gay liberation activists would need to directly counter these attacks.

Following the 1969 Stonewall Uprising in New York, cities across the nation founded Gay Liberation Fronts. The Los Angeles chapter proclaimed "unity with and support for all oppressed minorities" and joined forces with the local Peace and Freedom Party, whose office later housed the LAGLF.[15] While activists self-identified with the New Left, many also harbored an affinity for traditional liberal ideas. Don Kilhefner remained deeply touched by his experience in the Peace Corps and listed Franklin Roosevelt and John F. Kennedy as his political heroes.[16] Jon Platania was a strong supporter of liberal urban redevelopment plans and had worked for the U.S. Department of Housing and Urban Development (HUD) in the Bay Area and in Los Angeles.[17] Never making a clean break from the liberalism of the 1960s, these activists molded gay liberation within their own political imaginations. Much like Black Power, gay liberation could be a "plastic concept."[18] Housing was a natural concern, since many members were or had been homeless. Joining resources, gay men rented a duplex on the corner of Sunset and North Hoover called the Hoover Street Commune and began to experiment.

The Hoover Street Commune housed many of the white male leaders of the LAGLF. Don Kilhefner, Jon Platania, Rand Schrader, and Stanley Williams were all residents, and Morris Kight was "in and out on a daily basis." Lesbians were invited to commune events, but it was largely a male domain. An abundance of energy and marijuana transformed the commune into "a hothouse of emerging gay-centered consciousness" and planning.[19] Over communal dinners and highs, activists became disillusioned with the disorganized LAGLF. When a gay phone hotline was established, activists were hit with "a wave of telephone calls" reporting unaddressed discrimination. "Losing apartments, jobs, alcohol, drugs, I mean you name it," one recalled. It was time "to start thinking about gay *people*" and not just "a movement."[20] Many lesbians reached similar conclusions. Former LAGLF member Del Whan encouraged the Los Angeles Women's Center to begin posting housing and job opportunities specifically for lesbians.[21] In the summer of 1971, she founded the Gay Women's Center in Echo Park in hopes of providing additional social services to lesbians.[22] The shift toward social services was common among New Left activists. As the scholar Dan Berger put it, "the 1970s was a time when [social justice activists] felt they had to walk their talk."[23] In Los Angeles, organizations such as the Watts Labor Community

Action Committee and the East Los Angeles Community Union turned their attention to social service activism.[24] Gay liberation developed alongside these movements. While some have characterized this as a shift from "gay liberation" to "gay liberalism," many activists viewed the transformation as a mere *extension* of their politics.[25] "If we were going to succeed, we could not just continue with radical political work *per se*," an activist explained. "We needed, as Chairman Mao taught, to transform gay revolutionary consciousness into service to the people."[26] Providing housing was a logical first step.

Over the next two years, six liberation houses were established for low-income lesbians and gays. Activist and former HUD employee Jon Platania utilized his personal experiences to develop the program. Having earned a degree in urban studies, he felt a strong connection to President Lyndon Johnson's antipoverty and urban renewal initiatives. By 1969, Platania was engaging communities with urban renewal projects. When he was entrapped by Los Angeles Police Department vice officers in Griffith Park in 1970, he lost his job and became a passionate housing activist. Gregarious and popular, Platania raised funds from middle-class and wealthy gay men. He also signed leases for houses, since he was one of the few activists who had credit history.[27] Reliance on private fund-raising, however, produced a "very, very tight" budget that precluded staff salaries.[28] At the height of the program, six houses served the communities of Greater Los Angeles. They were mostly concentrated in the Hollywood and downtown areas but served a geographically diverse group of people. At one house in 1973, individuals came from Watts, downtown, and Northridge. Some came from elsewhere in southern California: one man made the journey from Lake Elsinore, another came from San Luis Obispo, and one woman came from Riverside. Outside California, new arrivals traveled from Moss Point, Mississippi; Portland, Oregon; Cincinnati, Ohio; Hope, Indiana; and Honolulu, Hawaii.[29] This wide geographical pull strengthens scholarly assertions that California was a gay magnet in the 1960s and 1970s.[30] As much as activists claimed to be inclusive, houses were overrepresented by white men. One 1975 report revealed that 69 percent of residents had been white; 62 percent were male. Most residents were young, and virtually all shared the unifying characteristic of poverty.[31] By 1972, just a year after the program had been initiated, activists claimed to have housed "over 200 gay women and men" but confessed that "scores of gay people of all ages [were] turned away due to a lack of space."[32]

By design, liberation houses offered both physical and emotional shelter. In an era of heated discourse surrounding the politics of "family," they demonstrated how family could be queerly constructed at the grass roots.[33] "It wasn't a homeless shelter," Platania maintained. "I wouldn't have managed a *homeless shelter* for love or money." Liberation houses, he insisted, were "run like a family."[34] Upon acceptance, residents chose new clothes and were taken to a county free clinic. A medical examination protected against the spread of sexually transmitted diseases within houses, and residents were given a contract that outlined rules and guidelines of the house. The program was not free, and rent was set at $2.50 per day, $15.00 per week, or $50.00 per month.[35] Most rents, however, were adjusted by income (in the end, most paid about a dollar per day.)[36] Residents were assigned chores to "share in the day-to-day maintenance and cleanliness of the house."[37] These "warm, supportive living environments" combated both emotional and economic poverty. Activists stressed that this approach would "offset the high incidence of hospitalization, imprisonment and suicide among the members of the gay community."[38] Within houses residents might find economic, emotional, and sexual opportunities that were desperately sought after. This connected the program with earlier homophile efforts, such as the Knights of the Clock, ONE, and the USM. As liberation houses expanded they blossomed into the GCSC, which would provide services from "womb to tomb."[39] Like others, activists soon realized that political alliances and public financing were central to their efforts.

Financing a Queer War on Poverty

While historians usually associate Johnson's War on Poverty with the 1960s, the ambitious initiative continued to evolve in the 1970s. The Economic Opportunity Act "poured millions into job training" and provided "much-needed services to impoverished communities" throughout the nation.[40] Although conservatives such as Ronald Reagan ridiculed the investment, it nurtured countless local social justice movements. Indeed, a central component of the act was the Community Action Program, which offered grants to a range of community organizations across the nation. In Las Vegas, black women took control of local antipoverty organizations, while Black Panthers in Oakland designed the first free-breakfast programs for children.[41] Lesbian and gay activists also sought support. Martin Meeker, Jonathan Bell, and Christina Handhardt have documented efforts to recast poverty in queer ways in mid-1960s San Francisco.[42] These were impressive but short-lived.

The political developments for lesbians and gays in Los Angeles, however, were not. In addition to funding through established programs, lesbians and gays made use of new social welfare opportunities, especially Community Development Block Grants (CDBGs) and Comprehensive Employment Training Act (CETA) programs to implement gay social services. Often cast as a decade of struggle against homophobic backlash, in Los Angeles the 1970s was a decade defined by dramatic state support for queers.

The GCSC resembled other social service organizations in Los Angeles, including the Watts Neighborhood Improvement Association and the East Chicano Community Union. In founding documents, organizers offered a structural explanation for homelessness and poverty, what Alice O'Connor has called "poverty knowledge."[43] Martin Meeker traced the origins of "queer poverty knowledge" in San Francisco, but Angelenos added even greater complexity.[44] Young gay migrants, they explained, fled to Los Angeles hoping to partake in a "fantasy that never existed." Arriving with "a lack of financing" and "few marketable job skills," many became trapped in a downward spiral of "disappointment, drugs, lack of funds," and "prostitution." More insidiously, "the lack of housing and employment among adult gay men and women" placed "them in positions of continuing economic insecurity." Taken together, these impediments created an "unending cycle between the streets, the jails, the clinics, the hospitals, and prisons." For many lesbians and gays, Los Angeles was "a nightmare of fear and self-depreciation."[45] To rectify the situation, activists argued, the state needed to fund gay activists. Such aid was by no means a given, but the 1974 election of Ed Edelman to the Los Angeles County Board of Supervisors proved to be a game changer. While Timothy Stewart-Winter found that "the path to lesbian and gay political power led through city hall" in Chicago, in Los Angeles it was the county that offered the breakthroughs.[46]

Aides and supporters believed Edelman to be "a new type of Democrat."[47] Part of a cohort that included Jerry Brown, Alan Cranston, and Tom Bradley, Edelman constructed his liberalism in what Jonathan Bell described as the "crucible" of California's "diverse mosaic."[48] Bridging Great Society liberalism with the New Left, Edelman touted his support for union rights and affordable housing while he criticizing the Vietnam War and defending personal privacy rights. In populist rhetoric, he promised to represent marginalized "underdogs, outsiders, [and] neighborhoods" and lambasted "downtown interests," including "land owners, developers, oil companies," and "big businesses," that refused "to open up government to the people." His "philosophy of inclusion" promised "equal rights in housing, education, and employment to all persons, regardless of age, sex, religion, race, or sexual orientation."[49] During the 1974 election, opponents tied Edelman to the gay community. To the surprise of many, he welcomed the connection and condemned "gay-baiting" as "sad and unfortunate." Activists rightly saw opportunity in his election. "The County's five supervisors wield sultanic [sic] power," an observer in The Advocate noted. "Ranging from hundreds of appointments to appropriations totaling $2.6 billion, how such funds are spent sets policy."[50] After his victory, Edelman did not disappoint. He quickly hired David Glascock as his personal gay liaison in order to "raise the level of consciousness in County Government to the needs of all, including gay people."[51] This partnership shaped and financed gay activism. As a GCSC insider, Glascock fielded constituent mail, prepared weekly briefings, and located funding opportunities for GCSC programs.[52] His position gave lesbians and gays an important ally in the halls of power. In one note to Glascock, Kilhefner confided, "'Praise the Lord' that you are where you are and doing what you do. We love you."[53] That love was well deserved.

Edelman was elected at a fortuitous moment. The county had always been more powerful than the city, but two new federal programs enhanced its clout.[54] Largely ignored by historians, CETA programs offered radical possibilities to grassroots activists. Signed into law by Richard Nixon in 1973, CETA provided grants to community service organizations and created thousands of new jobs. Nixon thought that it would "consolidate the many manpower programs that had been started during the Kennedy and Johnson administrations," but CETA actually expanded those programs.[55] For African Americans and Chicanos, one scholar has argued, it was the "most significant federal jobs program in the 1970s."[56] Since grants were awarded at the local level, county supervisors held enormous power. Once aware of the program, activists began spreading the word "that the County [was] funding organizations that [were] helping poor people."[57] Lesbians and gays joined a diverse mosaic seeking funding including the Greater Los Angeles Community Action Agency, which emerged from the ashes of the Economic and Youth Opportunities Agency and empowered working-class African, Mexican, and Jewish communities.[58] Thanks in part to Glascock and Edelman, by the summer of 1976 over $300,000 in CETA funds were flowing annually to the GCSC. These provided salaries, funded social programs, and linked gay rights with racial minorities. The funds also created jobs with the city such as Mayor Tom Bradley's gay liaison, which dramatically expanded possibilities for gay activists.[59]

The Housing and Community Development Act of 1974 also offered prospects through CDBG programs. A gift of President Gerald Ford, CDBGs were admired by liberals and conservatives alike. The former applauded urban investment, while the latter celebrated local community control (as well as the inclusion of private developers within the program). CDBG allocations could be made for public infrastructure, housing, administrative planning, public services, economic development, and property acquisitions. Those categories were deliberately vague in order to maximize local control. Beginning in 1975, GCSC organizers submitted grant proposals to the county on a regular basis. "Whenever we got requests for proposals we applied," an activist remembered. "Nobody else [in the country] was doing that, but *our* government was supporting gays." Grant writing could be unpredictable and cumbersome, especially since most "didn't know anything about writing proposals."[60] In truth, some had experience: Kilhefner had written grants as a graduate student, and Jon Platania had done so while at HUD.

In grant applications, activists stressed a grassroots approach to urban renewal. Applying to one CDBG program, they stressed that since "no other public or private agency in Los Angeles County [was] providing" services to low-income lesbians and gays, the GCSC could address a complicated problem. "By offsetting the high incidence of hospitalization, imprisonment, and suicide among the members of the gay community," the GCSC promised to "save the general public large sums of public funds." Queer housing programs, in other words, made "a direct impact on the general welfare" of all.[61] Of course, reliance on public funds carried risks. In the summer of 1976 funding was curtailed countywide, which placed GCSC programs in jeopardy. Here the relationship with Edelman paid great dividends. Activists reached out to Glascock, who convinced Edelman to intervene. As a county supervisor, he could bestow discretionary funds to organizations at will; in this instance he sent the GCSC $40,000.[62] He justified these awards as necessary, since many gay constituents lived in his district, but also believed that the GCSC was a strong partner in the fight against homelessness. Within a few years, CDBG funds allowed the GCSC to "grow from a dream housed in a few funky rooms on Wilshire Boulevard into an important community agency providing services." In a letter to Edelman, activists admitted that "the continuing support which we have received from you has played a critical role in [our] development. Several important programs are now closely connected with that of County government [and] we are deeply appreciative for the ray of sunshine which you have become for our community."[63]

This funding relationship transformed gay politics. As a well-respected and powerful Democrat, Edelman could pressure political allies and did so often. This proved especially necessary when it came to Councilwoman Peggy Stevenson and Mayor Tom Bradley. Both supported the GCSC but were tepid endorsers of "gay rights." When a liberation house opened in Stevenson's district, some neighbors complained. The councilwoman suggested that gays ought to "solicit [neighborhood] support" before they move in. Activists took her response to Edelman, who urged Stevenson to support "the import work of the [GCSC]" and encouraged her to reverse her decision. She did.[64] It was a similar story when it came to Mayor Bradley. When activists applied for funds under the Blue Ribbon Revitalize Hollywood Program, they promised to "do our part in making this City a better place to live for all of its citizens" and requested $300,000 to combat "blight" and contribute to the "beautification of the neighborhood."[65] After three months of silence, activists complained. "The Plan makes sense to us as we work in Hollywood," they argued. "We see daily deterioration of the community and could be the pioneering group to make the plan work."[66] Glascock suggested that Edelman "call [Mayor] Bradley and indicate how important it is to respond to the needs of gay citizens" because "he needs a gentle push."[67] What exactly Edelman said to Bradley is unknown, but the GCSC's application soon received approval. Years later, an aide described Edelman as having a special ability to "bring Mayor Bradley to a place of support" regarding gay issues.[68] For activists, having a powerful county supervisor as an ally was a plus.

With surprising speed, the GCSC became a politically powerful and publicly funded social services agency in Los Angeles. While funds were secured from other sources as well, Los Angeles County remained the most consistent and steadfast benefactor. By 1976, Glascock calculated that over $600,000 had found its way to the GCSC, with more grants outstanding.[69] During one funding cycle, Edelman dipped into his discretionary budget three times: to secure $75,000 for the GCSC Venereal Disease Treatment and Education Program; to provide $10,000 for the Prisoner, Probation, and Parole Program; and $25,000 for emergency housing programs.[70] Kilhefner estimated that the GCSC took in "four million dollars [in County funds] over the whole period." As is often the case, local success enabled greater rewards. The largest was a three-year National Institute for Alcohol and Alcohol Abuse grant for $1 million. While activists were just as dedicated in other cities, Angelenos accessed state resources in unprecedented ways. Within the social mosaic, gay rights were rarely funded equally, but it was significant that lesbians and gays were now a part of the welfare state. "They thought they could divide up the pie anyway they wanted to," Kilhefner bragged, "but we forced them to allocate some of that money to us."[71] This financial reliance helped embed gay rights firmly within the statewide and national Democratic Party in heretofore underappreciated ways.

Gay Politics and Public Policy in the Carter Era

By the mid-1970s, the most influential gay political organization in Los Angeles was the Stonewall Democratic Club (SDC). Through the SDC, activists encouraged Democratic politics to change and diversify in California. With the election of Jimmy Carter in 1976, they also hoped to impact federal policy with an ambitious gay rights plank outlining necessary changes to eradicate sexual discrimination and improve economic opportunities nationwide. While the born-again Carter appeared culturally conservative, historians have documented how feminists made gains within his administration.[72] So too, lesbians and gays impacted the direction of Carter's social agenda and helped reveal cracks in the straight state. Ironically, they achieved success as liberals continued to develop punitive policies directed against other social minorities in the nation.

The success of GCSC programs won immediate political allies. As early as 1973, *Los Angeles Times* columnist Art Seidenbaum praised the organization and its activists. "My visit to the Gay Community Services Center," he wrote, "persuades me that dignity is being fostered there." The GCSC addressed "needs that have not been met heretofore in this city" and earned "respect from the larger community because it helped spread human understanding rather than antagonism." A representative of the Sons of Watts Assistance and Rehabilitation Project commended the "untiring efforts" to "provide vital services to persons in need, such as counseling, job referrals, [parole] applications, and emergency housing." Noting that many gay residents of Watts were in need of those services, he wished the GCSC "much success" and encouraged organizers to "hang in there!" The Southern California Prison Coalition supported the attention on gay prisoners and parolees. "There are all too few organizations operating in our society today to help ex-convicts adjust to living again in the community," a representative wrote. The GCSC instituted "constructive efforts to help our most disadvantaged citizens who need so much support. . . . You can be assured that you have our support." Los Angeles city attorney Burt Pines believed that the GCSC offered a "chance" for those who "otherwise had none," making it "vitally important to the city." A representatives of the East-Los Chicano Education Training and Research Organization admired the "refreshing and innovative . . . step in the right direction," and a black activist in Watts was "encouraged to see the progress [the GCSC] has made in providing services to a previously neglected segments of our population, specifically black gays and females." The Asian Women's Center was impressed by attention to women's issues and the "diversity of [GCSC] programs."[73] These letters admired gay activists and also acknowledged queer needs within their own communities. The GCSC lifted all boats.

Established in 1975, the SDC sought to capitalize on these political partnerships. The very name of the organization implied its left-liberal orientation. "Stonewall" identified the SDC with gay liberation and the New Left, while "Democratic" signaled its willingness to work within the liberal establishment. *The Advocate* took note of this in a cartoon: during an SDC meeting, a young demonstrator held signs reading "2-4-6-8, Register as Democrate [*sic*]," and Morris Kight kindly explained, "Now that we're establishment, dear brother, we're just not sure we'll be picketing with signs anymore."[74] Overall, the SDC embraced more a shift in strategy, not ideology. "In recognition of a new awareness within the Democratic Party" to "fully and equally represent Gay People," founders labored to "make the Democratic Party responsive to and responsible for the needs of *all* people." The SDC prioritized the low-income populace, emphasizing "welfare rights" and the empowerment of "single and lower income persons."[75] In doing so it joined other grassroots Democratic clubs in California in order to push liberalism leftward.

The 1975 gay rights plank outlined how this could be done. An all-out indictment of the "straight state," it identified structural forms of discrimination and offered detailed remedies. Since the tax system "victimized single persons and same-gender couples," it ought not to use sexuality as criteria. Moreover, Congress needed to draft "legislation to enable persons covered by Social Security and all federal pension programs to designate whomever they so choose to receive benefits." Importantly, the language insisted on plural possibilities and did not clearly define what gay families would consist of. In demanding the right to choose *whomever* they wanted as beneficiaries, activists hinted at multiple familial possibilities. They also claimed solidarity with women's liberation, calling for the immediate passage of the Equal Rights Amendment (ERA). When it came to housing, activists specifically targeted HUD and FHA policies and demanded changes to encourage "all persons to choose housing and living arrangements in accordance with their own preferences." This necessitated ending "discrimination against gay people in public housing projects, federally guaranteed housing loans, and in all other areas under HUD's jurisdiction."[76] While they did not explicitly call for the redefinition of family, implicitly they did. How else could policies be changed? Reforms in HUD, the tax system, and immigration policy logically implied that sexuality and family not be tied to citizenship or welfare rights.

Alongside gay political clubs in the Bay Area, the SDC helped to incorporate gay rights into the California Democratic Party swiftly. Edelman endorsed the gay rights plank without reservation, and many left-leaning Democrats voiced support as well. These included Sabrina Schiller and Tom Hayden, both of whom pledged to author legislation to enact the plank.[77] If Democrats rejected gay rights, the SDC attacked. When Joe Montoya ran for a California Senate seat and refused to endorse the plank, activists informed Democratic leaders that he was "*not*, to use the word loosely, favorable to our cause" and threatened to support his opponent.[78] Beyond Los Angeles, activists won statewide approval. Jonathan Bell argued that the California Democratic Council helped push liberalism leftward in the 1950s and 1960s.[79] Progressive Democrats such as Alan Cranston, Phil Burton, and Jerry Brown succeeded thanks to council endorsements and support. In the 1970s the SDC continued this legacy. At the 1975 California Democratic Convention in San Jose, Morris Kight and David Glascock served as delegates.[80] On the evening of November 17 they introduced the gay rights plank, which was approved without debate. "The Democratic Party in California," the California Democratic Convention announced, "now affirms the right of all persons to define and express their own sexuality. . . . We pledge an end to all social, economic, legal and psychological oppression of gay people."[81] Activists had indeed "taken gay and lesbian issues from the streets to the halls of government."[82] The *Los Angeles Times* marveled at the "growing respectability of the gay rights movement in Democratic political circles."[83] While many memories of 1970s California highlight the Briggs Initiative and homophobic backlash, below the surface a political transformation had unfolded. At the national level, change could also be detected.

In 1976 the SDC plank was sent to all Democratic presidential contenders, including Hubert Humphrey, Jesse Jackson, Sargent Shriver, Birch Bayh, Fred Harris, and Jimmy Carter.[84] For many liberals, Carter's triumph proved confusing. The Democratic standard-bearer was often a sphinx. He disappointed progressives on many fronts and, according to some, implemented economic policies that exacerbated an "age of inequality."[85] At the same time, Carter expanded CETA and named avowed leftists (including many feminists) to key positions of power. The former governor of Georgia was an evangelical Christian who read his Bible nightly but, as Randall Balmer suggested, was cut from progressive evangelical cloth.[86] While Carter held moral anxieties regarding homosexuality, he thought that poverty and homelessness were greater sins. During the 1976 Democratic primary in California, he actively courted lesbian and gay voters. During one Edelman fund-raiser for Carter, SDC leaders pressed him on sexual discrimination in housing, immigration, military policy, and civilian contract employment. Carter pledged to end discrimination in all areas except military policy.[87] Pleased, some members rallied around the Georgian and founded Gays for Carter.[88] When Carter condemned racist housing and employment practices in a California speech, they wrote to clarify that this "also extended to sexual minorities." A Carter aide replied that the candidate was "opposed to discrimination in all forms, including discrimination because of sexual preference."[89] Yet in another letter, an aide confessed that "Governor Carter is not entirely comfortable with the issue of homosexuality."[90] Carter could endorse nondiscrimination but not gay pride. The breakthroughs that would unfold during the Carter administration would therefore need to be surreptitious.

This was certainly the case when it came to housing policy. Although largely overlooked by historians, in May 1977 HUD officials radically rewrote the definition of family. Shortly after Carter's election, the SDC sent copies of the gay rights plank to HUD and urged a new policy to allow "all persons to choose housing and living arrangements in accordance with their own preferences."[91] It is unclear how impactful this action was, but it likely found a favorable audience with HUD secretary Patricia Roberts Harris. A graduate of Howard University, she gained stature in the Kennedy and Johnson administrations as a civil rights and Democratic Party organizer.[92] A liberal, Harris was also a vocal supporter of the New Left, especially women's liberation and Black Power. Under her leadership, HUD moved in a decidedly feminist direction.[93] Indeed, televangelist Pat Robertson considered her an "avowed enemy" of conservatives after she labeled the Moral Majority "dangerous, intolerant, and polarizing."[94] Considering the heated cultural atmosphere of the mid-1970s, the policy change was subjectively ingenuous. "Any stable family relationship," HUD spokesman Tom Bacon explained, was now eligible to apply for housing subsidies. He did not mention gays, nor did he define "stability." When reporters asked if gay activists influenced the decision, he insisted that "the change was not made in response to pressure from any group." HUD was not "trying to get a particular group in. We are simply trying to expand the eligibility of low-income housing for *all* families."[95] Regardless, what HUD administrators decided to do was radical: they had in effect *destabilized* any definition of family. Theoretically, a *stable* queer family might be eligible for subsidies, while an *unstable* heterosexual one might not be. Stability was in the eye of the beholder. According to HUD, family was not beholden to marital and biological constraints. Historians have argued that the New Right and the Moral Majority coalesced around "attacks on the family" in the 1970s.[96] The 1977 HUD decision allows us to better understand the context of those fears.

The press reported the policy change as an issue of gay rights. A *New York Times* editorial declared that "the government [was] opening public housing to homosexual couples."[97] At a press conference, reporters asked President Carter if homosexuals could be families. Homosexuals did not form "normal interrelationships," he replied, but "I don't see homosexuals as a threat to the family either."[98] Across the nation, lesbians and gays expressed excitement and confusion. One woman celebrated but wondered "what does a 'stable family relationship' mean?" If "each public-housing authority" could "determine whether a couple fits the new description," then the law was "endlessly vague," she worried. *The Advocate* reported that HUD had finally decided that "gay people need roofs over their heads, too." Opponents recognized the potential of the new policy as well. In Congress, HUD's budget was threatened when two representatives proposed an amendment that barred lesbians and gays from subsidies. This caused headaches and a Democratic rumble in the Senate. As it reviewed the House amendment, "the usually stolid Appropriations Committee became a forum on gay rights." Two Democratic senators supported the amendment and argued that since "there is a waiting list for public housing . . . traditional wife-husband stable family relationships should have preference." Yet, two Democrats fought back, opposing the amendment on constitutional grounds. "Such language would put Congress on record favoring discrimination," they stressed. "We don't want to get caught up in some temporary hysteria and start mashing people's constitutional rights all over the place." The antigay language was removed; in its place, lawmakers emphasized that "eligibility would be determined" by local authorities on a case-by-case basis. This allowed Congress to approve the appropriations bill "without a whisper of gay rights" but did nothing to alter the nature of HUD's policy change.[99] Historians have not been terribly kind to Carter's urban policy, yet the 1977 HUD policy change was significant and opened housing to previously excluded people.[100] The victory did not belong to Angelenos alone but was certainly assisted by them, as was the White House Conference on American Families, which fittingly concluded in Los Angeles.

When Carter ran for president in 1976, he promised to bring Americans together for a conference about "the family." By 1977, he began speaking of "families" in order to "recognize the pluralism of family life in America."[101] His insistence on *pluralism*, like HUD's insistence on *stability*, allowed for the possibility of queer inclusion without deliberately saying so. Conference planners organized three regional meetings in Baltimore, Minneapolis, and Los Angeles. As the conference neared, the politics of family became volatile. Nevada Republican senator Paul Laxalt introduced the Family Protection Act in 1979 that, among other things, would have "banned federal support for any form of gay rights."[102] While the measure failed to win congressional support, it evidenced the growing power of the Moral Majority. The White House Conference on American Families did not. In Baltimore, the conference descended into a fierce struggle. Conservatives accused Carter of building "the worst record for family issues for any president in history."[103] Conference attendees, however, voted to endorse the ratification of the ERA and offered support for gay rights.[104] Antifeminist Phyllis Schlafly decried the results and stormed out. In Minneapolis, conservatives fought back and voted to "exclude homosexuals in the definition of family."[105] The conference was now ideologically confused. Los Angeles settled the debate. There, attendees voted to approve the ERA and "outlaw housing laws that would discriminate based on sexual preference" and reversed the exclusion of lesbians and gays from the definition of family.[106] Often a quiet supporter, Carter spoke more boldly after the conference. Families, he explained to reporters, were "networks of relationships, rooted not in blood but on shared experiences, shared joys and sorrows, and most of all, a shared love that crosses vast distances." He warned Americans against conservative fantasies. "Americans often feel nostalgic," he counseled, "about a past that seems to be simpler and sometimes seems to be better. We can learn from the past, but we must not limit our vision of what a good family *is* just to what a family *was*."[107] Through liberation houses, the GCSC, and the SDC, lesbian and gay Angelenos had made the same argument. HUD and the White House Conference on American Families represented but two breakthroughs in the Carter era. Others, such as the decision to remove homosexuality from the list of mental illnesses in 1979, were equally significant.

Ironically, as liberal policy makers moved in more progressive directions for lesbians and gays in the 1970s, punitive measures targeting racial minorities were enacted with more vigor, severely limiting the possibilities of reform. Elizabeth Hinton and Julilly Kohler-Hausmann have both detailed how liberal policy makers came to embrace draconian "law and order" policies that resulted in the mass incarceration of racial minorities. Even in Los Angeles, Mayor Tom Bradley courted the law and order vote at the expense of traditional economic liberal orthodoxy.[108] Thus, while it would be tempting to view the growing political power of lesbians and gays within a liberal progression narrative, in reality liberalism was suffering from very uneven development in the 1970s. That is an important caveat to this story. So long as they coexisted alongside policies limiting the socioeconomic possibilities of racial minorities, liberal gay achievements would benefit whites above all others. So long as the liberal pathology of the black family remained unchallenged, the growth of new queer families would be stunted. In other words, the important reforms detailed in this essay occurred in a liberal house that had already begun the process—unconsciously or not—of excluding many from the premises. As is so often the case in American history, progressive breakthroughs were tempered by new reactionary limits.

Still, the work of lesbian and gay activists in the 1970s began an important process of demolishing the straight state. Through housing, social service, and political activism, lesbian and gay activists in Los Angeles helped destabilize heteronormative welfare policies that were foundational to breadwinner liberalism. Working through established political channels, they helped remold liberal policies in more inclusive ways and at the very moment when religious conservatives were attacking them. Above all else, they showed that a strong welfare system was a necessary and vital partner in the quest to create a queerer world. In the tumultuous political environment of the present, this is a lesson worth remembering.

CHAPTER 3

Making Sexual Citizens

LGBT Politics, Health Care, and the State in the 1970s

Jonathan Bell

"One of the original precepts of the gay/lesbian civil rights struggle was that we want to get the government out of our lives," wrote National Gay and Lesbian Task Force lobbyist Jeffrey Levi in April 1986. "AIDS has transformed that and certainly made our relationship with the government more complicated. We have gone from asking the government to stay out of our lives to demanding that it step in and help save our lives. That requires a very different political strategy."[1] The notion that the American state in all its forms had historically been inimical to the interests of sexual minorities was widely shared across a range of activist networks with diverse political outlooks, uniting establishment Washington lobbyists such as Levi with radical gay liberationists. One libertarian radical pamphlet from 1979 argued that there was no place for radical queer politics in "the neat, ordered world of social democracy and central planning, where everything distinctive is blended in the great egalitarian Mixmaster of the State apparatus." In this worldview, attacks on sexual minorities, such as the attempt in California in 1978 to ban gay teachers and their supporters from the profession, highlighted that "the real enemy of the gay community, and of all minorities everywhere—State Power—had finally come out of the closet."[2] On the Left too, international solidarity politics bred an inherent hostility to state power as actually practiced in many parts of the world, as did leftist campaigns against efforts to persecute LGBT people at home.[3]

It was hardly surprising that a view of the American state as hostile to sexual dissidence had gained widespread traction by the end of the 1970s.

As Margot Canaday and others have shown, most state action in relation to LGBT people had historically been an exercise of police power, regulating their private lives, denying access to public benefits available to heteronormative citizens, casting them as illegitimate and medically unfit in federal immigration policy, and forcing them to live their lives in fear of arrest and persecution in every aspect of their lives.[4] The state at all levels in the twentieth century paid far more attention to defining and enforcing categories of deserving and undeserving, normative and deviant, in policy and law than it did to playing a positive role in the lives of all citizens. Yet the period from the late 1960s to the end of the 1970s also marks a time when LGBT activists became involved in local and national party politics for the first time. At the local level, an increasing interest in service delivery for LGBT clients directed activists building a network of support services to look to governments for some financial and political backing. Local and state governments in turn began to regulate LGBT health clinics and other social projects, and those using the services often fell back on government welfare programs such as Medicaid. At the national level, new organizations such as the Gay Activists Alliance (GAA) and the National Gay Task Force (NGTF) sought to enter and influence the national political scene, mostly in the Democratic Party and the Jimmy Carter administration, in order to challenge the "straight state" and integrate sexual minorities into the realm of legitimized citizenship. These processes of political mobilization and legitimation involved more than a demand to be free of the punitive force of state power. The intersections between LGBT activism and the levers of governance in the 1970s reveal the ways in which different political strategies could reify or erase socioeconomic and class disparities within the discrete elements of the loose coalition of lesbians, gay men, trans* people, and bisexuals. A functioning state-supported clinic could be the difference between a lesbian receiving the health care she needed or not. Conversely, a national lobbying strategy that privileged civil rights issues designed to remove LGBT people from government oversight often erased class, racial, and gender contexts of queer lives from public debate.

In this essay I contrast local activist politics predicated on health, welfare, and social service advocacy with a national gay rights politics increasingly in harmony with a Democratic Party gradually shedding a vestigial interest in social inequality. A focus on the local allows us to see the close relationship between sexuality and the state that highlighted questions of poverty, inequality, and race and gender privilege as central features of the American social contract in the 1970s. By then shifting focus to national gay organizing politics from the mid to late 1970s, we see how activists emphasized policy demands that downplayed or even erased these questions in favor of issues of individual rights that would play well with a post–Great Society liberal political worldview. While not all of those involved in GAA and NGTF lobbying were middle-class white cisgender males, it was that archetype that would shape much of the relationship between LGBT advocacy and national-level politics by the end of the decade. Understanding this in the context of the socioeconomic division within LGBT politics in local communities allows us to conceptualize more completely the changing dynamics of American liberalism on the eve of the Ronald Reagan era as well as explain the unpreparedness of LGBT national activism to appreciate the multiple levels on which the AIDS crisis operated in the 1980s. Local-level health activism in the 1970s created sexual subjects due to the varied health needs of the different sexual minority communities, whereas national gay rights politics tried to subsume sexual identity behind a respectable face of normative citizenship in which sexuality was essentially irrelevant.[5]

In making these arguments, I appreciate the important scholarship that emphasizes the limited options open to gay rights activists at a time when mainstream politics was only beginning to recognize, in very limited ways, the legitimacy of sexual minorities as rights-bearing subjects. Cities with increasingly organized and vocal queer networks were much better equipped to offer local social services reflective of a socially diverse population and a social democratic view of health and welfare politics than were activists seeking to operate at a national level. As Claire Bond Potter and others have shown, NGTF operatives seeking to gain access to the Carter White House needed to portray themselves as political insiders with uncontroversial, reasonable demands that would sit comfortably with the moral and economic conservatism of the administration. Issues of federal employment discrimination and immigration reform were feasible, incremental goals that could give activists traction at the federal level in ways that policy demands related to class and racial inequality could not.[6] And casting LGBT identity as a civil rights matter, in which complex gendered and racial differences were smoothed out to create a simplified narrative for wider political consumption, allowed activists to maintain and reframe their battles for recognition as the heady furor of the New Left and gay liberation years faded away.[7] The success of Anita Bryant's Save Our Children campaign in Miami and the wave of anti-LGBT legislative and ballot initiative efforts across the United States in the late 1970s from California to Oklahoma to Texas demonstrated clearly the obstacles that gay activists faced in their efforts to secure political citizenship. LGBT Americans continued to face significant persecution by the state at the same time that they were starting to gain access to its protections and resources in limited ways, so it is unsurprising that many chose a political strategy that would apply pressure at the points where the state would be most likely to yield.[8]

Yet if we place the national strategy of the NGTF in the 1970s alongside the local realities of sexual minorities in serious need of social services, it becomes clear that the emerging cautious relationship between elite gay activists and Carter Democrats was about more than mere strategic calculation. Activists entered into dialogue with national politics in the mid-1970s using a language of self-empowerment and individualism that dovetailed neatly with a liberal political class keen to turn their backs on antipoverty politics of the 1960s and break the association of Democratic Party politics with welfare dependency. Had NGTF activists attempted to reflect the lived realities of the range of LGBT populations in communities across the country in their national political strategy, they would have been forced to make the link between sexual dissidence and the ramshackle and unstable social safety net that shaped so many queer people's experience as sexual beings. The white middle-class leaders of the national campaign for LGBT rights rejected the narrative of "punks, bulldaggers, and welfare queens" that lay beneath the rights agenda they articulated, just as they calculated that the Carter administration and the national Democratic Party would reject it. The dynamics of national activism were as much ideological as strategic and form part of a wider story of the delegitimizing of social equality politics in the United States that began well before the Reagan era and long outlasted it.

Making Welfare Queens: Local Health Politics in the 1960s and 1970s

By the end of the 1960s, San Francisco had established itself as home to a wide variety of activists and social service organizations devoted to queer communities. Groups such as the Mattachine Society, the Society for Individual Rights (SIR), the Committee on Religion and the Homosexual, and the Tavern Guild formed a network of support for the ever-growing number of LGBT people settling in the City by the Bay.[9] To a greater or lesser degree, all of these organizations saw themselves as service providers for minority populations and were deeply embedded in antipoverty politics of the Great Society. SIR operated a community center, a twenty-four-hour telephone service, and a referral service for housing, legal aid, employment, and medical assistance.[10] Its thirteen board committees included a community services committee "in charge of health problems and related projects such as VD [venereal disease] prevention and cure, psychological and psychiatric referrals, the conducting of related sociological, sexualogical, psychological surveys" and "community service projects such as blood donating, hospital visiting, money raising campaigns for worthwhile charities," a remit that required SIR activists to cast sexual minorities not simply as individuals but also as part of a collective with specific socioeconomic needs.[11] Although the title of the group and the central message of its founding statement of purpose stressed the need for society "to give heed to the needs and aspirations of the individual," SIR also called for "the creation of a responsible social fabric that will contain all aspects of a worthwhile, open, unharrassed life for the self-respecting homosexual."[12]

The availability of federal Great Society antipoverty funding through local offices of the Office of Economic Opportunity gave activists in SIR and other queer organizations the material they needed to define a "responsible social fabric." A coalition of individuals from SIR, Mattachine, Daughters of Bilitis, the Glide Memorial Church, and the Committee on Religion and the Homosexual formed the Central City Citizens Council (CCCC) in late 1965 in order to lobby the city's Economic Opportunity Council (EOC) to designate the Tenderloin—a deprived neighborhood home to transient queer youths and transgender people—as a target area for Great Society funding.[13] Activists toured the streets and alleyways of the area by day and by night before writing reports and policy proposals to justify expanding the remit of the city's antipoverty effort into the queerest of neighborhoods. These reports made explicit the connection between sexual dissidence and economic marginalization in the Tenderloin and also articulated class and other social divisions bisecting queer communities that necessitated government action. "Within the Tenderloin area of downtown San Francisco a fairly large group of troubled and often transient youth and single young adults between the ages of 12 and 25 years reside," stated a CCCC paper titled "The White Ghetto." "These persons, most of whom are men, form a sub-culture that is generally ignored or condemned by middle-class oriented society." The report painted in lurid detail the activists' portrayal of the lives of hustlers, junkies, and homeless kids who stalked the area's streets, making the case for government funding of a range of social services, including a health clinic, a halfway house, a legal aid center, and paid social workers. The authors argued that "there is *no* agency existing in San Francisco at this time which is prepared to work with the Tenderloin youth on the basis of his whole person. The fact that no realistic work is being done with the young people of this area is something we will be paying for heavily for years to come."[14]

In making their plea for state sponsorship on these terms, white middle-class gay activists mirrored the language and political worldview of the Great Society bureaucrats in their association of poverty with delinquency and their inattention to hierarchies of race and gender. In a funding proposal submitted to the EOC by the San Francisco Mattachine Society, the Tenderloin was described as "truly a human ash heap which spawns every sort of sexual expression, but more sadly, it has become a cancerous sore which, if not recognized and treated, will not remain contained—it will spread throughout the metropolitan area and influence other young men and women." The authors reported an "utter lack of intellectual and spiritual development, responsible and productive citizenship and social and mental health [that] is shockingly apparent everywhere." In seeking to use EOC funds to enable two Mattachine staff members to work in the neighborhood every evening, Mattachine activists emphasized the role of Great Society programs as arbiters of social behavior and architects of normative social identity. The Mattachine program would "seek to eliminate preoccupation with sex to the detriment of its more proper role in the total personality, thereby freeing the individual to pursue other attributes necessary for growth and development into full adulthood: Education, earning a living, creativity, cultural and social values, etc. This would free those 'hung up' on their sexuality to help themselves in other ways—including unselfish service to others."[15] At no point did the report or indeed any of the documentation produced under the auspices of Mattachine, SIR, or the CCCC acknowledge the significant transgender population in the Tenderloin by name, nor did they highlight simple poverty and inequality as central factors driving social dislocation in American cities. Activists tailored their portrayal of the marginalized poor to the narrative of social improvement and integration into normative society, which they thought agencies of the state would understand and support.

At the same time, however, the interplay between the Great Society and grassroots gay activism encouraged these self-appointed community leaders to engage with the diversity of LGBT lives, however crudely. A focus on social service activism brought grassroots queer politics into negotiation with the state, a development most evident in San Francisco, where a vibrant LGBT movement grew in tandem with an increasingly sympathetic city government. By the mid-1970s the city's health department had established the Gay Health Project, funded by a one-year federal government grant, that provided sexual health and wider health services to sexual minorities, including information and referrals on mental health, women's clinics, and social service agencies as well as treatment for sexually transmitted infections (STIs).[16] The massive increase in STIs in the city in the wake of the sexual revolution of the late 1960s encouraged the San Francisco Department of Public Health to recalibrate public policy to recognize the diverse social mosaic of the population, recognizing "that the Gay community is not being reached by many of the traditional approaches to health care."[17] San Francisco was not alone in this respect. In the late 1970s, the New York State Department of Health Education Unit collaborated with the Gay Men's Health Project to fund and produce a booklet, *Gay Men and STDs*, a six-page description of the different STIs that could result from same-sex activity along with advice for seeking treatment, adding that "every major city in New York State has free, confidential health clinics, staffed by professional people who don't care about your sexual preferences. They just want you and your partner to stay healthy."[18] In parts of the country amenable to positive state interaction with sexual minorities, the creation of gay people as political subjects because of their health needs made possible a broader conception of the state's role in the rights revolutions than the antigovernment animus of many liberationists had suggested.

Nowhere was this fact more obvious during the 1970s than in the rapid expansion of a nationwide network of sexual health clinics and gay community centers. These clinics depended on a mixture of private donations, the free labor of volunteers, and some state funding to provide services for LGBT people. Examples included the Los Angeles Gay Community Services Center, established in 1971, and the FAN Free Clinic in Richmond, Virginia, established in 1970 to "provide health care and health information in a way that is considerate of the needs of people who have difficulty obtaining their health care from other facilities," that received "significant support thru contracts with the City of Richmond, the Virginia Department of Health, and the United Way of Greater Richmond."[19] Volunteer health activists discovered as the decade progressed that demand for their services rapidly outgrew the ramshackle walk-in clinics and community centers they had set up and that injections of public funding were necessary to maintain them. The Fenway Community Health Center in Boston, for example, started life in

1971 as a project of leftist antipoverty activists but by the end of the decade had become a free-standing medical facility with sixty staff, licensed by the Massachusetts Department of Public Health. What began as a single Gay Health Night at the clinic on Wednesdays soon grew into the full-fledged Gay Health Collective of over fifty self-identified queer staff, who in addition to providing a range of sexual health services also applied for grants from both public and private sources in order to expand its remit. In making a bid to fund an outreach education program in 1977, the collective stressed its mission to "provide quality health care at low cost" and "that health care is a right, not a privilege," and argued that developing health programs around sexual minorities raised awareness of the diversity of LGBT populations both to LGBT people themselves and to the wider society, especially health care providers.[20] The debate over how to promote the mainstreaming of sexual minorities in society took place at the local level in tandem with economic questions of access to health services.

In Greenwich Village, New York, a nonprofit collective called Gay Is Health Inc., founded by a network of people who met through the city's Gay Men's Health Project, set up an STI treatment center in 1980 "with substantial support from the Department of Health of New York City" and also put together a bid to the Borough of Manhattan for over a quarter of a million dollars for "the Christopher Street Multiservices Center." The center would offer anyone "gay or straight, with a community or social service need," a free referral "to the organizations that have resources to deal with their particular need(s)." The authors of the grant proposal were careful to set out how the emergence of professional associations of LGBT businesses and community leaders meant that in the "1970s, the gay movement has moved away from the radical mood of the 1960s," but in essence the rationale for the new community center strongly echoed that of the Tenderloin project in 1960s San Francisco over a decade earlier. "In order to understand the multiservices center's impact on both gay and straight communities," they argued, after painting a lurid picture of a local demimonde of drug dealing and social dislocation, "it is important to recall that the nature of gay oppression is to cause alienation and a sense of being outcast." Many sexual dissidents heading to Christopher Street "still conceal their sexual preference from employers and families and lack any resources to resolve legal, health, emotional, alcohol or drug-related problems should they exist." Creating social service structures, it was argued, would help clean up neighborhoods while at the same time integrating sexual minorities into mainstream society.[21]

The evident relationship between local health activism and antipoverty politics created an arena in which sexual and socioeconomic inequalities intersected, exposing the variety of lived experiences concealed beneath the LGBT umbrella. Many health care activists noted the double bind affecting many sexual minorities: many health care providers were ignorant of their health needs and were often deeply prejudiced, but in any event many LGBT people were on the economic margins of society and were also unable to access the heteronormative welfare state, leaving them without access to quality care. The president of the Women's Alternative Health Services Inc. in San Francisco noted that "members of two devalued minorities—women and gays—lesbians are facing serious problems getting quality care from our sexist, homophobic and expensive health care system."[22] This organization, set up to provide quality affordable care for women at San Francisco General Hospital, explicitly tied the process of coming-out as a lesbian to economic status: "Lesbians suffer not only from sexism but perhaps even more severe economic inequity than women in general. In a Bay Area study last fall the average income of 148 lesbians was found to be $525 a month, as compared to a national average of $734 for women in general during the same time frame." In addition, lesbians struggled to find affordable care in settings not centered around "gynecological, maternal, and birth control needs."[23] Women's health clinics made the issue of access central to their mission, often requiring activists to frame the health care needs of minority populations in ways that reified the class and gender dynamics of the rights revolutions and pitted them against the privatized social safety net. "Since women and young families have relatively low incomes," argued a member of the New York Women's Health Abortion Project in 1969, "they can't afford to pay for adequate care. . . . A strong women's health movement . . . could begin to initiate the demand for free and complete health care as the right of every citizen."[24]

The question of how to access the privatized health care system was equally as acute for those seeking medical procedures related to their transgender identity. A transgender activist painted a stark picture of the consequences of a private health care system that usually excluded trans* people from care, making volunteer clinics a lifeline: "Since most insurance companies have explicitly written us out of their policies, most of us find it difficult to seek health care through these avenues, even if they are available to us. . . . Unless we can find sympathetic health care workers, we are often at the mercy of the big money insurance companies."[25] The Erickson Educational Foundation (EEF), a trans* advocacy organization founded by wealthy female-to-male Reed Erickson in Baton Rouge, Louisiana, in the 1960s, published a list of gender-identity clinics and surgeons in 1972 and listed the fees and charges payable, which ranged from about $3,000 to at least $15,000.[26] The EEF also produced a helpful brochure detailing how to access the health care system, in which financing issues were front and center. Since most private insurance carriers refused to pay for sex reassignment when explicitly named as such, trans* patients were forced to redefine themselves as medically diseased in order to secure payment for surgery or treatment: "Best results have been obtained when the condition (transsexualism) is presented as 'a neuroendocrinological or psychohormonal disorder,' absolutely requiring and responsive to surgical and hormonal treatment." The brochure added that some "health insurance policies state that the holder is covered only for 'necessary treatment of an injury or disease process.' In such a case, the physician should represent transsexualism as 'a distinct, medically definable disease entity, for which treatment is required.' In every instance, it is advisable for you and your physician to examine carefully the wording of your policy, for indications as to how he should frame his diagnosis."[27] For transgender people, seeking medical attention represented a coming-out process framed by stigmatization and economic marginalization, subjecting them to the objectifying gaze of the medical and insurance establishments. As we shall see, these were not narratives that would gain much traction in national-level gay rights politics.

When seeking gender reassignment surgery or other treatment, transgender people faced an uphill battle to access Medicaid or Medicare too, as some states in the late 1970s did pay while others did not, leading to a number of court cases and a review by the U.S. Department of Health and Human Services during the Carter administration. In 1981 under a new conservative federal regime, the department banned the use of government funds for sex reassignment, citing "the lack of well-controlled, long-term studies of the safety and effectiveness" of the medical procedures.[28] The health care access debate in the 1970s at the local level created sexual subjects through a very different dynamic to the individualist paradigm of gay liberation. At its heart, sexual health politics was about who pays for sexual dissidence, inevitably leading to a debate over the role of government in advancing the rights revolutions in a post-1960s age. LGBT politics at the grass roots often overlapped with other arenas of health and antipoverty activism in ways that revealed multiple aspects to—and divisions within—the sexual equality movement and its relationship to the state.

Beyond the Blue Denim: National Gay Rights Activism
and the Democratic Party

At the same time that local sexual health activism was playing a major role in
the LGBT rights movements during the 1970s, a national activist movement
was coming of age. Organizations such as the NGTF and the GAA took their
demands for equal rights for sexual minorities to the Democratic Party conventions of 1972 and 1976 and lobbied presidential and congressional candidates during the 1976 election cycle. NGTF lobbyists famously gained an
audience with the Carter White House in March 1977 and by 1980 were an
acknowledged part of the Democratic Party coalition.[29] On its face, the sustained campaign of the gay rights movement to gain traction in mainstream
politics in the 1970s rested principally on an appeal for nondiscrimination
in law, building explicitly on comparisons with the African American civil
rights movement. "For many of us, the most moving moment of the 1976
Democratic National Convention was the sight of you and Coretta King,
two gentlepeople of the American South, celebrating an end to second-class
citizenship for the nation's largest minority," wrote cochairs of the NGTF to
Jimmy Carter shortly after he had secured the party's presidential nomination. "We invite you to become the champion of first class citizenship for this
nation's second largest minority. We invite you to welcome and encourage the
decline of an even older madness, hatred for and oppression of human beings
because they have acknowledged their capacity to love other human beings
of the same sex."[30] Leaving aside the questionable historical chronology and
reductive construction of a single identity for sexual dissidence, the letter was
one of many to presidential candidates in 1976 aiming to stake a claim to
legitimacy through seemingly uncontroversial appeals to "the right to privacy . . . [and] the right to pursue a personal lifestyle without fear of harassment," rights given heightened resonance in the context of the civil rights
campaigns of the recent past.[31] The strategy had its effect: of eight declared
Democratic candidates for the 1976 nomination, all but two expressed some
support for nondiscrimination against gay people in federal law, including
Carter, who wrote that he opposed "all forms of discrimination against individuals, including discrimination based on sexual orientation. As President,
I can assure you that all policies of the federal government would reflect this
commitment to ending all forms of discrimination."[32]

The focus on individual civil rights allowed gay activists to articulate
a simple message that played well politically while also touching on key

issues—federal employment, the extension of the 1964 Civil Rights Act, and immigration law—of direct concern to the federal government. This focus also marked a way of highlighting the self-assurance of lobbying organizations keen to shed the image of gay rights as a radical throwback to the 1960s. Bruce Voeller, while recalling the origins of the NGTF in 1973, argued that "if we were to have a viable national movement, it would need to have meaning for all gay people, not just the largely countercultural left who had been so effective in beginning our movement. . . . Blue-denim elitism had founded our movement, but it had in fact lessened its appeal to many talented people with skill in public relations, law, media, legislation, fund-raising, etc. We needed, and continue to need, both militant activists and more conservative movement members."[33] Speaking to gay journalist Randy Shilts at the Democratic National Convention in New York in August 1976, Carter press office aide Charlie Graham said, "I only have so much time in my life to be politically gay. The movement has to understand that there are those of us who want to work the establishment side of the street." Arguing that backing a political winner, Carter, would lead to far more political progress for minorities than any other strategy on offer, Graham argued that gay "people are so used to being oppressed, they have a hard time being anything else."[34]

Yet it was not so much a convergence of strategy that brought together gay rights advocates and the Democratic Party at the national level in 1976 as it was a shared emphasis on policy issues tied to middle-class respectability and individualism. A centrepiece of national Democratic strategy that year was a commitment to welfare reform and the value of productive work as the marker of citizenship. A draft advert for Daniel Patrick Moynihan's Senate campaign in New York, which explicitly tied his candidacy to the Carter-Mondale ticket, proposed to "help you make ends meet again" by reducing "the property tax burden of the working homeowner" and getting "welfare off your back" by shifting its cost entirely to the federal government (a policy that Reagan would later endorse) to facilitate "a national rate of payment to discourage migration into areas where welfare benefits are more generous." A further pledge, one of "cutting off welfare to any person able to work who declines a job," was clearly seen as too brutal and was amended in the draft to read "requiring welfare recipients able to work to take a job."[35] But the overall direction of travel of the 1976 campaign was clear. The New York State AFL-CIO published a campaign leaflet with the banner headline "Jobs, Not Welfare" across the top.[36] Moynihan aides wrote a campaign speech for a labor audience in August to swing the vote away from more left-wing primary challenger Bella Abzug, arguing that "among the causes of New York's crisis is this state's welfare system, which places a crushing burden on our cities and counties and most of all on our families. It is a burden which has in the end hurt every working man and woman in this state," a burden that Abzug was unwilling to lift in not endorsing Moynihan's welfare reform plans.[37] Moynihan's campaign launch appealed for "a government that begins to recognize its own limits, to stop acting as if the American people were one huge social problem, and to start treating us as the competent, creative, and energetic people that we so manifestly are."[38]

Encoded in what historian Robert Self has termed "breadwinner liberalism" was a simplified archetype of the self-sufficient worker, buffeted by strong currents of economic decline, bloated taxes, and inflation.[39] Its erasure of social and class differences allowed politicians such as Moynihan and Carter to integrate an undifferentiated category of "gay people" into a broader narrative of individual rights free from the intrusion of the state. The federal government, argued Moynihan in an exchange with NGTF member Robert Livingston in October 1976, "should treat gay people no differently from anyone else; both in its employment practices and in the guarantees extended to other citizens by federal law. And it means that the right to privacy of all American citizens must be upheld."[40] The right to privacy paradigm offered certain gay rights advocates a route to respectable citizenship in which their identity as political beings shaped by marginalization and exclusion could be shrouded from public view. "Almost everything of any significance [for gay rights] is being done behind the scenes," argued *Advocate* publisher David Goodstein in early 1976, by people who wished to divorce queer politics from the radical performative protest of earlier years; he claimed that self-appointed activist leaders "appear unemployable, unkempt, and neurotic to the point of megalomania," a nod toward the pathologized trope of the "welfare queen."[41] Goodstein had earlier claimed that the "gay population is diversified but tends to be more conservative than the average" and confirmed his status as the bête noire of national gay politics with the statement in *The Advocate* (reproduced in an article in *Gay Community News* deeply critical of Goodstein) that most "homosexuals are upwardly mobile. Oh, there are a few angry losers, but most are affluent. . . . You [*Advocate* readers] are employed and a useful, responsible citizen. You have an attractive body, nice clothes, and an inviting home."[42] It is important to stress that Goodstein, almost a caricature of the rich, well-connected political player, was widely disliked by many of those trying to forge a path to influence in the Democratic Party, not just by the "unemployable and unkempt."[43] Bruce Voeller of the NGTF sent the critical *Gay Community News* piece about Goodstein to Carter's domestic policy aide Midge Constanza, suggesting that it "accurately reflects the attitude of a wide part of the gay community towards Mr G."[44] Nevertheless, the concept of the queer American as a "useful, responsible citizen"—who would fit into a larger narrative of the modern liberal worker and member of the "middle class"—would recur when gay rights activists took their political message into the White House in 1977.

Making Healthy Citizens: LGBT Politics in the Carter Years

The NGTF's overtures to the Carter campaign paid off when his domestic policy liaison Midge Constanza was given the green light to invite a group from the NGTF to the White House in March 1977. Constanza, former vice mayor of Rochester, New York, and an integral part of Carter's successful campaign in the Empire State, seemed an ideal figure to raise the profile of issues concerning gender and sexual dissidence.[45] The planks that she put forward to the Democratic Platform Drafting Committee prior to the 1976 convention had mostly concerned issues of social and economic inequality, including the need for quality day care with subsidies for low-income women; federally funded family planning services, including the use of Medicaid funds for abortion; universal health coverage "without regard to sex, age, color, employment, or economic circumstance"; and support for gay rights by adding "affectional or life-style preference" to each protected category of the Civil Rights Act.[46] Of these, only the pledge for universal health insurance made it into the platform, but Constanza's evident commitment to gender and sexual equality suggested new possibilities for gay rights on the national stage inconceivable just a year earlier.[47] Carter later wrote in his diary that he had "been concerned about her involvement in the abortion and gay rights business, but she takes a tremendous burden off me from nut groups that would insist on seeing me if they couldn't see her," but even this indication of Carter's bewilderment at the pace of social change at the time he assumed office still demonstrated an opening for gay rights advocates that they were quick to exploit.[48]

While the focus of the agenda for the meeting between NGTF leaders and Constanza and domestic policy staffer Robert Malson concerned employment, immigration, and civil service discrimination, the activists brought thirteen different policy issues to the White House on March 26, 1977, grouped under the relevant government department. "Health, Education, and Welfare" was one of the issues for discussion. Constanza's assistant predicted that the NGTF "will ask for more federal grants to go to Gay counselling, health and education groups. We can set up a meeting with policy secretaries in Education and Health parts of HEW [Department of Health, Education, and Welfare]."[49] Presenting on this topic was Sacramento-based gay rights activist George Raya, a California lobbyist who had been instrumental in the successful effort to repeal the sodomy statute in California state law in 1975. A twenty-seven-year-old former law student whose lobbying interests spanned Chicano rights and labor issues as well as gay rights, Raya had been "surviving on food stamps and income from blood plasma donations" before *The Advocate* began bankrolling his efforts to force the state legislature to reform its sex statutes.[50] His experience across a range of activist issues and his success as a lobbyist in California secured his place on the NGTF team.

In preparation for the White House meeting, Raya compiled letters and testimonials from a range of academic and social service contacts about the health needs of sexual minority populations. The director of the Kinsey Institute provided estimates of how many in the U.S. population were homo-sexual. An anthropologist at UC Berkeley reported hostility on the part of the National Institute of Mental Health and other federal agencies toward research into same-sex sexuality. A gay activist at Meals on Wheels San Fran-cisco wrote about the special needs of older gay people. Of particular inter-est for a presentation on health care were a letter from the director of the Washington, D.C., Gay Men's VD Clinic concerning chronic underfunding of STI research and treatment and a statement from a former staff member of a sexual health clinic in San Francisco funded by the city's Gay Health Project, a program sponsored by the Centers for Disease Control (CDC) but terminated the previous year.[51] Both the letter and the statement pointed to the importance of government funding if STIs were to be tackled effectively and also to the growing mismatch between a heteronormative state and the demands of sexual minorities beginning to gain political and legal legitimacy for the first time. The CDC provided "much of the funding and staff positions at [San Francisco] City Clinic. Most of the clinic's management comes from the CDC. They follow the CDC model for VD control—interviews, contact tracing, and paperwork. The model is used around the country regardless of community differences." Given that 75 percent of clients at City Clinic were gay men, contact tracing was ill-suited to the city's sexual health needs. "It makes about as much sense to trace [a] gay person's sexual contacts for gonorrhoea as his contacts for a common cold," argued the former clinic worker. The CDC needed to adapt its surveillance policies to reflect the needs of different population groups. In addition, its funding of the Gay Health Project had helped reach far more gay men through innovative programs such as a mobile VD unit, but the project's termination threatened to reverse the progress made in tackling STIs.[52]

In a chillingly prophetic warning, the director of the Washington clinic noted that the "drastic slashing of CDC funds for combating VD is paralyzing VD control across the country, and an inevitable plague will hit in less than five years and strike with greatest destructiveness gay men. . . . This foolhardy trend of 'saving' money must be radically turned around. . . . Gay men's VD clinics in every major city, with few exceptions, have had real opposition from local public health departments. Our clinic here is a dramatic case in point. We need a special department at CDC with massive funding to encourage the clinics presently in existence and assist in establishing others in every metropolitan center."[53] Integrating sexual minorities into the nation's public health infrastructure, in terms of both harnessing state funds and recalibrating health policy away from a purely heteronormative medical model, was the central message of gay health professionals on the ground, a message that they hoped would shape the discussion in the White House.

Yet Raya's report for the meeting with Constanza and Malson barely made any mention of these issues other than a brief reference to the need for HEW's Office of Volunteer Development to "begin an outreach program to counsel gay service organizations on maximum utilization of their volunteers." Raya's report noted that the massive reliance of LGBT people on volunteer groups was "created by the failure of existing agencies and programs," but he made no recommendation for a major injection of public resource into the sexual health infrastructure. Instead, Raya focused on the possibilities offered by government-funded research to dispel stereotypes of sexual minorities and to construct a positive public image of queer Americans. "The freedom of all of us is limited," wrote Raya, "as long as stereotypes about homosexuals persist and we do not feel free to do what we want for fear we will be thought to be homosexual." Research into different aspects of the homosexual experience (there was no mention of varieties of sexual dissidence) would help establish gay Americans as legitimate citizens, a political project requiring a focus on markers of respectability such as "job history and occupational performance," "family dynamics," and "personality factors." Raya urged HEW to develop a "taxonomy of homosexual experiences and behavior" that would "cover the total range of homosexual phenomena. This range should include homosexual individuals who do not come into contact with medical, legal, or other social control or treatment sources and who therefore have been least studied."[54] To Raya, health as public policy was as much about defining healthy, normative individuals as it was providing health care and understanding the special health needs of sexual dissidents. Indeed, a focus on treatment needs and on the inadequacy of the nation's cumbersome health care system for LGBT people risked perpetuating notions of sexual minorities as marginalized as well as effectively donning the mantle of the "welfare queen," heading to the White House as an economic supplicant. Such a focus would also acknowledge the reality of the sex act as a marker of sexual identity and highlight the variety of lived experiences of queer subjects carefully shrouded under the increasingly respectable category "the gay community."

Given that the NGTF aimed to pressure the Carter administration to end discrimination in areas such as tax policy, civil service employment, the Department of Defense, and immigration policy, it was imperative that the themes of respectability and normativity be stressed if they were to gain credibility. Carter aide Bob Malson's notes of the meeting simply reported that Raya "focused on the lack of sensitivity of HEW, and its inability to deliver social services to the gay community," but it was clear that those present— on both sides of the table—did not want to make sexual health a dominant theme.[55] The reports on the various policy issues, including Raya's, were "passed on to the appropriate people on the Domestic Policy Staff," but it soon became clear the HEW report would not occupy a central place in the administration's policy around gay rights issues.[56]

The NGTF meeting took place in the context of an administration increasingly wedded to "cost containment" as its flagship health care policy, to "welfare reform," and to cutting overall spending in an effort to combat high inflation. Carter had committed himself to some form of national health insurance during his campaign, and the administration periodically and hesitantly reaffirmed that commitment once in office, but it quickly became clear that the political and economic climate would not be favorable.[57] The President's Council of Economic Advisors produced a fairly damning assessment of HEW's lead agency memorandum launching the plan in May 1978, arguing that one key aim of the plan, that of "mandating a substantial and comprehensive increase in benefits and medical expenditures for noncatastrophic health care" to those ineligible for government programs but not covered by good health insurance through employment (a category into which a disproportionate number of LGBT Americans fell), was "relatively low on the list of immediate national needs."[58] Without votes in Congress to mitigate the divisions within the administration, HEW secretary Joseph Califano was left to devote much of his department's energy to efforts to force health care providers to curtail their prices, a fruitless effort dressed up as a way of saving money both for the government as the purchaser of health care and for private insurers and their customers ahead of a possible future push for national health insurance.[59] Much of this effort required Carter administration officials to court business leaders and to frame the health care debate "from the perspective and in the language of businessmen," portraying government as a facilitator of private initiative.[60] One Carter adviser painted hospital cost containment plans as a way of promoting "more vigorous market forces and expanded individual choice," and noted that Senator Edward "Ted" Kennedy's decision to challenge Carter from the left in the 1980 primary offered the opportunity to "clearly distinguish the President from the Senator's highly governmental approach, but more importantly, our approach could directly appeal to voters as a way to control costs, give them greater individual choices and, most important, get government out of their hair in a way consistent with the President's existing efforts at deregulation."[61] Different factions within the Carter White House disagreed vehemently over the extent to which meaningful reform of the health care system was possible or even desirable, but they all seemingly agreed that a state-centered approach ran contrary to the political currents of the time.

In this context, although the NGTF met representatives of the Carter administration several times between 1977 and 1980, and lobbied frequently for even more representation at domestic policy briefings and White House events, the March 1977 meeting was the first and last time health care was on the agenda.[62] A member of Carter's White House staff proposed in early 1980 inviting NGTF representatives to briefings, "the health insurance ones in particular," but the topics that the NGTF brought to the table in meetings at the White House in the fall of 1977 and late 1979 related to civil service and immigration discrimination, areas not only more likely to gain traction with the Carter administration but also better aligned to the promotion of gay Americans as productive citizens.[63] Certainly the administration saw its relationship with gay political advocacy in these terms. "Gay people are being drawn into the everyday routine decisions of government, are being accepted as part of the political community," argued domestic policy staffer Bob Malson in May 1980. He identified policy areas, such as federal employment, that linked political legitimacy to markers of middle class respectability. "The IRS [Internal Revenue Service] has granted tax-exempt and tax deductible status to gay organizations," Malson noted. "Though no changes in the regulations were required, the IRS had moved slowly on this until the Administration brought in a changed attitude toward gays. The IRS action has practical benefits and indicates the increased legitimacy with which gay organizations are treated."[64] NGTF leaders attending a White House meeting to present a petition on gay rights in December 1979 highlighted exactly the same issues, eliding important socioeconomic divisions within sexual minority groups. "I think that progress was made on important issues including employment, where the administration is now aware of a number of our concerns," reported Lambda Legal Defense and Education Fund President Margot Karle, who attended the White House meeting. "I think there will be significant policy and legal changes which will benefit all lesbians and gay men."[65] In a domestic policy meeting that same month, Carter officials wondered about making reference to sexual orientation in the 1980 State of the Union address, but in terms associating civil rights with individual freedom from state oversight: "where [the] speech addresses American goals for the 1980s, the language discussing the goal of a just society should specifically refer to lesbians and gay men. Alternatively, the goal of respect for individual right to privacy could be framed to specifically include freedom from intrusion by the government and private sector in matters that are based on private consensual behavior."[66] The transformation of Democratic politics from Great Society liberalism to individual rights liberalism was clear. The notion of "privacy" was a euphemism for a new closet, one that hid from view the varieties of sexual dissidence beneath a simplified paradigm of "gay rights."

Gay Rights and the Carter Campaign in 1980

The relationship between the Democratic Party and the national gay rights movement was cemented during the 1980 campaign. The NGTF and a set of other activist groups formed the National Convention Project to ensure that a gay rights plank was inserted into the party platform for the first time. The group produced a document, "Gay Rights Issues at the Federal Level," which listed only three items: federal employment, immigration and naturalization, and nongovernmental discrimination.[67] Recognizing the growing power of gay political operatives in California, and keen to ensure they delivered

Carter's renomination over Ted Kennedy, his domestic policy aides Allison Thomas and Bob Malson flew to the Golden State in May 1980, and noted the lack of ideological fervor of some of the key players, especially in Los Angeles.[68] The administration increasingly viewed prominent gay rights leaders still loyal to Carter as bound to him by their shared antipathy to the kind of redistributive left politics characteristic of the Kennedy campaign. Carter policy adviser Anne Wexler urged Vice President Walter Mondale to drop in on an American Civil Liberties Union gay rights dinner in Los Angeles, arguing that "the Los Angeles gay community is more sophisticated politically than the San Francisco community—fewer gays exist and those that are active are wealthier, more established (many are in the closet at work), and more conservative. What this means is that is that those attending the dinner will react more positively than a San Francisco audience to the Vice President and will listen to what he has to say." To allay fears that Mondale's appearance might cause divisions in the party, she noted that "our positions on issues relating to gays are based . . . purely on human rights" and were "to the right of Ted Kennedy and John Anderson."[69] In essence, Wexler viewed many gay rights advocates as easily seduced by promises of a seat at the political table and as suspicious of radical politics that could derail their steady march to respectability.

Wexler was right that queer communities with a longer history of access to political power and a strong association with wider minority and antipoverty movements, such as in San Francisco, were far less enamored by the Carter administration. The Harvey Milk and Alice Toklas gay Democratic clubs in the city published a rousing and forthright endorsement of Ted Kennedy ahead of the California primary, signed by some of San Francisco's most prominent gay figures, in which they explicitly tied their enthusiasm for Kennedy to Carter's failure to pursue liberal policies at home and abroad. The statement excoriated Carter for his stance on women's rights, including the thorny question of Medicaid funding for abortions for the poorest women, and attacked his record on social policy. "Candidate Carter, like any good Democrat, promised to support the cities, the poor, minorities, and labor. But President Carter's budget out-Republicans the Republicans, requiring massive cutbacks in jobs, social programs, and aid to cities," they claimed. "Senator Kennedy has been a forthright voice against the draft and nuclear power and in support of the poor, the workingperson, the disabled, and the elderly. He has fought for national health insurance, gun control and cuts in defense spending. He supports controls on wages, prices and profits to control inflation." The statement highlighted Kennedy's support for a gay rights plank in the party platform and for an executive order banning discrimination against LGBT people but only toward the end, viewing discrimination through a wider lens incorporating class as well as individual rights.[70]

This was a minority view among gay activists, especially once Kennedy was no longer in the race. The National Convention Project and most key figures in the NGTF tried to push the administration further on antidiscrimination issues by pointing out the political alternatives on the Right whose antigovernment message might include antipathy to overt discrimination. Carter campaign chairman Robert Strauss wrote to NGTF cochairs Charles Brydon and Lucia Valeska in March 1980 to seek their endorsement, and their response, while positive, lamented the lack of progress on civil service reform and the absence of an explicit gay rights plank. They noted the candidacies of wildcard liberal Republican John Anderson and Governor Jerry Brown of California (oddly ignoring Kennedy) and argued that Reagan "has a record of actively defending gay teachers during the unsuccessful 1978 California antigay rights campaign (the Briggs initiative). We believe that it is in the interests of lesbians and gay men . . . to carefully evaluate the positions of all candidates and make a decision on the basis of both performance and rhetoric."[71]

Thomas Bastow, cochair of the National Convention Project, went further, writing to the research director of the Carter-Mondale campaign in April that gay voters were disillusioned with Carter, an assertion that Bastow claimed to prove by enclosing an editorial from *Gay News* titled "Reagan for President?" The editorial qualified the sensationalist headline but argued that "Ronald Reagan is no worse than the others. After all, 'getting government off our backs' is the implicit argument in sodomy law repeal."[72] Bastow portrayed gay voters as political consumers who needed to be targeted as respectable citizens with individual rights. "Most gay people do not perceive Ronald Reagan as a threat even though he has assiduously courted the right-wing fundamentalist vote," he wrote. "I have found a widespread appreciation within the gay community for Reagan's personal, forthright and articulate opposition to California's Proposition 6. . . . Reagan supporters argue that gay rights advocates would fare about the same under Reagan as under Carter: the President would maintain a hands-off attitude, and some appointees—in this case libertarians rather than liberals—would make headway against discrimination."[73] Left unspoken was the privileging of cisgender men, who fit the mold of the middle-class employee whose sexual identity could be hidden from view more easily than other sexual dissidents.

From Carter to Reagan

The election of Ronald Reagan as president in November 1980 marked the dramatic acceleration of a political assault on the nation's rudimentary social safety net that had already begun in the late 1970s. The Reagan administration slashed federal contributions to Medicaid, including implementing the ban on transgender treatments; tried to dismantle the social security system; and eagerly expanded efforts to throw thousands of people off the disability benefit rolls. The Reagan budget chronically underfunded agencies such as the CDC. The political context in which the AIDS crisis unfolded could not have been worse for those needing treatment. The advent of AIDS forced gay activists to embark on a new and urgent political campaign that centered the health needs of sexual minorities and highlighted the homophobia of both public and private health systems determined to limit their liability for tackling the crisis. New activist groups such as the Gay Men's Health Crisis and Mobilization Against AIDS lobbied the federal government to devote more resource to AIDS research and treatment. The NGTF formed an AIDS program in late 1982, hired Washington lobbyist Jeff Levi, and soon claimed to have "achieved notable breakthroughs in persuading the executive branch of the federal government—specifically the Department of Health and Human Services and its relevant subdivisions . . .[—]to increase allocations for AIDS research."[74] LGBT politics now needed the state to step in if a major public health crisis was to be tackled.

As we have seen, however, the question of the specific health needs of queer Americans was not new in the early 1980s and had shaped a good deal of gay activist politics at the local level over the preceding decade or more. The NGTF was hardly ignorant of health care issues: founding member Howard Brown had worked as New York City's health services administrator under Mayor John Lindsay, and Walter Lear worked in the Pennsylvania Department of Health, founded the Caucus of Gay Public Health Workers to lobby the American Public Health Association, and solicited support for the caucus in a letter in the late 1970s claiming that the "gay health movement is coming out of the closet. Local gay health groups and gay health services . . . are the core of the gay health movement."[75] The growing network of clinics and community centers required local, state, and federal funding and served often underprivileged populations. There was an undeniable bridge from antipoverty politics to the politics of sexuality in the 1970s that helped maintain a spirit of 1960s radicalism in cities such as San Francisco and suggested that LGBT politics could be a crucible of leftist activism and a challenge to neoliberalism.

Gay activism gained traction in the Democratic Party at the national level at the very moment the party was moving away from Great Society liberalism and recovering from the disastrous presidential bid of George McGovern in 1972. NGTF leaders mirrored the Carter White House in downplaying questions of poverty and inequality in favor of notions of individual civil rights and respectability as productive citizens. The image of the gay American as a model consumer citizen extended to their political identity by the 1980 campaign, as the NGTF portrayed the choice between a range of right-wing candidates for national office as a case of picking the one who promised to enhance their personal rights and remove state sanctions over their individual freedoms. The mainstreaming of gay rights on the national stage took place in the context of the delegitimizing of the welfare state and the rise of antigovernment animus in American political life. This partially explains the slowness of much AIDS activism to recognize the racial and class dimensions to the AIDS crisis, with one activist in 1991 claiming to be "stunned that ACT UP has sat back and not reacted to the budget cuts in Medicaid in New York State. . . . Poor people, children, people on Medicaid—that's who's not getting care. The [ACT UP] insurance committee doesn't want to deal with it because it's too messy."[76] The emphasis on respectability and the NGTF's role as a responsible political broker in its dealings with the Carter White House and the Democratic Party were hardly surprising, given Carter's religious beliefs and the continued popular antipathy toward sexual minorities. Questions of health care rested on LGBT people as sexual beings, something that the administration was reluctant to consider, rejecting what it termed "homosexuality as a lifestyle."[77] Contrasting local queer health politics at the local level with national activist strategy in the Carter years demonstrates the ways in which the dwindling ambition of American liberal politics damaged the prospects for many sexual dissidents to gain a voice in political debate. Very few LGBT Americans were represented in the mainstreaming of "gay rights" at the dawn of the Reagan era.

PART II

Confronting AIDS

CHAPTER 4

AIDS and the Urban Crisis

Stigma, Cost, and the Persistence of Racism in Chicago, 1981–1996

Timothy Stewart-Winter

In the 1980s, as gay men and intravenous drug users began to die in growing numbers following the mysterious collapse of their immune systems, America's cities, already suffering from the combined effects of deindustrialization, white flight, and the tax revolt of the 1970s, bore the brunt of this new catastrophe. At the same time, AIDS was not simply an emergency that happened to unfold in cities but was also an aspect of the broader urban crisis shaping the late twentieth-century United States. This essay uses Chicago as a window onto how the politics of the early years of AIDS looks different when we focus on local and state political responses in three ways. First, AIDS involved exceptional stigma, and fear and disgust became key drivers of the policy process. Second, AIDS imposed exceptionally high financial costs. In these two respects, AIDS confronted local and state government with new and distinctive problems. In a third respect, however, political contests over AIDS at the local level represented an intensification rather than a departure from the broader trajectory of late twentieth-century urban and metropolitan history. As it played out on the ground in Chicago, the politics of the AIDS crisis very much reflected the overwhelming feature of the political culture of Chicago as well as much of urban America in the late twentieth century: intense black-white racial conflict, with newly empowered African American leaders facing virulent white backlash.

State, county, and municipal officials acted both to incite and codify panic and also—sometimes simultaneously—to curtail it. For example, Chicago's police department in 1984 recommended that officers wear latex gloves when coming into contact with persons who might be infected with AIDS, a policy quickly rescinded when activists pushed back and local public health experts took their side.[1] Similarly, an arbitrary policy that excluded women patients from the AIDS ward at Cook County Hospital, known as "County," was quickly changed in 1990 after members of ACT UP/Chicago dragged fifteen mattresses—representing the number of empty beds there, which women were being excluded from occupying—through city streets.[2] Adopting the vantage point of big-city municipal government enables us to look both "upward" and "downward" and see how the city was the crucial mediator between on one hand federal and state policy and on the other hand the ground level—the neighborhoods, hospitals, and grassroots organizations—that was the scene of sickness and death, resilience and mourning.

HIV/AIDS, which remains understudied by historians, was a new disease, and this has made it at first blush a profound historical rupture. It challenged the confidence, even arrogance, of postwar medicine; as one scholar put it, "the myth of our perceived conquest of infectious diseases was shockingly pierced."[3] Beyond its medical dimensions, studies of HIV/AIDS as policy history have tended to focus on the federal level. The crisis occurred at a moment of profound conservative ascendancy in the federal government. Yet the texture of the AIDS crisis in the United States was disproportionately and specifically urban. The most popularly influential account of the AIDS crisis in the United States remains *And the Band Played On* (1987) written by the journalist Randy Shilts, whose two major arguments are that homophobia determined the Ronald Reagan administration's neglectful response and that gay male sexual excess made the crisis inevitable.[4] Jennifer Brier has complicated the first prong of this argument, arguing that the Reagan administration was in fact deeply divided about how to respond to the epidemic and also usefully challenging distinctions between AIDS service organizations and protest groups, instead referring to both as "AIDS workers."[5] Some of the most important work on the politics of AIDS has been written by political scientists including Cathy Cohen and Deborah Gould, who analyzed the boundaries of black politics and the trajectory of ACT UP.[6]

More recently, AIDS historiography has developed in important directions beyond national politics and AIDS activism per se. Still, only a few monographs by academic historians exist. Phil Tiemeyer has offered a powerful critique of the second prong of Shilts's argument while situating the AIDS crisis in the context of the evolving contests over gender and labor, specifically through the figure of the male flight attendant.[7] Kevin Mumford has shown how black gay men experienced and responded to AIDS, locating it in the evolution of black gay political history.[8] Emily Hobson has connected AIDS to the movement against U.S. policies in Latin America, while Katie Batza has pointed to an important thread of continuity by tracing the emergence of gay health networks developed in the 1970s that then became the front lines in responding to the crisis in the following decade.[9]

Moreover, the federal response to the crisis was characterized by broad indifference at the highest levels, and there were tensions with the Reagan administration between social conservatives and public health authorities, especially Surgeon General C. Everett Koop.[10] But it was not solely *explicitly* AIDS-related federal policies that mattered; also crucial was that city governments were strapped in the 1980s because of the Reagan administration's cuts to federal aid. Moreover, the epidemic's particularly urban political dynamics have been neglected, with most historical writing about the crisis focusing either on the coastal gay meccas or on the federal government.[11]

From 1981 to 1990, AIDS created tensions between urban city and county governments as well as between local officials and their counterparts in state capitals and at the federal level. This essay takes as its case study the city of Chicago, a stronghold of African American political power. The case of Chicago helps brings into focus the municipal political economy of AIDS, emphasizing a racial analysis and thereby building a framework that can serve to render black queer lives and deaths more analytically central. Renslow Sherer, a doctor at County who went on to become Chicago's best-known AIDS specialist, believes that in 1982 he saw his first AIDS patient there: a young black gay man "who could no longer do his daily six-mile run."[12] By 1987, gay people of color made up fully 70 percent of AIDS patients at County, according to Sherer.[13] At a deeper level, the case of Chicago illuminates how profoundly the stalemate between black insurgency and white reaction diminished the policy-making capacity of local government.

Chicago's trajectory was typical—far more than New York and San Francisco—of sixteen U.S. urban areas that Congress recognized in the Ryan White CARE Act of 1990 as polities upon which a public health emergency, requiring federal funds, had been visited. This law specifically framed the problem of AIDS as analogous to a geographically confined natural disaster. As in New York and San Francisco, AIDS activists in Chicago targeted greed on the part of drug companies, insurance companies, and doctors, as in the coastal cities; a group called Chicago for AIDS Rights disrupted the 1988 annual meeting of the Chicago-based maker of pentamidine, a drug widely used to treat *pneumocystis* pneumonia, after the company quadrupled its price.[14] But compared to San Francisco and New York, caseloads were lower and radicalism a less potent dimension of political contestation.

Beyond federal policies not simply being implemented from the top down, national politics was not simply determinative of local controversies but instead was taken up, recycled, and reframed at the local level. Consider an episode in which the Chicago Transit Authority (CTA) refused an AIDS prevention advertisement that showed a naked man with his arm around a woman holding a condom package, calling it too sexually explicit. In responding to the CTA's decision, AIDS activists linked it to former first lady Nancy Reagan's controversial antidrug campaign, calling it "a useless 'Just-Say-No' approach to the problem."[15] There was thus a complicated interplay between the national and the local. To understand how this works, we now turn to policy dimensions of the crisis that were distinctively local.

Fear, Disgust, and the Politics of Panic

It is nearly impossible to exaggerate the stigma that surrounded AIDS in the early years. Crucial to understanding the politics of AIDS is the degree to which stigma led to concealment and avoidance. "It is imperative that the word AIDS be printed in my obituary," wrote one young gay man in his last will and testament. "If I die from some other unrelated cause, say that I had AIDS."[16] For the first fifteen years of the crisis, before protease inhibitors became available in 1996, the public's response to AIDS was rooted in the sense that it was always fatal. Everyone diagnosed with AIDS was forced to confront the likelihood of a gradual decline in their immune system followed by death from an opportunistic illness.

These deaths were often extremely painful. The most common opportunistic infection that AIDS patients faced—present in 64 percent of Chicago's AIDS patients up to the end of 1985—was *pneumocystis* pneumonia. This typically required the extensive use of mechanical ventilators during end-stage care.[17] A nurse with years of experience reported that she burned out on working in the medical intensive care unit at County, which handled most of Chicago's AIDS inpatients. "There were some nights when I would feel as if I was doing nothing more than torturing them," she recalled. "I was wishing that I didn't have to suction them and cause them pain, even though I had to, to take out the secretions so they could breathe."[18]

At every level of governance, political responses to AIDS were shaped by fear and disgust. People with AIDS were viewed as vectors of contamination. Consider the micro level: Not long after taking a job as a housekeeper at County, Jewell Jenkins realized that she could switch to a coveted day shift if she volunteered to work on the AIDS ward. "At the time, nobody wanted to work up there," she recalled.[19] A restaurant owner in a neighborhood known as a gay enclave told columnist Clarence Page that his customers—especially tourists—did not want to be waited on by gay wait staff. "Y'know. Fear of AIDS and all that," the man said.[20] AIDS also was met with antigay violence and vandalism. Indeed, in 1987 a *New York Times* article reported on the extent of this antigay backlash in Chicago, focusing on episodes in which gay bars and other gay-friendly businesses in the city's most visible gay enclave, on the North Side near Lake Michigan, were defaced with obscenities and the word "Die!"[21]

Churches, hospitals, extended-care facilities, and funeral homes all tried to distance themselves from the devastating, painful, terrible suffering of people with AIDS. Parents in Chicago as elsewhere fought to keep children with AIDS out of their schools: "Our hearts are sick with worry over the ruling to place a child with this most deadly disease called AIDS in our school without our voices even being heard in the decision," wrote a Chicago parent who objected viscerally to the decision of the Chicago school board even after it was clear that AIDS cannot be transmitted by casual contact.[22] In late 1987, the board of Cook County Hospital removed a doctor diagnosed with AIDS from seeing patients, then reinstated him following criticism from civil liberties groups and experts. In response, the board forced the hospital to adopt a policy—over strong objections from the American Medical Association and the state's public health director—giving patients the right to refuse to be treated by people who had tested positive for HIV.[23] Even homeless shelters, officials from one agency reported, were "unprepared to manage the panic of staff and residents" should it become known that someone present was infected with the AIDS virus.[24]

Crucially, there was not *one* major means of transmitting HIV but *two*: one involving sex and the other involving drugs. The epidemic's urban trajectory was shaped by the particular shades of stigma and political powerlessness attached to the two populations, or what came to be called "risk groups," most strongly associated with the virus. Each was highly stigmatized by the dominant culture and encoded with moral meanings that varied dramatically among American subcultures. Also important, even after it became possible to test for HIV antibodies in 1985, the two modes of transmission remained clinically indistinguishable. Doctors had to ask their patients how they become HIV-positive. At the federal level, the very name of the Ryan White CARE Act—the name of a white Indiana teenager with hemophilia who had become an unlikely symbol of pediatric AIDS—reflected stigma and fear, as activists chose as the face of the virus one of the few people with AIDS whose seroconversion had *not* involved sex or drugs.[25]

Fear and disgust shaped the logic of the authorities as well as the stigmatized constituencies affected by the virus, who were not only geographically dispersed but often did not themselves wish to "touch" each another. A neglected aspect of the epidemic was the increasingly widespread conflation by the second half of the 1980s of race with "risk group." This conflation made especially invisible the black and brown men who seroconverted as a result of sex with other men by fostering an impression that people with AIDS were either white gay men or black drug addicts. More than 80 percent of AIDS cases diagnosed in African Americans up to mid-1987 and reported by the city health department were attributed to sexual transmission between men.[26] Yet the very same health department nonetheless reproduced this conflation in a 1988 request for proposals.[27]

Illinois state legislators' responses to AIDS primarily centered on fear-motivated surveillance and punishment. State lawmakers often proved more eager to pass mandatory HIV testing—a proposal strongly resisted by gay activists—and criminalize HIV transmission than to appropriate public funds. Indeed, Illinois lawmakers considered some of the most draconian repressive AIDS legislation of any state. In mid-1987, the legislature passed a complicated package of laws dealing with AIDS. In a progressive vein, the package included financial incentives for nursing homes to accept AIDS patients and a provision guaranteeing the confidentiality of test results. But other provisions were more complicated.[28] The bills passed included mandatory antibody testing of all applicants for marriage licenses, hospital patients between thirteen and fifty-five years of age, prison inmates, and persons convicted of sex crimes and a statewide registry with names and addresses of anyone diagnosed with AIDS or who tested positive for HIV.

Some of these measures were known to be effective in dealing with diseases such as syphilis that had once similarly been both untreatable and sexually transmitted. But as Harold Washington's gay and lesbian liaison Kit Duffy wrote in a memo, "There are a number of traditional methods used by the public health systems which, while they may appear applicable to any sexually transmitted disease and are being proposed to deal with AIDS, will not in fact work because they will meet with such intense resistance from the risk group most affected by this disease." Duffy argued that the very strength of this resistance would make them ineffective and unworkable.[29]

AIDS activists had reason to fear that these measures would infringe on the civil rights and privacy of people with AIDS; indeed, one of the proposals before the Illinois legislature represented the most aggressive AIDS quarantine law passed by any state legislature during the AIDS crisis. It would have mandated contact tracing of the sexual partners of anyone diagnosed with AIDS for the past seven years and creating a mechanism for officials to seek a court order to quarantine someone with AIDS deemed to be at a high risk of transmitting the virus to others.[30] In Illinois, the quarantine provision had been advocated by Penny Pullen, a social conservative associated with Phyllis Schlafly, whom President Ronald Reagan had appointed to his commission on HIV and AIDS. After members of the direct-action group Chicago for AIDS Rights chained themselves to the gate at Governor Jim Thompson's house, Thompson vetoed the bill requiring testing of prisoners and hospital patients, which would have cost the state millions of dollars annually to enact, as well as the contact tracing bill with its quarantine provision, which was the measure that AIDS activists found most outrageous.[31]

Thompson's veto of this measure, however, blocked only the most coercive of the measures passed by the legislature. Other measures did become law, and social conservatives did not give up on the enactment of more aggressive legislation. Thompson also signed into law a less coercive measure, which soon proved to be a failed experiment, requiring marriage license applicants to show proof that they had obtained (at their own expense) an HIV antibody test. Two years later, the policy yielded hardly any positive test results but had measurably driven down the marriage rate in Illinois, pushing couples living near the state's borders to cross the state line to marry in towns such as Kenosha, Wisconsin; the law was deemed a total failure and repealed legislatively without controversy.[32] In 1988 another proposal was passed, again at Penny Pullen's behest, to allow the secret testing of patients' blood without their knowledge by their doctor; this too did not become law.[33] Most important, in 1989 Thompson signed one of the first state laws criminalizing the intentional transmission of HIV.[34]

Conservative policy responses, in short, were not limited to the relatively well-known instance of the federal Helms Amendment, which cut off AIDS funding for any organization that promoted or even described gay sex.

A Unique Fiscal Burden

AIDS was uniquely and shockingly expensive. "Because of the complex, multiorgan involvement in AIDS, the cost of care was high—double that of other infectious diseases," Guenter Risse observed in his history of American hospitals.[35] By depleting the resources available for medical care in central cities, the conservative movement of the 1970s set the stage for the greater suffering of the 1980s as these areas confronted a devastating public health emergency. It was at the local level that debates over AIDS policy played out on the ground, and they did so increasingly in a climate of austerity.

The unique U.S. private employer-based health insurance regime, dating to the post-World War II era, led to many patients with AIDS losing their health insurance. The *Chicago Tribune* editorialized against any special provisions for people with AIDS, arguing that state insurance regulators should not follow the lead of those in the District of Columbia who had limited the ability of insurers to require residents to take HIV antibody tests before offering them policies. Having HIV, argued the paper, whose editorial page was among the nation's most conservative, should not protect someone from aspects of the insurance marketplace to which the general public remained subject.[36] AIDS also reflected and magnified the bifurcated regime of federally funded health care spending enacted in the 1960s that included "separate and unequal programs for the elderly and the poor," with the latter program administered by states, many of which chose to sharply curtail eligibility.[37]

In the 1970s and 1980s, as manufacturing jobs left the city, Chicago's South Side and West Side black ghettoes had grown increasingly segregated and poor and also increasingly cut off from health care.[38] At the same time, as newly emboldened conservatives worked to roll back the expansion of federal health care spending during the 1970s, their targeted cuts hit teaching hospitals "especially hard because of the large number of poor patients in inner-city areas where many teaching hospitals are located."[39] A resulting series of hospital closures had disconnected residents of large swaths of Chicago's South and West Sides from health care and treatment for drug and alcohol dependency.[40] In hypersegregated cities such as Chicago, with African Americans (and increasingly Latinxs) infected disproportionately from the very beginning of the epidemic, the dynamics of AIDS were embedded in the problems of industrial decline, unemployment, poverty, and addiction.

The trajectory of the crisis was shaped by the conservative ascendancy in Washington not only in terms of its impact on medical research but also because of the way the Reagan administration's cuts to social services played out in cities. In 1986, big-city health commissioners whose jurisdictions included nearly three-quarters of the nation's diagnosed HIV infections gathered in Chicago to discuss how to deal with AIDS.[41] At this moment, municipal health departments faced significant pressure to cut their budgets even as poor neighborhoods were increasingly devastated by entrenched poverty.

Before 1990, when Congress stepped in to enact the Ryan White CARE Act, the AIDS crisis imposed major expenses on municipalities, and that also grew, rapidly and unpredictably, from year to year. Chicago's first mayoral liaison to the gay and lesbian community, Kit Duffy, appointed by Mayor Harold Washington in 1985, laid out the problem starkly in a 1987 letter to a top mayoral aide. While the need for direct services for people with AIDS was growing rapidly, she said, money from the federal government was available to the city only for "educational programs of questionable effectiveness." Most importantly, Duffy said, "CDBG and other funding sources the city might use have been cut"—a reference to Community Development Block Grants, one of the relatively few remaining vestiges of Lyndon Johnson's Great Society and among the most flexible forms of federal aid to cities, which the Reagan administration reduced sharply in the 1987 and 1988 budget years. The State of Illinois, for its part, was "earmarking most of its funds for antibody testing."[42]

To be sure, there were failures that were specific to local government. A gay newspaper reported as early as 1984 that "'red tape' has kept the city from hiring two AIDS researchers, even though federal funds for their salaries [were] available." In her 1987 memo, Duffy warned that people with AIDS and the gay and lesbian activists who were increasingly organizing on their behalf might not view the predicament of city government sympathetically. Activists, she predicted, would "look at the difference between the corporate budget for tree trimming and that for AIDS, and remember that no one died last year from catching Dutch Elm disease."[43]

But the broader fiscal context was overwhelming. In the 1980s most people with AIDS died in hospitals, often public hospitals that were in serious financial trouble. The local public sector bore a tremendous burden as a result of AIDS care. County, a sprawling, deteriorating West Side facility, was the city's only public hospital. It had long been the provider of last resort, a place that had long taken uninsured patients, most of them African Americans, that other private hospitals would not accept. It was there that the first AIDS clinic in Chicago was founded in 1983 by Ron Sable and another doctor, who later recalled being told by hospital administrators that "a new disease is not welcome here. There's not enough space for the ones we've already got, and there are too few resources."[44] By early 1992, the director of County's trauma unit reported that 10 percent of patients presenting with trauma injuries requiring surgery at County and 5 percent of the overall patient population were HIV-positive.[45] Moreover, the facility was treating fully one-third of all people with AIDS or HIV in Illinois. This percentage included 80 percent of the women and 40 percent of the children with AIDS or HIV in Illinois.[46]

Lacking capacity for large-scale interventions to confront the crisis, the city sought small-bore measures. Ron Sable, a doctor at County who was also an advocate for progressive health care policies and AIDS funding, complained that "the city's perception of its role is not as a service provider, rather as an educator and provider of seed monies for care-provision," which, he noted, "is also the role most foundations envision for themselves and so care-providers are getting lost in the shuffle."[47]

Besides Cook County Hospital, small grassroots organizations and non-profits became the other major provider of direct AIDS services. In Chicago, the Howard Brown Memorial Clinic, established by medical students in the 1970s for gay men seeking a more gay-affirming alternative to private doctors and public clinics for obtaining treatment for sexually transmitted diseases, represented a small infrastructure of gay-identified community-based outpatient health provision that was crucial in dealing with patients whom most doctors avoided. Chicago House, an eight-bedroom house for people with AIDS who had lost their jobs or homes, accepted its first two patients in a North Side lakefront area in February 1986.[48] In 1989 Open Hand Chicago was founded, delivering meals to people with AIDS, mirroring a similar program begun four years earlier in San Francisco.[49]

Howard Brown found itself stretched thin even as it expanded to respond to an increasingly expensive crisis.[50] The epidemic had hurt business in the bars whose owners often funded local gay movement organizations and decimated the male membership of such groups. The entertainment industry became a crucial source of revenue, and Broadway and Hollywood stars played a pivotal role in raising funds to support AIDS charities. In the fall of 1987 an unprecedented fund-raiser in Chicago, emceed by Angela Lansbury and starring Chita Rivera, Peter Allen, and Oprah Winfrey, raised $1 million for the AIDS Foundation of Chicago.[51]

AIDS also strained existing municipal resources in other areas, especially housing, as cases rose sharply in the second half of the 1980s. When a Chicago alderman proposed using vacant Chicago Housing Authority units as a housing option of last resort for indigent people with AIDS, Francine Washington, the agency's director of security, complained that its resources were already stretched to the breaking point: "I don't have nothing against AIDS patients, but I'm already in trouble with the rats and roaches. I ain't got time for AIDS." Remarkably, she continued, "Anyway, these people need a clean environment . . . like Lake Shore Drive. Put 'em there." Her invocation of Lake Shore Drive, where the city's most expensive real estate is located, does at least reflect an accurate perception that people with AIDS, because of their susceptibility to opportunistic infections, required a clean and sterile environment.[52]

Racial Inequality, White Reaction, and Structural Constraints on Black Organizing

The second half of the 1980s—between the development of the antibody test in 1985 and the passage of the Ryan White CARE Act in 1990—was a crucial period in the history of AIDS. To the extent that local government plays a role in existing accounts, it is most often San Francisco, which was important precisely because it was unique. At one point early in the crisis, nearly a fifth of the entire amount of money spent fighting AIDS in the United States was paid by the city and county of San Francisco.[53] The San Francisco "model" of HIV/AIDS care developed there became the gold standard that activists elsewhere pointed to. The model included the establishment of the first dedicated AIDS wards at a municipal hospital as well as a highly developed system of home-based care, palliative care in outpatient settings, and other services that sharply reduced both the strain on the public hospitals and the overall cost of the epidemic. San Francisco also possessed a compact geography and strong public support for progressive causes as well as a uniquely gay-friendly political environment, with both openly gay elected officials and local gay activist organizations that had already successfully lobbied for legislation and backed candidates. In short, gay political empowerment at the local level was uniquely powerful there. Most cities were more like Chicago—where not as high a proportion of AIDS patients were gay-identified white men—and the quest for cost-effective, high-quality AIDS care proved more elusive.

Black gay and lesbian Chicagoans, like white Chicagoans, responded to the crisis at the grassroots level. In September 1983 Max Smith organized a weekend discussion of AIDS at Martin's Den, a black gay bar on Chicago's

South Side. "From two to four we'd have our workshop, then at four o'clock people would stick around and buy drinks, so they benefited from having an early crowd," he recalled.[54] Later, African Americans organized the Kupona Network, a tiny South Side volunteer-based organization that sought to work through black churches to raise awareness about AIDS and connect affected people with available services. Though Kupona struggled and the organization became deeply divided in 1986 over whether or not to partner with Howard Brown in an effort to seek federal funds, it offered critically important services to African American people with AIDS and a crucial form of community-based resistance to their marginalization.[55]

Compared to the predominantly white gay enclaves on the North Side, Chicago's black neighborhoods had far fewer material resources available for responding to AIDS, compounding the extraordinary material consequences that typically accompanied a diagnosis. As I have argued elsewhere, the crisis made the gulf between African American neighborhoods and the mostly white gay enclaves on the city's north Side—with respect to organizational infrastructure, political economy, sexual cultures, and customary networks of care—more consequential than they had previously been.[56] Most of those diagnosed with AIDS in the epidemic's first five years lived on the North Side—74 percent of those diagnosed by mid-1987, compared with 20 percent living on the South Side and 6 percent on the West Side.[57] City surveillance data showed that white men living on the North Side and concentrated in and around the lakefront New Town neighborhood made up the largest cluster of HIV and AIDS diagnoses, while African Americans living on the South Side made up the second-largest cluster. After County, the hospital with the next highest number of AIDS diagnoses in the early years was St. Joseph Hospital in Lincoln Park, on the North Side, because of its proximity to the Lakeview gay enclave.[58] In 1987, the Howard Brown clinic served almost two-thirds of patients living on Chicago's North Side but just over one-third of those living on the West and South Sides.[59]

The location of most of Chicago's AIDS service organizations on the predominantly white North Side worsened an already fragile tie between black political organizations and gay ones. "Volunteering to help agencies such as Horizons or the Howard Brown Memorial Clinic is a sign of status," reported the *Chicago Tribune* in 1987, illustrating the public attention disproportionately afforded AIDS treatment organizations on the North Side.[60] "When an IV drug user is diagnosed with AIDS, he is often referred to a gay clinic on the North Side for help," said Curtis Winkle, an urban planning professor at the University of Illinois at Chicago, in a 1988 interview. "If he is straight and from the West Side or she is a mother with a sick baby, he or she might not feel comfortable going there or have the transportation to get there."[61] Indeed, over time AIDS added another strand to the growing bundle of cultural markers that signified homosexuality as an element of the urban landscape whose proper location increasingly seemed to be prosperous, mostly white enclaves. Meanwhile, because the county, *not* the city, controlled the only public hospital (Cook County Hospital), conservative elected officials from Chicago's nearly all-white suburbs controlled an institution serving a predominantly poor black and/or Latinx population. As a county rather than a municipal agency, the hospital depended on the support of the Cook County Board of Commissioners, where Republicans and conservative Democrats from suburban areas of the county exerted strong influence.

Importantly, even among white gay men, the AIDS crisis disproportionately affected the poor and economically vulnerable. Strikingly, as of mid-1987, fully 70 percent of patients with AIDS treated at the Howard Brown clinic, the largest provider of outpatient AIDS services, survived only on Social Security payments and public assistance.[62] This contradicts Shilts's notion that AIDS struck primarily "fast-lane" wealthy white gay men.[63] Injecting drug users were more likely to lack health insurance or access to regular medical care before they ever contracted HIV, but for many middle-class gay men, AIDS rapidly drained their savings, sooner or later cost them their jobs, and led their insurance companies to cancel their insurance plans. People with AIDS frequently lost their jobs and health insurance and experienced family rejection and sudden downward mobility.[64] The urban experience of AIDS was not simply a matter of affluent whites and poor black and brown people.

But even when the Howard Brown clinic made efforts to secure the participation of people of color in its treatment and research programs, the history of white racism, exploitation, and experimentation on communities of color nonetheless created barriers to success. Shelton Watson advised the clinic on the recruitment of African American volunteers for a trial that began in 1993 of a live, attenuated vaccine. Participants in the trial would not seroconvert, but the vaccine posed a risk that it could lead participants to generate anti-HIV antibodies and thereby test positive on the HIV test. "You know, people still remember Tuskegee," he recalled. "And they do not want to be part of a trial that's, if they go get tested for a job, [will make them] come up HIV-positive on the test."[65] Here yet again, AIDS represented a moment of continuity, not rupture, in public health history.

In Chicago, moreover, AIDS created tension between a newly ascendant class of black political leaders and the gay community who had made the leaders' entrance into municipal politics possible. As in other cities in the urban North, as I have argued, gay activists in Chicago gradually began to win political power in the 1970s and 1980s, partly by joining liberal electoral coalitions that flourished as African Americans gained power in municipal politics.[66] Following the election of Harold Washington in 1983 as the city's first black mayor, black political leaders were eager to cement their newfound power but faced a virulent reaction from white city council members who sought to stymie Mayor Washington at every turn.

The intensely racist white reaction against Mayor Washington's ascent to the mayoralty made racial politics the all-consuming axis of municipal policy disputes. This reaction created a situation in which it was politically diffi- cult for Washington to fire his health commissioner, Lonnie Edwards, who was black, despite a response to the epidemic that AIDS activists increasingly considered grossly incompetent in the second half of the 1980s. Edwards drew mounting criticism beginning with a 1986 press conference in which he discussed AIDS largely in terms of the risk of infection faced by men patron- izing female prostitutes (a risk experts that thought was negligible in the United States) while broaching the possibility of quarantining HIV-positive persons deemed at high risk of infecting others.[67] By the spring of 1987, the city had failed to make payments to agencies with which it had signed con- tracts to provide AIDS services.[68] Edwards's failings even created an open- ing for gay Republicans—otherwise marginal in a Democratic-controlled city—to mount a credible attack on the administration.[69] By May 1987, the members of Washington's Committee on Gay and Lesbian Issues believed that the health department's delays in disbursing both federal and state funds posed a major and needless difficulty for the city's AIDS service organiza- tions.[70] The board president of Kupona Network—then the city's only black gay AIDS agency—defended Edwards privately, claiming that he "has been very responsive to Black people," though without any public statement.[71]

Although it is not entirely clear why Washington declined to replace a health commissioner widely seen as problematic, the context for that deci- sion was an all-out unending conflict to retain control of the city council on the part of an insurgent black-led coalition. Following Washington's sudden death late in 1987, his successor Eugene Sawyer, who was also black, kept Edwards in the job, and Edwards continued to be harshly criticized for the inadequacy of his handling of AIDS.[72] The failures of the Washington and

Sawyer administrations to respond adequately to the crisis placed significant stress on the distinctive coalition between progressive white gays and lesbians and black political leaders during this period. Richard M. Daley, eldest son of the city's longtime late political boss, cultivated the gay vote in 1989 by castigating Edwards's incompetence in his successful 1989 bid to oust Sawyer.

In Chicago, the election of Richard M. Daley as mayor in 1989, like the election of white Republicans Rudy Giuliani in New York and Richard Riordan in Los Angeles, was a symbolic restoration of white control over the city and led to an intensification of harsh policing and punishment in communities of color. Yet even though Daley had worked to win the votes of gay and lesbians with harsh criticism of the health department, he too stumbled repeatedly in handling the politics of AIDS funding. Partly because of the growing radicalization of AIDS activists nationwide, tensions between Chicago officials and gay activists became even more explosive after Daley reneged on a promise to increase the city's budget for AIDS.[73] In November 1989 furious gay activists summoned him to a public forum at a gay-owned restaurant, where the chairman of his ostensibly nonpolitical Committee on Gay and Lesbian Issues declared that he had been told he should focus solely on reelecting the mayor. The specific charge evidently touched a nerve in Daley, who had struggled mightily to distance himself from his father's reputation for corruption and patronage politics. He stormed out of the meeting while activists chanted against him.[74] Daley soon essentially capitulated to all of the protestors' demands and embarked on a long-term strategy to win over and incorporate gay and lesbian Chicagoans to his political coalition. As he solidified his standing with whites and Latinx voters—though notably not black voters—the possibility of a progressive politics in Chicago faded.

* * *

The AIDS policy landscape shifted with passage of the Ryan White CARE Act, which was pitched to Congress as a form of disaster relief for urban America. Its Title I provided direct aid to the cities hardest hit by the epidemic. In the law's initial five-year cycle, Chicago's CARE award under Title I during the first year was $3.2 million.[75] In its first two years, the law provided "$847 million to fund AIDS services nationwide," altering the fiscal environment in which direct service providers for people with AIDS operated by establishing a federal responsibility to address the ballooning costs.[76]

The 1990s saw public funding of AIDS improve somewhat. In 1990, the Ryan White CARE Act changed the structural relationship between the gay movement and the state, bringing many AIDS service organizations into a permanent relationship with state power. That same year for the first time, more blacks than whites were diagnosed with AIDS in Chicago, as the epidemic continued to become even more disproportionately a disease of women, children, and men of color living in poverty who may not have had a gay identity even if they had sex with men.[77] And after the election to the presidency in 1992 of Bill Clinton, who was viewed as far more sympathetic to funding AIDS than Ronald Reagan and George H. W. Bush had been, radical AIDS activism declined.

But what is striking about the trajectory of HIV/AIDS in the 1990s is the degree to which, despite significant improvements in funding and later in the medical possibilities, the epidemic's course was also marked by important continuities. In the 1990s, AIDS organizations competed with one another—and with gay and lesbian political organizations seeking legal reform and electoral clout—for private funding, which seemed to grow scarcer as more men became sick, lost their jobs, and died.[78] AIDS continued to cause racial tension in gay communities around funding for prevention and services.[79] And the problems caused by the spatial concentration of AIDS services on the North Side also continued. The transportation needs of South Side residents who needed to access AIDS care on the North Side remained often unmet. In 1994, assessing how the landscape of service provision had changed under the new law, researchers noted that three-fourths of people with AIDS who fell under the IV drug user category required health transportation under the act, compared with less than half of gay men. Moreover, these researchers noted that "African Americans and especially Hispanics/Latinos are significantly more likely to have needed housing in the last six months than are whites."[80]

Even as the discovery of protease inhibitors in 1996 finally began to abate the toll of suffering and death caused by AIDS in the United States, racial and economic disparities in access to health care remained perhaps the most notable feature of the AIDS-specific medical landscape. The new class of drugs dramatically improved HIV/AIDS survival rates, and today the life spans of many will approximate those of the larger population. Indeed, access to prescription medications became a new vector of inequality. African Americans benefited significantly less than whites from the new drugs, whose costs could range into the tens of thousands of dollars annually.[81]

Viewed in broad perspective, the experience of AIDS in the United States was characterized by important ruptures and discontinuities, as we have seen, because of stigma and cost. Equally striking, however, is remarkable continuity evident across the thirty-five-year sweep of the epidemic's American history—with racial and economic inequality when it comes to health care an enduring constant.

CHAPTER 5

"Don't We Die Too?"

The Politics of AIDS and Race in Philadelphia

Dan Royles

In 1981 doctors reported the first cases of what would later become known as AIDS, which appeared as an outbreak of strange infections among groups of gay men in New York, San Francisco, and Los Angeles. Before long, cases began to appear in other cities as well, including Philadelphia. In August 1982, the city had six confirmed cases of the new disease; a year later, that number had quadrupled to twenty-four. By the end of 1984, over a hundred AIDS cases had been reported to the Department of Public Health. As the epidemic grew, gay men and their allies in Philadelphia organized to do something about it.[1]

Unlike New York and San Francisco, which have anchored much of the literature on AIDS in the United States, Philadelphia is not a gay mecca, nor is it a global capital of finance and culture.[2] However, Philadelphia is a major city, home to over 1.5 million people. Moreover, its response to the AIDS crisis in the 1980s illustrates the ways that the postwar fate of American cities shaped a growing epidemic. Like other urban centers in the Northeast and Midwest, Philadelphia was scarred by segregation, white flight, deindustrialization, and disastrous urban planning schemes, which left the city with an eroded tax base and dwindling coffers on the eve of the AIDS crisis. Cities such as Philadelphia would be the epicenters of the early epidemic, but thanks to systematic abandonment and disinvestment, Philadelphia lacked the resources to mount an effective response.[3]

At the same time, as was the case in other cities, a vibrant gay and lesbian scene flourished in Philadelphia during the decades following World War II.

Downtown Philadelphia emerged as the nexus of local gay life, particularly for men drawn to cruising areas in Washington Square and Rittenhouse Parks and to gay bars along Spruce Street. For this reason, the area encompassing several blocks south of Market Street and east of Broad Street came to be known as the "Gayborhood." Here during the 1960s and 1970s, gay men and lesbians in Philadelphia began to organize for sexual freedom. In the early 1980s, they successfully lobbied the Philadelphia City Council to add sexual orientation as a protected category under Philadelphia's Fair Practices Ordinance. They also formed an increasingly visible voting bloc within the city's Democratic Party political establishment, helping to elect W. Wilson Goode, the city's first African American mayor, in 1983.[4]

However, the "city of brotherly and sisterly loves" was divided along racial lines. The downtown gay scene comprised mainly white men, while black gay men and lesbians instead set up their own social clubs in West Philadelphia. When black gay men ventured downtown for a night of dancing and drinking, they tended to go to one of a handful of bars that catered to men of color because "the music was always better" and they were made to feel unwelcome at or were actively excluded from the bars frequented by white gay men. As a result, gay men in Philadelphia developed overlapping but distinct racial and sexual geographies. Black and white gay men tended to live, work, and play in different parts of the city, or at least in different clubs downtown. Even when they did share a dance floor or browse the shelves at Giovanni's Room, the city's gay bookstore, those spaces took on different meanings for black gay men versus their white counterparts.[5]

The geography of the Gayborhood also took on a class dimension as gay men helped to gentrify Center City and the surrounding neighborhoods beginning in the 1960s. As they moved into the area around Washington Square and along the South Street corridor, they drove out residents who tended to be disproportionately black and working class. Gay men were not the sole participants in the "back to the cities" movement that brought young upwardly mobile professionals to the urban core. However, newspaper coverage about gentrification framed the new urban residents as gay and bourgeois, describing the "quiche-and-fern bars" that they brought to rapidly changing neighborhoods such as Queen Village, which bordered Center City along the Delaware River.[6]

Through both discrimination and gentrification, white gay men marked their downtown enclave, along with the rest of the central business district and surrounding neighborhoods, as a space for affluent and middle-class whites.[7]

In a city already known for its neighborhood divisions, this would have significant consequences for the way that African American residents, especially black gay and bisexual men, understood their risk for AIDS. With a cash-strapped city and with state and federal officials largely unwilling to address an epidemic associated with gay men and drug users, groups rooted in the Gayborhood took on the work of responding to a crisis that might have otherwise been handled by public agencies. The whiteness of early AIDS groups in Philadelphia also reinforced the idea within the city's black communities that AIDS was primarily a *white* gay disease. As the disproportionate impact of the new disease on African Americans became clear, activists challenged local AIDS groups to improve their minority outreach. In the so-called AIDS wars that followed, public health became a battleground in the struggle over identity and the limits of community in postindustrial Philadelphia.[8]

* * *

As in other cities, Philadelphia's first response to the AIDS epidemic came from within the predominantly white gay community, centered on the downtown bars, bathhouses, and bookstores where gay men came out, met friends, and had sex. In 1979 gay health activist and regional health commissioner Walter Lear founded Lavender Health, a gay and lesbian community health group, that was renamed Philadelphia Community Health Alternatives (PCHA) in 1981. The following year as news of a new and deadly "gay cancer" began to spread, PCHA members formed the Philadelphia AIDS Task Force (PATF), a volunteer group dedicated to fighting the disease. Task force members distributed educational materials outside gay bars, operated an informational hotline, and provided "buddy" services to those who had become sick and had trouble caring for themselves.[9]

The downtown gay enclave in which PCHA and the PATF emerged was in many ways a segregated neighborhood and was perceived as a specifically white space by both black gay men who felt excluded from it and at least some of the white gay men who lived, worked, and played there. As public health reports began to show that a disproportionate number of African Americans were affected by AIDS, PCHA and the PATF came under fire for not doing enough to address the epidemic in Philadelphia's black communities.[10]

Among the most significant and contentious sites for AIDS education in Philadelphia were the city's gay bars, specifically those understood to be *white* gay bars. These were not entirely white spaces, but bar owners and staff certainly tried to limit the number of black customers. At the door, a bouncer might ask black gay men for multiple forms of identification while letting white gays who appeared to be underage enter freely. Black gay men who did get inside reported being served last by bartenders and ignored by white patrons. The problem was not limited to Philadelphia; black gay men in other cities described similar experiences with racial discrimination.[11]

In Philadelphia, these complaints were confirmed in 1986 by the release of a two-year study undertaken by a coalition of gay community groups. The study found "pervasive racial and sexual exclusivity in Greater Philadelphia's lesbian and gay bars" and noted that "many patrons tolerate this kind of racial and sexual discrimination." As a result, a handful of bars catering mostly to black gay men had cropped up in Center City by the early 1980s, including Smart Place near 10th and Arch, Pentony's near 13th and Arch, and Allegro II at 21st and Sansom. However, as black gay activist Arnold Jackson noted, "if blacks think they are escaping oppression by going to these bars, they are truly mistaken." Black gay men decried the bars' owners—who were all white—for their "apparent refusal to spend money on upkeep." Philadelphia's gay bars, it seems, were both separate and unequal.[12]

Moreover, the treatment that black men received at the city's gay bars was emblematic of a racial tension that suffused the community as a whole. Black gay men in Philadelphia reported that their white counterparts viewed "blacks as being inferior or less intelligent or sex objects." Others reported being made to simply feel invisible. Joseph Beam, a black gay writer who lived in Center City, described being ignored by his "mostly young, white, upwardly mobile" neighbors, except when they wanted to see "if I had any reefer."[13]

Black gay men and lesbians felt similarly marginalized in local gay politics. In a 1986 letter to the gay newspaper *Au Courant*, Don Ransom, a black gay man, criticized the "plantation mentality" in Philadelphia's gay and lesbian community. He pointed to the lack of local black gay speakers at a protest organized by the Philadelphia Lesbian and Gay Task Force (PLGTF) in response to the U.S. Supreme Court's decision to uphold state antisodomy laws in *Bowers v. Hardwick*. The group had invited Gil Gerald of the National Coalition of Black Lesbians and Gays, based in Washington, D.C., to speak at the event, but Ransom saw this as evidence that the PLGTF "had to go out of town and find someone who wouldn't know about their behavior or their exclusionary policies."[14]

Discrimination and exclusion in the Gayborhood shaped the way that black gay and bisexual men understood their own risk for AIDS. By the middle of 1984, it had become clear that African Americans in Philadelphia were suffering from the new disease.[15] That year, the PATF launched its One New Case Per Week campaign to highlight the shifting demographics of the epidemic, with posters featuring three different faces—one white, one black, and one Hispanic—along with a tagline about the rate of new AIDS diagnoses in the city. Perhaps in a deliberate attempt to push their message beyond Center City and transcend the city's neighborhood divisions, they placed the posters on Philadelphia's subway system.[16] Tyrone Smith, a black gay activist in Philadelphia, remembers:

> They used to have on the subway these posters up, and it would be how many folks had become infected within that week or with that month. And I started seeing these white faces, and then I got appalled one day when I saw black faces there. I thought it was the enemy, I thought it was a trick, I thought that if anybody was to get AIDS, it would be the black children who fucked with white men.[17]

As Smith's story suggests, in the early days of the epidemic some black gay men saw themselves as being insulated from the new disease. Jose de Marco, a black queer Philadelphia native, similarly remembers that "gay black men thought this only happened to nasty gay white boys because [they] do nasty, dirty things. But in reality, a lot of black men and white men were having sex."[18] For black gay men, deflecting the identification of AIDS as a gay disease onto gay white men may have been a way of showing their frustration with racism and segregation in the downtown gay community, a way to counter the historical association of blackness with hypersexuality and disease, or both.[19]

The One New Case Per Week campaign angered other black Philadelphians for the same reason. One woman called the PATF to say "you have a lot of nerve showing a Black person on that poster." Agency president Nick Ifft defended the campaign to the *Philadelphia Tribune*, the city's black newspaper: "Many of the calls we received suggested that we are doing something which is not true, but our reason for using three different images (Black, white and Hispanic) is because all people can get AIDS." African Americans viewers, or at least those who objected to the posters, saw them not as evidence of the disease's morbid equanimity but instead as a white organization's attempt to demonize blacks by associating them with the burgeoning epidemic. Given their initial relief—in the words of local AIDS activist Linda Burnette—that "finally it's something that's not about black people," the revelation that African

Americans were also at risk would seem to be a terrible reversal of fortune. As Smith suggests, some saw it as a "trick," possibly one masterminded by some powers that be to pin the blame for the epidemic on black people.[20]

The PATF also worked with the Philadelphia chapter of Black and White Men Together (BWMT), an interracial gay men's group, to produce "Respect Yourself!," an educational rap single about AIDS and aimed at African Americans. The record was funded by a grant from the U.S. Conference of Mayors and released in 1985, with an initial run of five hundred copies to be distributed to radio stations and dance clubs frequented by black gay men. The project would come to be viewed as something of a flop: commercial radio stations in Philadelphia never played "Respect Yourself!," and the PATF stopped selling copies at cost out of its Center City office, although a spokesman claimed that this was not an indication of the record's failure. Don Ransom of Philadelphia BWMT thought that the record's lyrics had been too explicit, while others thought that "Respect Yourself!" had been too much like "a Sesame Street rap," with the lyrics

Be you a butcher, a baker, a candlestick maker,
AIDS don't care about the color of your skin.
You gotta keep your body strong.
Respect yourself and you will live long.[21]

Later, in the midst of a public battle over funding for minority AIDS outreach, David Fair would accuse PCHA executive director Thomas Livers of sitting on money that had been left over from the U.S. Conference of Mayors grant because, in Fair's words, the PATF "never took the rap record project seriously."[22]

When PCHA and the PATF did make good-faith attempts at minority outreach, their efforts could easily be short-circuited by larger racial tensions. When Len Bost, a black gay man and PATF volunteer who coproduced "Respect Yourself!," tried to distribute the group's AIDS education literature at the city's black gay bars, he was rebuffed. Some bars turned him away outright, while others threw the materials away as soon as he left. Although Bost himself was black, this was apparently not enough to overcome the PATF's reputation for not being "integrated," as one black gay bar patron asserted, or its association with discrimination in the Gayborhood as a whole.[23]

Critics also saw these efforts as insufficient: some posters and a song would hardly make a dent in the burgeoning AIDS epidemic among black Philadelphians. As the impact of AIDS on Philadelphia's black community and on black gay men in particular became clear, local critics called on PCHA and the PATF to improve their minority outreach efforts. Some worked within the organizations. These included activists such as Tyrone Smith, who joined Interpreting Minority Perspectives for Action (IMPACT), a volunteer committee within the task force that aimed to expand AIDS education directed to communities of color in Philadelphia. Rashidah Hassan, a black Muslim nurse and infectious disease specialist, also joined the task force as a volunteer around 1984 and was elected as vice president of PCHA's board in May 1986. Around the same time, she and Wesley Anderson, a public health professional with experience working on sexually transmitted diseases, founded Blacks Educating Blacks About Sexual Health Issues (BEBASHI), one of the nation's first black AIDS service organizations. Others criticized PCHA and the PATF entirely from without. They included David Fair, who was a member of BWMT and worked as secretary-treasurer of District Local 1199C of the National Union of Hospital and Health Care Employees. Members of the union, who were mostly black, had encountered some of Philadelphia's first cases of AIDS while working in the city's hospitals. Fair, a white gay political firebrand, often found himself at odds with the city's gay community leaders over what he saw as their racism and classism.[24]

From within and without, critics of PCHA and the PATF demanded greater minority representation among the groups' clients, volunteers, and staff. They argued that the agencies, which were made up primarily of white gay men, should look more like the AIDS epidemic in Philadelphia, where more than half of all people who had been diagnosed with AIDS were nonwhite. However, critics sought more than token representation of African Americans at PCHA and the PATF. They felt that shifting the agencies' demographic composition to better reflect racial disparities in the epidemic would yield more effective AIDS services for people of color. For example, if the PATF recruited more black operators to its AIDS hotline, African Americans would be more comfortable calling and more likely to believe the information they received. Similarly, they noted, black volunteers for the buddy program would be more sensitive to the needs of black people with AIDS. Tyrone Smith recalls that gay white men with AIDS

> were the Center Citiers, the Main Liners; they were the affluent who were being stricken with this disease. And what was being said to them is, we want you to live a normal life, as normal as your life has been. Well going to brunch was common for them, but going to

brunch wasn't something my boys did. They just wanted a couple of dollars to go to a movie and basic stuff like that. So it was us who had to say to institutions, "Okay, well, but this is what these guys need." He wants a hoagie! I mean, he doesn't want truffles and luffles and luffles. He wants a hoagie, and he wants it where he wants it from.[25]

Here Smith frames the difference between black gay men with AIDS and their white counterparts in terms of space and class, while his comment about "truffles and luffles" recalls the gentrifying "quiche-and-fern" set. To be sure, not all gay white men with AIDS took home hefty paychecks or lived in upscale parts of the city. That Smith associates white gay men with the Main Line, a wealthy white suburb not known for having a visible gay presence, reveals the overlapping geographies that shaped black gay men's sense of where they did—and did not—belong in the city. This in turn shaped their relationship to PCHA and the PATF.

Indeed, the debate over *whom* the agencies represented was linked to the question of *where* their efforts should be concentrated. Critics and allies alike framed this not just as a problem of racism in the Gayborhood but also in terms of how racial, sexual, and class identity mapped onto Philadelphia's physical geography. David Fair saw this as part of the problem of a local gay "movement" concerned only with advancing the interests of those who already enjoyed proximity—literally and figuratively—to power: white middle-class affluent gay men and lesbians in Center City. As Fair told Dan Daniel, host of the local radio show *Gaydreams* in 1985,

The fact is that in Center City if you are gay, you can get information on "safe sex" and you can get information on AIDS[.] But if you're a black kid who lives up at Broad and Columbia, or if you're a white kid who lives in Roxborough or K&A [Kensington and Allegheny], you can't get that information. . . . And we need to do something about that . . . because people are dying as a result of our racism, people are dying as a result of our elitism, and they're dying as a result of our lack of courage in being able to develop real strategies and real commitment, to involve people outside of the barriers that have been set up for us so far.[26]

Fair criticized the city's gay political leadership for spending time, money, and political capital addressing the needs of gay "yuppies" in Center City while ignoring working-class and minority neighborhoods to the south, north, and west. Whether minoritized gay people had been shut out of the downtown area by historical segregation, high rents, or an unwelcoming atmosphere, they remained outside the orbit of PCHA and the PATF. For Fair, the failure of local gay rights and AIDS groups to reach beyond the Gayborhood evinced a deadly lack of political will rooted in bias. Like Smith and other AIDS activists, Fair challenged PCHA and the PATF over questions of whose interests they represented and how their resources should be distributed.

The AIDS activists who attended BEBASHI's meetings around this time reflected this sense of division between a mostly white downtown, including the Gayborhood, and the rest of the city. Two extant sign-in sheets from BEBASHI meetings show that only about one out of six of those in attendance lived in Center City, while most of the rest lived in West or North Philadelphia. The location of the meetings is unclear, but around this time BEBASHI was using office space in the headquarters of David Fair's National Union of Hospital and Health Care Employees at 1319 Locust Street, in the heart of the Gayborhood. Thus, it seems reasonable to assume that the location of the meetings does not explain the relatively low number of attendees from Center City.[27]

As the number of AIDS cases in Philadelphia grew, pressure for change at PCHA and the PATF mounted. However, even those who agreed that a problem existed did not necessarily agree on a solution. Cei Bell, a black transgender journalist who reported on charges of racism at the PATF for *Philadelphia Gay News* in April 1986, suggested organizing within the gay and lesbian community. Bell proposed that "there are enough black gays around to create a serious change in how our community works." She noted that bringing black gay men into an organization such as the PATF would be challenging but stressed the importance of black and white gays alike laying aside their differences to work toward common goals. "It is not as though," she warned, "there are so many of us (both black and white) or as though we are so invulnerable we can not be eliminated en masse." Bell saw AIDS as bringing a "bizarre equality to the gay world that has never existed" by striking down people regardless of class, education, or race. In this new context, she argued, "we can no longer afford the luxury of fighting with each other."[28]

Rashidah Hassan, quoted in Bell's piece on racism at the PATF, took a different stance. For Hassan, the epidemic reflected and reinforced patterns of inequality, as evidenced by the disproportionate number of African Americans living with AIDS in Philadelphia. Nevertheless, she allowed that the exclusion of people of color from the agency "[had not] been intentional" but instead resulted from blindness to the experiences of homosexually active men outside their downtown enclave. The PATF had structured its response to the epidemic according to the social milieu of its staff and members, inadvertently putting its efforts outside the reach of some of the most affected. Moreover, Hassan argued, becoming involved with a gay-identified organization could put black men in a precarious position: "Once you step out you label yourself. If you separate yourself from the black community, where does that leave you? In the black community, what affects one of us affects all." She argues now, as she did then, that "it's not like saying, 'Oh, we'll go to the Gayborhood.' There's no black Gayborhood, so I've got to do the whole community, to make sure the most at risk hear the message." According to Hassan, AIDS educators would have to canvass the entire African American community in order to reach not only black gay and bisexual men but also those who had sex with men but did not identify as gay or bisexual as well as their potential female partners, who were also at risk of contracting HIV.[29]

David Fair similarly framed the issue of racism at the PATF as a function of spatial and structural exclusion rather than as the result of malicious prejudice on the agency's part. As a solution to the group's minority outreach problem, Fair insisted that Executive Director Tom Livers hire someone "with proven community organizing skills in Philadelphia's black and Hispanic communities." Anything less would amount to nothing more than "pious proclamations" and would indicate that the PATF failed to take seriously the needs of minorities in Philadelphia. For this reason, Fair remained reluctant to cooperate with Ifft and Livers in recruiting black volunteers to the PATF. In March 1986 Fair announced at a meeting of BWMT for Education, an AIDS education group for people of color that he cochaired, that he had been meeting with thirty-five black members of his union "who were angry at having lost . . . lovers, friends, or family members to AIDS." When asked why he "kept those people in his hip pocket" while calling for the PATF to improve its minority relations, Fair replied, "I don't believe that the structure of the gay and lesbian community works for black people, and I will not input them into that structure."[30]

Bell, Hassan, and Fair each presented a somewhat different diagnosis of the PATF's minority outreach problem, along with a different solution. Bell saw racism in the gay community as a problem of interpersonal relations: some white gay men were certainly racist, but closeted black gays should overcome their personal misgivings so they could join the out gay community in addressing a terrible crisis. Hassan and Fair argued that by concentrating its efforts in the Center City gay community from which it emerged, the PATF failed to reach gay men in the city's minority and working-class white neighborhoods, although Fair tended to be more vitriolic in his indictments of the agency. According to Hassan, openly gay black men risked separating themselves from the rest of the African American community and its networks of social support and care if they openly identified themselves according to their sexuality. Since black gay men were also excluded from or unwelcome at many of Philadelphia's downtown gay commercial establishments and were largely lacking their own autonomous spaces, the best way to reach them would be to canvass entire black communities. By contrast, Fair sought a movement by and for those who fell outside the white middle-class model of organizing presented by the downtown gay community, even as he pressed Ifft and Livers to hire someone to coordinate the task force's minority outreach.

Critics of the PATF also used the question of funding to challenge the group's focus on AIDS education in the Gayborhood. They argued that because the agency received money from city contracts and block grants, it should serve people with AIDS across lines of race, gender, sexuality, and neighborhood. A week after running Bell's piece on racism at the PATF, the *Philadelphia Gay News* reported that Fair's union was considering a lawsuit against the group under the 1964 Civil Rights Act, which prohibits discrimination by institutions receiving federal funding. Similarly, a leaflet titled "Don't We Die Too?"—which may have been produced by Fair's union—accused the task force of not using $100,000 of received public funds (a number disputed by Ifft) to "serve the needs of the majority of people with AIDS" in a city where over half of the AIDS caseload was nonwhite. At a public meeting hosted by Local 1199C to discuss the pamphlet, Darlene Garner, who served with Fair as cochair of BWMT for Education, proposed that concerned people of color could continue to press the PATF on minority outreach while setting up parallel services through black churches. To this Gwendolyn Johnson, the chair of the meeting and a Local 1199C member, responded, "We don't want to do that. The Task Force has money. We want to get our share." Johnson stressed her concern with the PATF's funding sources and client population because, she said, "It's our tax dollars, too."[31]

Some white gay men who volunteered with the PATF took exception to the criticism. In a letter to Ifft published in *Au Courant*, David Wentroble, a Presbyterian minister in Devon, a township outside of Philadelphia, criticized Fair's allegations of a "racist attitude" at the agency, which he viewed "as a personal insult and an affront." Wentroble, who identified himself as a "suburban white middle-class gay professional," wrote that he had become involved in the PATF "to help my community." His reaction to the people he served as a buddy trace the boundaries of his initial sense of his community. Wentroble had at first been paired with a young black man, who had passed away, then with a two-year-old black boy and the boy's family. He wrote that he had been "apprehensive at first" but was "blessed" to "have had my eyes opened about how people much different from myself live." When Wentroble described wanting to help his community by volunteering with the PATF, these had not been the people he had in mind.[32]

Wentroble's letter indicates the source of complaints against the PATF and to white gay men's lack of understanding and anger in response to the criticism. His lack of familiarity with his clients' culture and lifestyle—by his lights "much different" from his own—speaks to the lack of and need for specific services for people of color with AIDS. Wentroble framed his volunteer work as providing an opportunity for personal growth, but how did the people with whom he was paired experience the encounter? Perhaps they sensed his wariness at working with them. For critics, this was evidence of racism at the task force, but for Wentroble, his own story belied charges of bias. For him, racism would likely have meant denying services to African Americans, which the task force clearly did not do. As a volunteer and part of the task force's "community," Wentroble took the charge of racism personally, and Fair's allegations in particular left him "infuriated."

By the fall of 1986, the two sides in the fight over minority AIDS education in Philadelphia had reached an impasse. Although the PATF planned to hire a minority outreach coordinator, Rashidah Hassan had grown tired of fighting for change within the organization, where she often felt like the agency's "colored poster child." Hassan decided that she would publicly resign from the PCHA board in September 1986 during her speech at a rally following the city's first candlelight AIDS walk. She thought about the text of her speech that day as she bought a huge candle for the event—black in contrast to everyone else's white and large enough to make a statement. That evening she marched through rain showers with over 2,000 others, many holding signs stenciled with numbers to represent those who had died, to LOVE Park, where the assembled crowd waited to hear from a slate of speakers, including a woman who had recently lost her son to AIDS. Hassan felt guilty; as the mother of two young boys, she had some insight into the other woman's pain. Hassan recalls that she approached the other woman near the podium and explained, "I had a very painful task that I was assigned, and that nothing that I was going to say should reflect negatively on her son, or her grief, and that I understood what she was going through, but that there was a socio-political statement that I needed to make in order to save the lives of others." According to Hassan, the woman hugged her and replied, "We all have to do what we have to do."[33]

When her turn came, Hassan stepped behind the podium, placed the giant black candle in front of her, and laid into the city's AIDS services establishment. She directed her criticism at the PATF and the white gay community it represented: "Our people—minority, those differing comparatively to the population—have the right to be educated, have the right to have resources committed, have the right to stand here with you and say that we are dying from this disease and you are making it our disease."[34] Since the PATF "didn't, couldn't, haven't, won't provide education for the minority community," she had founded her own group, BEBASHI, to do so. Hassan and her BEBASHI colleagues had worked with the PATF to improve the older organization's minority outreach but to little effect. In her speech she warned, "If in your presentations . . . you don't remember the Hispanics and you don't remember the blacks, I guarantee you—I guarantee you we will be there to haunt you for it." She knew that her criticism of the PATF, which provided much of what little local services were available, would anger some, but she told the audience "I want you to be upset, [and] turn that energy to committing yourselves to seeing that minority people obtain the same treatment, the same empowerment to suffer from this disease and get away from it, to have health care, as you have." She ended on a conciliatory note, adding "I want you to remember that while you're fighting, there are those who are different from you who need to have a voice in how things are done . . . because they do not recognize that it is not just a white gay disease, and I ask your help and your support in trying to provide that information to the community."[35] Today Hassan remembers this as her "Malcolm X speech," an "intense" piece of oratory that "was a little graphic about bending black butts over and feeling free to bang them without giving them the information or the protection they needed." However, an extant video recording shows that the speech contained no such language; Hassan appears forceful and resolute but not bombastic in her criticism of the city's AIDS establishment. In the video at least some audience members appear to cheer her on, shouting "Tell 'em about it!" and "That's right!"[36]

Looking back on that moment through the turmoil that came afterward probably makes it seem much more contentious in retrospect and helps explain why Hassan now frames it as "the skirmish of the war" for minority AIDS education in Philadelphia. After she split from PCHA and the PATF to pursue her own work with BEBASHI, Hassan drew fire for "creating division within the community." As a greater number of specialized AIDS groups came on the scene, she eventually became the target of the same criticism that she had once leveled at others.[37]

Although the crowd at the vigil seems to have been vocally supportive, the negative reaction to Hassan and her speech was almost immediate. A week after the march the *Philadelphia Gay News* ran an angry editorial by Bill Whiting, a white gay visual artist who had designed the PATF's "One New Case a Week" posters. Whiting criticized the event as a whole and Hassan in particular for her "intolerable" speech. He questioned the route laid out for the marchers, which began north of Center City outside the state office building at the intersection of Broad and Spring Garden Streets before heading south to Benjamin Franklin Parkway and City Hall and finally to JFK Plaza for the candlelight rally. The starting and ending points for the march were meant in part to draw attention to the lack of city and state funding for AIDS services. However, the route also intentionally avoided Center City; women on the march planning committee objected to the idea of planning a route along Spruce and Pine Streets, which cut through the heart of the Gayborhood, because those streets were "too white gay male." With statistics showing the disproportionate impact of AIDS on Philadelphia's minority communities—including minority women—march organizers wanted to disentangle the disease from its close association with homosexuality and portray the epidemic as "a growing concern that would effect [*sic*] everyone, not just gays."[38]

In comments to an *Au Courant* reporter for a separate piece, Whiting insisted that the Center City neighborhood the march organizers had avoided was in fact diverse, with residents comprising "blacks, whites, men and women, gay and straight, and families of a variety of ethnic backgrounds." From his perspective, a Center City route would have reached people from different walks of life without sacrificing the need to "remember our own in the setting where they had lived most comfortably." Instead, the march had gone "past bombed-out building sites, industrial warehouses and vacant lots," where "few people worth reaching live." He saw this decision as yet another example of Philadelphia gays "trying to be all things to all people at all times," lamenting, "we couldn't even do this thing right and remember our own in the setting where they had lived most comfortably."[39]

By "we," Whiting meant the PATF and Center City's largely white middle-class gay community. Though he excoriated many of the rally speakers as "blathering, ill-prepared, and often destructive," he heaped special scorn on Hassan, who in his view "proved to be no friend to either the gay or the black community by acting out her own therapy at everyone's expense." He painted her as an interloper at PCHA and the PATF whom he had only recently become aware when she "[appeared] on the scene to unleash venom for an unclear purpose," despite his having worked with both organizations for four years. He compared her to David Fair, "Philadelphia's own version of the Reverend Jim Jones," and warned readers parenthetically, "I advise that no one accept Kool Aid from either of them."[40]

Although Hassan and Fair criticized the PATF for not allocating resources in accordance with the demographics of the epidemic in Philadelphia, Whiting insisted that the group used half of its time and money "to help blacks." He meant this point not as a defense of the group but instead as a criticism—another example of the downtown gay community trying to be "all things to all people." Given that most of the volunteers at the PATF were white and that "the monies donated by middle class white gay men . . . carried the financial burden of AIDS in Philadelphia," he argued that the group had a greater claim to AIDS prevention and services, based on their collective access to wealth. To drive home his point, he asked readers "When was the last time that half of the monies and efforts by any black organization were used to further the health and welfare of whites?"[41]

For Whiting, the AIDS epidemic in Philadelphia was synonymous with its Gayborhood. For that reason, he felt as though the decision to hold the walk and vigil elsewhere, along with Hassan's critical speech, betrayed the memory of friends already lost to AIDS. But Whiting was either blind to or willfully ignorant of the constellation of factors that produced the Gayborhood as a white space. Those same factors in turn marked AIDS as a white gay disease, which made it difficult for PCHA and the PATF to reach black gay and bisexual men, much less the rest of Philadelphia's black community. His reaction shows that even if statistics showed that people of color were disproportionately dying of AIDS, white gay men in Philadelphia *felt* the epidemic most strongly in the ways that it cut down friends and lovers in the prime of life and threatened their own lives. Meanwhile, the epidemic raged in the city's poor and black neighborhoods outside of Center City.

In BEBASHI's 1986 annual report, released a few months after the walk, Hassan laid out a view of AIDS in Philadelphia that overlaid race and sexuality with urban space. She argued that PCHA and the PATF had been unable to overcome their limitations as groups "centered in a gay community that is overwhelmingly white, educated, and employed" and that worked through members' "highly personal networks and . . . existing gay community structures, most of which have little connection to the city's poorer neighborhoods." Those neighborhoods, Hassan argued, looked rather different from the downtown Gayborhood in the ways that residents understood the relationship between race and sexuality: "For the most part, black communities do not segregate themselves by lifestyles; instead, people of all types and conditions live together in one community." According to Hassan's argument, race—not sexuality—structured black gay men's lives as well as the spaces and places in which they moved. For this reason, Hassan argued, she would need to canvass Philadelphia's entire black community with AIDS education messages. This would have the added benefit of reaching not only black gay and bisexual men but also black men who had sex with men but identified as straight, black drug users, and black women.[42]

Over the years following her resignation from PCHA, Hassan and BEBASHI enjoyed the support of Local 1199C as well as David Fair, first as secretary-treasurer of the union and then as the first director of the city's AIDS Activities Coordinating Office. In 1988 BEBASHI also won a grant from the Centers for Disease Control. However, Hassan and Fair continued to draw criticism from other AIDS activists, who claimed that BEBASHI failed to reach black gay men and who charged Fair with patronage for directing city funds to Hassan's organization. In spite of that support, BEBASHI struggled financially, especially compared to PCHA and the PATF, which enjoyed much greater financial support from the city's gay community. This dimension of the political economy of AIDS—fund-raising and budgetary vulnerability—deserves greater attention from scholars. In 1993, BEBASHI sought bankruptcy protection amid financial troubles; Hassan resigned as executive director the following year and was replaced by Gary Bell. In contrast, since the 1980s PCHA has grown into the Mazzoni Center, a large-scale LGBT health provider and community organization offering a wide array of services with over $17 million in revenue during 2018.[43]

* * *

During the 1980s, AIDS exploded across the nation in cities that had been shaped by the political, economic, and cultural shifts of preceding decades.

These included white flight, deindustrialization, and urban gentrification as well as the emergence of visible and politically active gay and lesbian communities and the rise of an urban black political elite. In Philadelphia these groups had sometimes found common cause, but in many ways the Gayborhood excluded people of color, which made collective action on AIDS difficult.

In fact, this reality laid the groundwork for the conflicts that erupted between the predominantly white and gay AIDS establishment and its critics over minority AIDS education and services. For their part, white gay men largely downplayed the many ways that the Gayborhood was unwelcoming to people of color. These men saw the enclave as diverse and racially liberal but failed to reckon with the forces—both structural and personal—that had carved out a mostly white gay neighborhood in the middle of the city. They knew that their friends were dying and that few people seemed to care, but they did not see how many in the city's black community were dying and that even fewer people seemed to care about *them*.

If the shrinking pool of municipal resources seemed to exacerbate the AIDS wars in Philadelphia, the infusion of federal AIDS dollars that came with the passage of the Ryan White CARE Act in 1990 did little to quell them. By then groups such as BEBASHI had themselves come to be seen as part of the city's AIDS services establishment and came under fire from a new, more militant wave of activists for constituting an "AIDS mafia" that monopolized resources for the fight against the disease.[44]

More than thirty years after Rashidah Hassan stepped up to the dais in LOVE Park, racism is alive and well in Philadelphia's Gayborhood. In September 2016 a video of Darryl DePiano, the owner of a popular downtown Philadelphia gay bar and dance club, using a racial slur to describe black customers was posted online. Around the same time Philly Pride youth marshal Kemar Jewel, who is black, was turned away from another bar supposedly because his sweatpants and sneakers violated the bar's dress code. These and other incidents led to a public hearing on racism and discrimination in the city's LGBTQ community by the Philadelphia Commission on Human Relations, at which a former Mazzoni employee described the center as "a dehumanizing environment for people of color." Several months later in January 2017, the commission released a report recommending, among other things, implicit bias training for gay bar owners and staff as well as board members, managers, and staff at the Mazzoni Center.[45]

Over the next several months controversy engulfed the organization. Board secretary Michael Weiss, who was also the owner of several downtown gay bars, was implicated in the indictment of District Attorney Seth Williams on corruption charges. Weiss resigned from the board. The following month Mazzoni Center medical director Robert Winn was placed on leave after being accused of sexual misconduct. Employees staged several walkouts, charging that CEO Nurit Shein and the Mazzoni leadership overlooked not only Winn's misdeeds but also a discriminatory work environment. Under such pressure, Shein and board president Jimmy Ruiz both resigned.[46]

Meanwhile, HIV and AIDS continue to disproportionately affect black Philadelphians by a wide margin. As of 2017, African Americans made up 44 percent of Philadelphia's population but just over two-thirds of newly diagnosed cases of HIV in the city. Black gay and bisexual men also have the highest prevalence rate of HIV of any measured group in the city and are around twice as likely to have HIV as their white counterparts. The disparity is likely even greater for black transgender women; although the Philadelphia Department of Public Health does not count them as a separate category, one study found that 56 percent of black transgender women are living with HIV. This reality is likely mirrored, if not amplified, in Philadelphia's HIV epidemic.[47]

Now as then, vulnerability to HIV is determined not merely by what people do but also by their access to space, power, and resources. In the early years of the epidemic, the fight for equitable HIV prevention and services raised thorny questions about who the Gayborhood—and Philadelphia more broadly—was for. Thirty years later, those questions remain unanswered but are no less urgent.

CHAPTER 6

Black Gay Lives Matter

Mobilizing Sexual Identities in the Eras of Reagan and Thatcher Conservatism

Kevin Mumford

Against all odds in the face of pervasive cultural stigma, immobilizing individual isolation, and routine physical violence as well as the disproportionate impact of the AIDS crisis, into the 1980s black gay men pioneered a new sphere of identity. Appearing almost as if out of nowhere after James Baldwin's meteoric rise and declining almost as suddenly, the new generation drew on a longer activist tradition that fought against insult and collective denial and discovered a range of tactics with which to raise their voice in a culture increasingly hostile both to diversity projects and cultural agendas for social change. Speaking directly to a pervasive power of normalization that silenced and erased, queer people of color defended against both psychological and bodily violence by building a series of important organizations, withdrawing from white institutions, and constructing literary and erotic representations.

Despite powerful conservative pressure on several fronts—indicated by the rightward turn toward family values and against civil rights in the Ronald Reagan era as well as the struggle over gay age of consent laws and racial immigration restriction leading up to the Margaret Thatcher era in Britain—neither of these rightward mobilizations produced a total backlash. Rather, a variety of factions, organizations, and collectives joined together to fashion alternative positions or definitions of black and queer identity. In this search for brotherhood and stewardship, building on inherited and shared concepts of Black Power and sexual liberation, African American as well as Afro-British and Asian British activists challenged conservative conventions while interacting, conflicting, and cooperating with each other across the Atlantic. This essay surveys the output of several groups at the tail end of the long civil rights movement, debates around immigration, and new definitions of cultural identity to understand the broader range of masculinity politics that unsettled, intervened into, and resisted the hegemony of 1980s conservative conventions of nationhood and manliness.

A Black Power Sexual Revolution

The key U.S. black publications, *Ebony* and *Jet* magazines, reversed course in the late 1960s and 1970s by dropping the rhetoric of respectability and joined what might be termed a black sexual revolution (parallel to but distinct from the transformation in mores and behaviors that swept the white mainstream in roughly the same period). First off, the editors at Johnson Publications decided to print more stories on questions of sexuality than ever before, tendering personal advice and covering new developments in sexology and psychiatry. Black Power mobilizations had ushered in a wave of political texts—both scholarly and fictional—as well as a new and influential genre, the so-called Blaxploitation film, all of which prioritized the expression of black male eroticism. Rhetorically rebelling against the historical threat of white sexual violence for desiring white women in the South, Eldridge Cleaver in a best-selling memoir, *Soul on Ice* (1968), advocated rape in the service of the revolution while not coincidentally declaring homosexuality to be a sickness of the black sycophant desiring penetration by his white master.[1] If activists and actors displayed sexual dominance over white women and by extension white society, mainstream social science reported on the benefits for black men and women of a healthy sexual release. Harkening back to the era of slavery rather than lynching, black social scientists such as Alvin Poussaint and Robert Staples defended the normality of heterosexuality and extolled the pleasures of the black body that inherited a deep well of eroticism from Africa.[2]

It was also in this period that readers of black publications would learn more about the distinction between gender role and sexual orientation through regular coverage of transsexuals and transvestites that now distinguished their conditions from homosexuals (*Ebony* did not employ the term "gay" yet). One learned reader wrote in to rebuke an author for implying that "homosexuals 'come out' by cross-dressing," which was "as stupid as it is misleading." Cross-dressing continued to signify homosexuality, but its presence did not justify familial rejection: "If your son, who has been the star of the football team, walks in one day wearing lipstick, a dress, and a rose in his hair, do not immediately call for the looney bin or a priest."[3] Key publications presented a variety of queer situations: a drag queen, a homosexual scandal, and the homosexual son deserving of compassion. No doubt homosexuality felt pathological to many and continued to carry a stigma. Into the 1970s, letters to the editor featured men anxious to convert and leave their homosexuality past behind, while others explained that they had "gone cold turkey" but feared a relapse into homosexual contact after they married. The advice was not for such a man to deal with his desire but rather to share fully his sexual past with a girlfriend or potential fiancée. This type of advice supposed a certain plasticity of desire while not yet recognizing the moral legitimacy of homosexuality.[4]

In this context, much of the public black discourse about homosexuality circled around the nature or nurture question—whether homosexuals were born that way or became that way due to a condition arising from experience and familial treatment—and here the issue of race influenced the dialogue. Just like one's hereditary background, some writers asserted, homosexuality was innate and embodied. Tending advice to the parent of a suspected homosexual, one author counseled, "Offer whatever help and understanding you can, and do not feel disgraced by something that may be a biological fact just as is the color of your skin or the shape of your nose."[5] By the late 1970s, the gay rights movement had exploded onto the national stage as major cities and towns debated the merits of passing legislation to protect homosexuals from discrimination in housing, accommodations, and employment. In hearing after hearing and in the backlash against passed legislation headed by Anita Bryant's Save Our Children campaign, advocates on both sides of the measures compared racial difference to sexual orientation as well as racist exclusion to the operation of homophobia.[6] The New Right denied the injuries caused by homophobia, and some black conservatives rejected the concept of a sexual minority that in any way could compare to the experience of a racial group.

Yet in cities and college towns across the nation, a range of liberal actors advanced a powerful case for extending the benefits of the rights revolution to homosexuals and, in the process, introduced for public consideration the notion that gays and lesbians deserved equal protection under the law like any other group defined by an immutable difference. Over the last quarter of the twentieth century this appeal to civil rights was continually championed by

African Americans, and eventually the case for gay equality persuaded many of its merits. In her classic studies of African Americans and gay or queer formations, Cathy Cohen has tended to find reason for pessimism much of the time. On the one hand, her survey of black print cultures found a high level of distrust of homosexuality, particularly when framed as a core personal identity that rivaled racial identification. On the other, Cohen argues that the coalescence of a queer political moment in the 1990s had overlooked questions of class and therefore excluded racialized others, especially marginalized black women. Although conservative purveyors of orthodox religion and respectability had long inveighed against homosexuality in black communities, by the 1980s the push for rights secured a level of recognition even in the church.[7] Heading into the first wave of the AIDS crisis, black gay men had mobilized a fairly extensive network, refusing to be left outside the boundaries of either gayness or blackness at a time in the United States when both sources of identity had surged as a source of metropolitan clout.[8]

A Utopian Brotherhood

In celebration of their one-year anniversary in 1981, the interracial gay social organization Black and White Men Together (BWMT) brought out the first issue of its monthly newsletter, *BWMT News*. Leading with a humorous story detailing antics at the anniversary banquet that boasted a "large turn out of close to one hundred participants," the paper listed reports from a number of committees—Publicity, Political Action, Group Services, Steering, and Welcoming—and announced the winner for the group's logo design competition. The newsletter promised a slew of new columns that would feature recipes, personal columns, classifieds, and "letters-to-the-editor column for those who like to express themselves."[9] Founded as a social organization that sought to bridge the racial divide among gay men, BWMT was soon drawn into a variety of political activities beyond picnics and the brotherhood.

Although the first BWMT chapter was founded in San Francisco, over the next half dozen years the major chapters mobilized on the East Coast and in key cities in the Midwest. The structures appear similar across the nation, but some of the later chapters dealt with more serious and entrenched racial conflict, particularly the fallout due to the larger black populations and the resultant racial conflicts. With a declining population of 1,688,210 in 1980, Philadelphia was among the largest cities with substantial black populations in the nation. At the same time, BWMT chapters developed a cosmopolitan outlook, seeking pluralistic formations and learned or scholarly practices regarding race and mobilizing external, indeed transnational, organizational connections.[10] The point was to press for international diversity where possible and to study the best practices, as it were, for advancing antiracism across the gay and lesbian communities. Designated BWMT members frequently traveled to conferences concerned with "Third World" affairs that included "Asians from Toronto, Hispanics from Los Angeles, Peru, and Chile. . . . Black lesbians from varied regional locations, professions, and political outlooks."[11] To an extent typically overlooked, these avowedly cosmopolitan groups took up political challenges. BWMT–New York, for example, was engaged in a lengthy battle against racial discrimination in gay and lesbian bars, and along with BWMT-Philadelphia, dozens of members worked in the "documenting racism project." Posing as racially mixed parties, they recorded incidents when black members in a party were required to produce identification or were otherwise detained and excluded, while white members often sailed past the front door. Soon the Chicago and Boston chapters organized similar actions to document and protest bar discrimination, initiating, for example, an "In Depth Study of the Boston Bars."[12]

By the early 1980s, additional chapters of BWMT had formed in Los Angeles, Cleveland, Denver, and Washington, D.C., while at the same time a Brooklyn chapter announced its closing due to "limited resources, funds, and manpower available to us," as did a number of others from the Midwest.[13] All along, various chapters complained of dwindling membership rolls and uneven commitment, with some reporting the attendance of far more white members (70 percent) than black members.[14] From its inception by a somewhat controversial white gay man often accused of objectifying black men to its proliferation within upwardly mobile gay neighborhoods, it would be fair to say that BWMT attracted more white than black members and therefore fostered a certain skepticism. By 1986 the increasing impact of AIDS illnesses and deaths reverberated across the chapters, and Chicago reported losing contact with BWMT/Connecticut, BWMT East Bay, BWMT Houston, BWMT/Omaha, BWMT/Raleigh, BWMT Richmond, and BWMT Tallahassee during the early to mid-1980s.[15] In the face of the crisis, however, BWMT entreated the readership not to "forget that we must continue to resist racism"—"let us not forget our reason for being."[16] In its final period of decline, BWMT extended its international reach with functioning chapters around the globe, including a chapter in South Africa.[17]

On the local level and even before the full-blown AIDS crisis, however, anecdotes (a letter to a close friend, an entry in a diary) suggested that black gay men approached BWMT with apprehension. There was an increasingly widespread sentiment among black men that the expansive, not to mention often elitist, gay landscape of bars, baths, and pornography had not fulfilled their desires but instead had left them feeling dejected. As a result, black gay organizing went against the grain of the 1980s, with its crass materialism and competitive individualism, and by contrast black gay churches, reading groups, and social outlets proliferated. In turn, many chapters of BWMT coordinated the operation of numerous workshops and clusters in which "growth, understanding, or just sharing of fellowship is possible."[18]

During BWMT's relatively brief tenure, the formation of BWMT chapters helped to air long-standing anxieties and resentments arising from the fraught, often objectified, relationships between white men who desired black men in the club scene of the 1970s and 1980s. There was a sense that they "competed" for the attention of a relatively few available black men in select bars, leaving some "disheartened" while others sought to "maximize their own individual options." Therefore, BWMT's key objective was to challenge stereotypes while promoting the "enlightening inter-racial brotherhood that truly brings us together!"[19]

BWMT sponsored a series of workshops that addressed issues ranging from visibility in media, prisoner outreach, and religion to "why there are no black bartenders" and "raising the political awareness of BWMT members." BWMT also sought to instill a deeper sense of racial history among its membership. At the national annual meetings, it was reported that "a special workshop was presented by a very special individual, Richard Bruce Nugent, who wrote the first overtly gay prose work by a Black writer in English." Here they referred to the openly gay author and poet of the Harlem Renaissance whose prose celebrated the beauty and eroticism of black men long ago in the 1920s.[20]

But the newsletters also attest to a collective imperfectly grappling with powerful stereotypes—often perpetrated by gay men themselves—that illustrated how personal desires could interfere with efforts to peel back layers of sexual racialization. One dimension of this imagery originated from the proliferation of gay pornography that typically featured all-white casts, while the far fewer interracial sexual scenes typically presented black studs ravishing passive blue-eyed boys. The newsletters referred to these problematic images of the "Mandingo hunk" alongside the "Yukon stud." In this sphere too often defined by erotic distortions, the potential for misunderstanding was often exacerbated by personal accusations of racism, such that even the founding group in San Francisco, perhaps the most progressive major city in the nation, reported that its chapter was "in serious danger of becoming a thoroughly racist organization if the membership permits domination by a small umber of whites, whose interest in blacks is paternal and who see them only as sex-objects."[21]

Yet more often, BWMT promoted the values of stewardship and sensitivity to the presence of societal racism. A striking number of black gay men volunteered and became involved with black prisoners, probably because of the far higher rates of black male incarceration. Some of the evidence comes from relatively obscure correspondence. Like many gay publications, *Chicago's BWMT Newsletter* received many letters to the editor. These sought out information about policy or health or requested the placement of announcements and classified advertisements. It is interesting to note that a sizable percentage of the correspondence was received from incarcerated men. Gay black and white inmates sought out publications of interest, and sometimes cell mates or subsequent occupants picked up a leftover, hidden-away gay publication and reached out to a published address for a possible connection, pen pal, or sponsor, regardless of their sexual orientation. One inmate complained that the State of Michigan prohibited gay magazines such as *In Touch*, *The Advocate*, and *Blueboy* while at the same time permitting *Playboy*, *Hustler*, and *Penthouse*, and he added that racism further complicated imprisoned gay desires. "Where black and white gays are found together in the prison setting, usually the black is subjected to such discrimination as commitment to indefinite segregation, and in most cases, transfer to a maximum security." But in the case of same-race relationships, "two blacks or two whites are generally left alone." He went on to explain that within the general population, however, most gay men faced violence, and their only recourse was a small number of protective custody cells or "administrative segregation," "no doubt jeopardizing further his sanity." First printed in Boston's *Gay Community News*, the letter circulated to Chicago BWMT, which asked the author for permission to reprint. "It is more than an honor for me to answer your request to reprint my letter," Bobby Lee Gordon replied. In an editor's note, "People have repeatedly said to me, 'BWMT/Chicago doesn't offer anything to get involved in. Well, the plight of our fellow BMWT'ers institutionalized and elsewhere gives us a perfect opportunity to start.'"[22]

Not infrequently, some of the membership became embroiled in painful disputes over nomenclature and personal misunderstandings of the meanings or consequences of racial difference. What was the distinction between a "preference" for one type of partner or group versus racial discrimination— were racially explicit personal advertisements an example of bias or permissible admiration?[23] It was in 1982 that the Chicago branch first announced the publication of Mike Smith's anthology *Black and White Men*, "with special emphasis on the Gay Black Experience" and publicized as the first effort of its kind.[24] The resulting volume of interracial writings sparked as much racial controversy as it sought to address, in part because of the unexpected emergence of a new network of black gay cultural activists around the same time. The black writers complained about the editor (and his whiteness in particular) and his decision to publish several photos of scantily clad or naked men posed as the black stud, while the book included no photos of whites, nude or otherwise. It is difficult to explain Smith's editorial decision, except possibly to see it as unconscious objectification that rested on genuine fascination with and desire for the black body and also as a betrayal of the rank-and-file black gay membership of BWMT who confronted the prevalent suspicions that the photos only seemed to confirm. On a historical level, it could be observed that Smith and others, despite their best intentions, were unable to transcend a long history of white supremacy that associated the eroticism of the black male body with white control. This fact alone sparked an onslaught of infuriated reviews and criticism and, more importantly, helped to inspire a new generation of black gay voices to start up their own project of representation and voice.

Black Men Loving Black Men

In relation to and in some cases as a direct rejection of BWMT chapters in the cities, a fledgling group of black gay activists coalesced to build a national organization for black gay and lesbian political and cultural advancement. By the 1980s, the National Coalition of Black Gays would meet routinely to formulate new strategies for visibility and rights. One major effort was to establish a national publication—*Black/Out*—to move beyond the localism that characterized much of the gay urban press (except for publications such as *The Advocate*). Both it and the gay urban press were heavily criticized for an almost exclusively white focus, even as key papers engaged some black gay journalists. Similarly, the key organizations, such as the National Gay and Lesbian Task Force and the Human Rights Campaign, were also criticized for their apparent racial homogeneity. As Washington-based activists formed the National Coalition of Black Gays and raised the revenue for a national publicity campaign, they employed Joseph Beam to edit *Black/Out*. As he explained in the premiere summer 1986 issue, *Black/Out* hoped to become the "voice of the new movement of Black Lesbians and Gays, one which bespeaks renewed Black pride and solidarity." Beam then rehearsed their familiar dilemma of feeling invisible: like the "outrageous drag queens who started it all," they were "relegated to 'color' supplements, minority task forces, and workshops on racism—rather than woven into the fabric." On the other hand, "in the Black press, our news is no news. In short, there has been a 'blackout' surrounding our lives, our visions, our contributions, which Black/Out seeks to end."[25]

Black men withdrew from white gay enclaves and circuits because of the racism that BWMT had documented and exposed for years, and they too arrived at the recognition that despite the complexity of their desire, they were often expected to enact a certain role of the black Stud that permeated gay pornography and bar culture. Obviously, the complaints about and indeed the gradual decline of some BWMT chapters attest to too many white members, despite their best intentions, manipulating, objectifying, and even harassing other black members. And like white gay men, black gay men also left to organize against the AIDS crisis—as one writer recalled, "Black men were just beginning to realize that this was not a white man's disease, despite the monochromatic images the Gay press was feeding us and continues to feed us." The physical departure mirrored or coincided with what might be termed a black queer Afrocentric turn, and this movement was signified by discussion of gayness in African cultures. "I left New York to teach at a regional teacher's college in one of the largest countries in Africa." His destination was Zaire, a nation sometime associated with and stigmatized as a source of the "AIDS virus." He interviewed a number of men who spoke of their coming-of-age in homosexual relationships, some of which "lasted beyond adolescence." Other tribes endowed homosexuality with a mythical or religious meaning, while the same structure might punish same-sex relations between women with death.[26]

In the end, the author found affirmation in his interviews and expeditions, in part because he identified a "gay love" that transcended mere physical contact. In his vision of African homo sociability he discovered a kind of queer diaspora, and he also reported on the intense danger that "our double brothers" faced under more conservative African regimes, where leaders routinely explained homosexuality as a white, colonial imposition that "does not exist in our country." It was true that in some cases, white elites secured younger African boys as servants and companions and reportedly shared them with one another. It was also true that a few African men had established long-term relationships that often mirrored heterosexual domesticity. In either case, the *Black/Out* piece reported that the "gay European presence in African cities has paved the way for the emergence for a truly African Gay subculture."[27]

Alongside the black lesbian voices that were published to feminist acclaim in the 1980s—Alice Walker, Audre Lorde, Gloria Naylor, and Barbara Smith—a lone black gay writer was featured in the mainstream black publications. Essex Hemphill was among a handful of black gay activists, or cultural workers as they sometimes self-identified, who had managed to publish consistently.[28] With a chapbook and other publications and a National Endowment for the Humanities Fellowship, Hemphill pioneered a black gay poetics throughout the 1980s–1990s. In the *Essence* piece, he declared his black gay identity (recognized at an early age) and then related his coming-out experience to his parents and his subsequent search for "dignity." Much of his energy aims to overturn stereotypes of gayness by demonstrating his strength, resilience, and courage and refusing a black homophobia that doubts his authenticity and *silences* his desire in the name of brotherhood. But he saves his harshest criticism for the gay rights movement that has rejected or downplayed black gay involvement, and therefore, Hemphill declared, "the Gay Rights Movement [is] an insincere human rights struggle." For a long stretch of black imagining of homosexuality, most speculation held that black gay men often acted like women to express their difference, their perversion, and that black gay men always desired white gay men. Although white gay men had promoted the objectification of the black gay stud, the transformations of the 1980s, particularly the ongoing development of black feminism, introduced black gay men to new ideas and forums. Speaking the language of courage and strength, dignity and community, Hemphill identified the tenets and tactics of the new black gay activism.[29]

However, by the mid-1980s as the number of dedicated gay bars gradually declined in many major cities, black gay men confronted a more dangerous society. Black artists and writers had spoken out against gay racism, while others had joined BWMT to mobilize for recognition and inclusion. But the AIDS crisis led others to form social and political organizations for black men impacted by alarmingly high rates of conversion, such as Philadelphia's Adodi.[30] In many ways this was too little, too late, as black gay AIDS activists suffered from a lack of access to both city hall and white-dominated support networks. In part because of the impact of economic inequality and spatial segregation, Adodi and other black gay collectives felt alienated from white gay cultures, and some even "took exception" to being labeled gay, which one member objected to because he identified the term with whiteness. They chose the name Adodi because of its Portuguese/African origins that denoted a "'homosexual Black man.'" After some months the enterprise had increased its membership, and at a "retreat" involving men from Philadelphia, New York City, and Wilmington, they were "present to talk and hear about their spirituality, and the creative ways they deal with being Black Gay men in our society."[31]

What might be called a queer Afrocentric impulse influenced the organization of the first Black Gay men and Women's Conference, involving activists based in Washington, D.C., and Philadelphia, that featured a keynote address by black lesbian filmmaker and writer Michelle Parkerson.[32] The 1983 event offered "workshops, a disco, a talent show, and numerous meetings," it was reported. Again, the idea for the event evolved in response to white gay-led efforts to convene a conference, signifying yet another moment of black queer withdrawal. This also reflected a rejection more specifically of BWMT Washington, in part because of internecine debates over the merits of a social versus a more political agenda. A new wave of activists believed that interracial sociability represented little more than "dinge queens," or white men who desired and presumably objectified black men. But it was noted that the Washington chapter, like those in Philadelphia and New York, had mounted a serious investigation into bar racism and brought antidiscrimination suits, and of special significance was the club Badlands. A number of black gay men reported difficulty in gaining entrance to the new club, which was located in what was once a black and Latino bar. The enterprise's owner at first ignored protests but changed course after BWMT filed complaints with both the human rights unit and the Alcohol Beverage Control Board that was in charge of issuing liquor licenses. As the Badlands owner was planning to open a fifth gay establishment and faced an investigation by city authorities, he moved swiftly to address the charges. It was reported that he sought a meeting with the conveners of the black gay conference and presented them with a $400 check, and "no one questioned it." Behind the scenes, the conference leadership debated whether or not to deposit the check, which they finally did in order to meet mounting expenses, and it was soon reported that plans for a picket at Badlands were scrapped. Later, the same owner donated a much larger sum to BWMT in exchange for withdrawing its complaint with the city. While the conference speakers went on to rally for renewed organizing "armed with the knowledge that our anger at racial and sexual injustice just fuel our faith"—the susceptibility of fledgling political groups to the lure of early settlement remained true for black gays and lesbians as well. The retreat of black gay men from white-controlled mobilizations signaled a new politics of black masculinity, of the sort brilliantly formulated by black British cultural theorists such as Kobena Mercer and Isaac Julien, that rejected the extremes of white homoerotic objectification while allowing for a guilt-free interracial desire to form freely. When Joseph Beam declared that black men loving black men is the revolutionary act of the 1980s, one gets the sense that he meant it, and yet he moved in spaces (public and private) in which black and white bodies continually touched and became somehow tethered.[33]

Yet toward the end of this moment later in the 1990s, the historical apogee of mobilizing masculinities for social change became the Million Man March. Scheduled for October 16, 1995, the march was organized as a day of atonement for black men to reflect and reimagine. The backers were a loosely affiliated network of cultural or nationalist groups. The original proposal stirred intense controversy that continued to the day of the event. Black radicals and liberals and especially black women denounced the formation, even as many acknowledged the need for and possible utility of a mass march especially to denounce worsening economic conditions, political exclusion, and incarceration.

The historical sociologist Michael West locates the march in a long history of black nationalist interventions, from rebellions to activist demonstrations to electoral campaigns. By the 1980s, however, the Reagan revolution had stifled civil rights gains of the previous decade and threatened to cut back on social programs and block other liberal causes. In response, Louis Fararakhan called for a march that urged men not to demand jobs and freedom but instead to seek "atonement and reconciliation" and repent their transgressions against black women, children, and communities, while black women were "urged to stay home" or were expected to remain on the sidelines or participate in the March of Absence. Though some critics decried the lack of focus or tangible objectives, the marchers understood the protest as a collective challenge to stereotypes, objection to conservative pundits and politicians, and a new regime of cultural domination. Implicit in the action was the sense that this new order relied with particular force on the subjugation of black men.

Though many observers criticized or misunderstood the rhetoric of atonement and responsibility, one obvious point was that this strand of self-help ideology offered the advantage of providing a platform of independence and social autonomy that relied on self-help and community development rather than lobbying the nation-state. In an insightful analysis of the Million Man March, Manning Marable compared the mobilization to the original March on Washington and declared that the exhortations of a few—notably Farakhan—were calling for self-recognition, not policy or state change, and yet this mobilization translated into increased black male turnout in the following election cycle. Despite pointed opposition from prominent figures such as Angela Davis and Julianne Malveau on the basis of its exclusion of women and from LGBT activists responding to a long history of black nationalist homophobia, the mobilization gained far more support than it lost.[34]

Ain't No Black Queer Here

In 1989, the black gay filmmaker Isaac Julien produced *Looking for Langston*. Abstract and romantic, the film presented a dreamlike meditation on the underworld of the 1920s Harlem Renaissance that was a fantasy of black-white homoeroticism. In the U.S. community, historian Eric Garber had published essays documenting the gay identities and bisexual aura of that moment when Harlem was in vogue. By the early 1980s, reports from Britain indicated an increasing prominence of black gay and lesbian voices, many of whom turned out to be inspired by their U.S. brothers and sisters, both past and present. But if black American gay activists joined a broad cultural Left mobilizing in the culture wars, in Britain such a Left was smaller and weaker, and black gay activists grappled with not only racism and homophobia but also xenophobia and ethnocentrism. In other words, incipient black gay activists on both sides of the Atlantic confronted similar barriers to full participation in society due to homophobia as well as a set of quite unique circumstances of ethnocentrism that prevented many from claiming their rightful place in the nation.

A 1982 British piece, "No Black Humour, Please," noticeably chafed at even a hint of grassroots diversity in satirizing an "ethnic minority" meeting designated for the topic of "black lesbians." The reporter went on to ask what "particular problems" they faced and supplied their (unsatisfying) answer: "Well, I think they may face discrimination and prejudice within the gay community because they are black." After sarcastically noting that London was to be declared Britain's first "'anti-racist zone,'" the reported quipped, "You have to laugh. The alternative is to lie weeping, under the pillow in a darkened room."[35] In response, a handful of black gays and lesbians gradually organized to voice their unique concerns, and again their presence initially sparked anxiety, presenting "a challenging profile on the problems of being a homosexual in Britain's black community." For the black community—in this case both Caribbean and Asian—the homosexual was a "taboo" and "regarded as a damning social stigma."[36]

Identifying itself as the Gay Black Group (GBG), first organized to pro-test against representations of Asian homosexuals in a film, *Eastern Eye*, the group presented at a forum in Leicester that sought to publicize some of the complications faced by gay people of color. The GBG complained about the film's assumption that "nothing of any real significance is being done within the Asian and Black communities on the issue of homosexuality and that only white gays can show the way forward."[37]

Early on, the GBG sought to establish itself as an organ for both black and Asian gays and lesbians, because "in Britain at least, the term Black applies equally well to those of Asian and African descent." Operating at complicated intersections, their early interventions sought to challenge a homophobia that forced many to "live in closets." And they expected easy sympathy from white gay and lesbian allies, but this was not always forthcoming. "Is it not enough that we should suffer the harassment and racism meted out to all members of the black community?"[38] As the GBG attracted public scrutiny, it confronted these sort of misunderstandings both in the public square and in print. After being interviewed by the straight-identified *Root*, members of the GBG wrote to complain about the their mistreatment in print. The reporter, who remained anonymous, had observed their immorality, printed "GOD" in boldface, and claimed that black gays "paraded" their "immorality" along with making "snide references to AIDS."[39]

The Root also ran a headline article titled "Black Gays Come Out," and again the tone betrayed a limited engagement or sympathy with gay poli-tics. Describing one subject as a "confessed Black homosexual," the reporter chronicled the tragic circumstances in which Vernal Scott loses the affection of friends and family alike, even though he never fit the stereotypes of carry-ing a purse or wearing perfume. On the other hand, the story discloses that some white gays practice racism, treating blacks like "the coffee" that they desire only because "they are different." The bulk of the story rehearses the

tragic coming-out narrative and concludes by praising his courageous triumph through telling the truth and being himself.[40]

During what was officially to be designated as an "antiracism year," gays
of color complained about various examples of homophobia in their home
communities, and one letter writer stated that "I think the black community
is unsympathetic to its gay members." Another letter criticized the article for
suggesting that black gays were motivated by "white decadence." Imploring
the black periodical *The Voice* not to "join with the rest of the establishment
in portraying gays in a bad light," the author of one letter reported that he
had "heard some of my mother's friends say exactly what they're saying in
America—that homosexuality is a sin against God and we will be punished."[41]

An apparently tenuous alliance between the Labour Left and "black politics" crumbled upon of the introduction of questions of homosexuality when
what were described as liberals in London introduced a cultural program
proposing a gay and lesbian studies module to be taught in the local schools.
Local activists faced off in the London neighborhood of Haringey, where
white educators proposed to introduce a progay study module for school-
age youths. The ensuing controversy exposed contrasting priorities—perhaps
more than fundamental opposing values—and yet the fallout possibly hard-
ened black opposition to gay politics. In a closed meeting drawing more than
two hundred black parents, a black government member with expertise in
education was said to blame "white councilors for Haringey's gay policies"
and characterized them as a "part of a racist conspiracy." The plan involved
the inclusion of so-called positive images of gays, but many in attendance felt
that the "gay policies were just the latest facet of oppression that blacks had
to face." Explained as a fear of diverting political power or resources to the
black community, a member of Haringey's West Indian Leadership Council
warned that "'we will go to any extremes to stop it.'"[42] It was later reported
that more than seventy passed a motion in opposition to the gay curriculum, and the fallout proved potentially divisive, with the press picking up and
publishing emotional comments and incendiary insults. "I would not have
my daughter taught in a Haringey school. I picked up a book in a Haringey
library that left me sick for days." One reason for the "bitter" opposition had
to do with the lack of prior consultation and the general sense that black
constituents were not consulted by the gay and lesbian activists behind the
proposed educational reform.[43]

About six months later, a letter signed by "The Lodge of Black Worker's Groups" set out to protest the publication of a "'Fairy Prince'" cartoon

that they described as "blatantly anti-gay." It was observed that the "black community" viewed this particular publication, *The Voice*, as an alternative newspaper "providing positive images of black people" and that the image represented an "unjustified attack on another minority group." They went on to demand an apology.[44]

On the whole, the steady emergence of gay activist politics continued to stir rifts among and between minority groups, in part due to concrete ideology but also indicative of a kind of turf battle on the margins of British politics. Again, these debates operated in some relation to U.S. sexual politics. For example, in 1987 Marcus Garvey Junior, a descendant of the early twentieth-century black nationalist leader, spoke to a "capacity crowd" about the "progressives" who promoted alliances with gays. "'Let me say now, I don't care who leaves this meeting, but homosexuals and lesbians are alien and cursed by our traditional African culture and I denounce all such practices." Attributing homosexuality to a "white western power system," Garvey declared that "we Africans reject this sickness and so we will not go down with the white West." Reports indicated that he concluded his address with a recollection of the 1950s Brixton riots, specifically a homicide—a "broad daylight murder"—that went unsolved. In his view, that level of racism persisted in contemporary England, which ought to be the sole target of reform for black Britain, not other issues of homosexual acceptance.[45]

Following on the trail blazed by Joseph Beam, UK black gay activists proposed a new editorial project to promote their visibility and combat homophobia, to be titled "Black/Out" according to a notice that was advertised in *The Voice*. Similar to Beam's project by the same name, the Black/Out Editorial Collective solicited "writings, poetry, fiction, interviews and letters."[46] Arriving after his death, Beam received a letter from a London address querying him on the terms of identity. Should we speak of ourselves as "black gay men" or "gay black men," the inquiry went. As indicated, key writers such as Kobena Mercer and Isaac Julien were working with a less homophobic and more flexible intellectual project of cultural studies, and from there they could forward a new critique of black masculinity. Their studies also engaged the ongoing controversy sparked by the publication of Robert Mapplethorpe's gay artistic work and the increasing attention it received. His avant-garde photographs featured a series of erotic shots of black male bodies, usually nude and positioned in highly objectified poses: a nude midrift, a penis protruding through a headless man in a three-piece suit, a bare behind jutting into the lens. The Mapplethorpe controversy incited a transnational conversation by and for

black gay men on the politics of representation and visibility. Beam's earliest
political inspirations were black feminism, but the rise of a cultural studies
perspective adopted by figures such as Mercer and Julien in turn impacted
him. It is difficult to assign more weight to one metropolitan site than another
and perhaps is not necessary, as the point here is to show the continual flow
back and forth through gay media, aesthetic practices and products, and local
activisms with ephemera, from newspapers to fliers to reports, that circulated
freely across gay sites. Into the 2000s, the mainstream black British newspapers recognized the trendsetting powers of U.S. gay cultures. One story
pointed to increasing numbers of black gay Americans—who attended some
thirty black gay pride events—and asked, "Gay pride in the U.S.: How long
before the UK is down?"[47]

Gay Asians spoke publicly for their place in their community but also
quite specifically against "white gay racism," to quote a three-inch headline
of the *Eastern Eye*. The immediate cause was the 1994 Gay Pride March of
160,000 in which "anyone looking across the sea of bodies would have been
hard-pressed to spot Asian faces among the throng." In a moving if also by
now familiar account, they entreated queers of color to challenge the perception that only whites were gay as well as the realization that "the white
gay community still looks at Asians as exotic." In response, many gay Asians
refused to enter white clubs, wishing to be "desired for who they are, not
what they are." As one Asian man remarked, after five years on the gay scene,
"they always comment on my black hair, brown eyes, and the colour of my
skin. . . . I don't mind but they then refuse to see me in any other light. I'm as
British as the next person." Reporting on the launch of a new pornographic
magazine, *Asian Gays*, the story presented several interviews with Asian gays
and lesbians testifying to a pervasive white misunderstanding or objectification. Rather than the black stud image so pervasive in gay U.S. culture,
Asians described white British gay tendencies toward exoticism of them as
the ultimate other.[48]

Because representations of gays of color were few and far between, those
that presented oversimplification and stereotype were subject to intense criticism when queer people of color had a voice. In 1989 the BBC presented
a documentary on the South Asian experience that suggested a community
united in opposition to homosexuality, drawing the ire of one critic who
countered that "Asian lesbians and gays can lead happy and fulfilled lives." Yet
around the same time, another letter arrived at the *Evening Mail* disputing the

notion that "British-Asians" viewed homosexuality as a "perfectly accepted norm" when, "on the contrary, it is a behavior of much stigma, and it is certainly not a component of the Asian culture." Like the black activists who opposed gay curriculum, this Asian writer called for a return to traditional priorities—"devoted to questions of a more general nature, such as racism, immigration, education, etc." Yet tolerant Asian voices also emerged, and one columnist even chided his ethnic kin for not being more out, quipping "the biggest question in multicultural Britain: do Gay asians really exist?"[49]

Yet as Asian gays constructed their own institutions and networks, they experienced a familiar backlash. By 1999 an *Eastern Eye* headline blared "Asian Gay Ball Sparks Outcry," which reported on the first attempts to put on an Asian gay gala that "whipped up a homosexual hooha." Billed as a celebration not unlike the events promoted by U.S. black gays more than a decade before, the purpose was to promote visibility and dispel stereotypes. In a refrain that defined the queer nation of the 1990s, the gay Asians proclaimed, "We're gay! We're Asian! We're not going away—get used to it!" The celebration was a fund-raiser to help people with AIDS, and opponents objected to having "their lifestyle being rammed down everyone's throats like this." On both religious and political grounds, the event sparked debates, and yet some moderates, though surprised by it, nonetheless supported an event "helping the gay community and not harming anyone else."[50]

In light of a long past of suspicion of if not outright hostility to gay issues, black and Asian leaders were called out for their biases. "Some of the worst prejudice can be found among the ethnic minorities," read one article. "Black homophobes are just as ignorant about homosexuality and seem never have to read the brilliant novelist, James Baldwin." Yet signs of encouragement, including the election of an openly black gay peer to the House of Lords, signaled the small but accumulated accomplishments of two decades of grassroots activism, even if religious fundamentalists too surged in opposition to homosexuality. By the opening of the twenty-first century, a columnist concluded that "race, religion, and multiculturalism have entered the fray, making the situation much more difficult."[51] At the same time, *The Times* reported that a leading Hindu religious leader, representing some 10,000 Hindus, came out against homosexuality in response to a four-day gay Asian cultural fair, arguing that "tender minds could be easily influenced by this." Conservative Asians called for the repeal of positive legislation and for mobilizing against any and all such progay activities, hoping to repeat the cancellation of a similar Asian celebration: the Gay, Lesbian, and Glitz Ball. At the same time, Asian gays sought out nightlife and social networks in increasing numbers, even if underground and out of sight. But now, as with black gays in the United States, the search for community became involved with the policy of safe sex and the prevention of the transmission of HIV. It was not clear from the reports if people of color were more likely to become infected—as was the clear case among black gay men in the United States—but the project of gay Asian community formation had the added incentive of advocating safe sex and health.[52]

Similar stories abounded concerning Caribbean attitudes toward homosexuality: in a profile of Mr. Black Gay UK, it was suggested that "being gay, and what's worse, being out, just isn't done in the black community." Black activists argued for honoring the winner of the annual contest as a way to reform homophobia based on religious values and cultural mores as well as to encourage more black gay men to come out. The story also covered the rise of a black gay activist network, the Blackliners that had formed more than a decade ago. Like the black gay impulse in the United States several decades before, black British gays argued for the necessity of coming-out and acceptance as "basic human rights."[53]

Yet in some ways, New Yorkers had always been prepared for the avantgarde and the spectacle of cultural transgression. The proximity of the world-renowned "Black Mecca" to the exceptional cultural riches of New York City's Broadway stages and downtown independent movie screens meant that African Americans were potentially exposed to images and stories of homosexuality well before other black urbanites. In the pages of the *New York Amsterdam News*, an approving review of *Beauty Shop*, the 1990 Broadway comedy featuring several black women, added that the role of the black homosexual was played "masterfully"—"a finger-snapping, head-rolling homosexual who just cannot keep his eyes off any male who strolls into the parlor." Rather than a cliché, the gay hairdresser fit in nicely with a company of women who dish out "serious gossip and shocking confrontation."[54]

With access to independent and typically obscure art house films, Harlem readers were exposed to the plot of *Fortune* and *Men's Eyes*, set in a prison, that showed the rigid sexual system in which ("having no other sexual outlet") the more seasoned men forced the weaker or younger men into "passive roles," while others were "gang raped" (as the review put it), and still others saved the latter from the former. Though featuring black characters caught in a brutal system, the reviewer noted that "gay people ought to see this one, along with prison officials."[55] In 1983, the Broadway plays *American Buffalo* and *Trade* both portrayed aspects of the downtown gay culture in which the "'faggot usually goes after and pays for . . . more macho-acting and whether Black, white, or Hispanic, usually from the underclass."[56] But the plot turned on lurid stereotypes nonetheless when a wealthy white john seeks to sample a farm boy, and "in the ensuing drug-filled act that begins to unwind, Mac, the 'wasp type,' takes a poker from the fireplace and beats Waldo to death."[57]

Advice columns in African American newspapers tended to change with the times, reflecting a gradual liberalization of attitudes and a softening of homophobia. When a young adult reported that he enjoyed his relationships with very muscular men but now considered seeking a heterosexual partner, a skeptical columnist noted his rather extensive sexual experience. If he did end up going the other way, she hoped that he would "find a woman with big muscles."[58] By 1985, for example, editors reported on the value of family counseling and marriage therapy, including for the "homosexual family."[59]

As a number of scholars have shown, the epidemic of AIDS disproportionately impacted black communities, especially given higher rates of incarceration. Warning of a "looming AIDS crisis" in the prison population, a *New York Amsterdam News* article reported that to control the spread of HIV, state prisons would provide masks and gowns for personnel, remove homosexuals from food handling areas, and destroy the "eating utensils and plates of AIDS victims."[60] By 1991, alongside the announcement that basketball star Magic Johnson was infected with HIV, reports acknowledged skyrocketing infection rates in minority communities, but few of these stories explicitly mention black gay men. Rather, the source of concern was intravenous drug users, not bisexual black men, though reporters were more informed about HIV issues than ever before.[61]

Despite the conservative turn in the United States and the United Kingdom, both nations' new radical social networks and their more numerous planned demonstrations belied the claims of total retrenchment by the leaders of the New Right. Indeed, people living on the margins and at the intersections discovered a new resourcefulness and pressed for greater recognition in urban areas, universities, local governments, and smaller presses and radical bookstores. They joined task forces, staffed human resource offices, and organized political and cultural gatherings. In other words, the age of Reagan was never hegemonic or totalizing, sparking as it did the rise of not only ACT UP but also Queer Nations in New York, San Francisco, Chicago, Los Angeles, and many more towns and cities and simultaneously inspiring similar inter-sectional activism in Britain. This remarkable energy and inventiveness was expressed through direct action, headline-grabbing protests, and powerfully creative graphics combined to redirect the political winds of the day. Gay liberation sprang from but was never limited to the United States. By the end of the 1980s, black gay activism had inspired Caribbean and Asian black men in the United Kingdom who in turn shaped ideas about race and memory in U.S. queer identifications.

PART III

Beyond Liberalism and Conservatism

CHAPTER 7

Gay and Conservative

An Early History of the Log Cabin Republicans

Clayton Howard

It did not take long for journalists to coin a new cliché when gay conservatives formed the Log Cabin Republican Federation (LCRF) in 1991. "Is gay Republicanism anything other than an oxymoron?" asked *Newsweek* in 1992. A writer in the *Chicago Tribune* exclaimed that same year "Republicans? Gay? Whoa. Hold on Here." A few years later *The Advocate*, a liberal-leaning gay magazine, noted that audiences frequently greeted the group's members with "boos and hisses" and that skeptics sarcastically asked, "So you're a gay Republican—isn't that an oxymoron?" Conservative *New York Times* columnist David Brooks meanwhile marveled at the "quixotic" attempt to bring gay rights to the GOP amid the political polarization of the 1990s. "Is it even possible to be a gay Republican?" Brooks wondered in 1999. "Or are the two labels inimical?"[1] Liberals and conservatives may have disagreed about many things in the 1990s, but bafflement at the alleged absurdity of gay Republicans seemed to bring them together.

This chronic bewilderment at gay conservatism reflected in part the common assumption that most lesbian, gay, bisexual, and transgender people shared liberal values and an allegiance to the Democratic Party. Since the early 1990s, few groups of Americans have more consistently supported Democratic candidates than self-identified LGBT voters. Pollsters have found that at least two-thirds of LGBT people supported Democrats in federal elections between 1990 and 2016. In 2016 just 14 percent of LGBT voters supported Donald Trump for president, and they were three times more likely to identify as "liberal Democrats" than straight-identified people.[2] Yet amid the "culture wars" over gay rights in the late twentieth and early twenty-first centuries, sizable minorities of LGBT voters have nevertheless identified as Republicans. In 2012 one out of five self-identified lesbian and gay voters described themselves as "conservative" or "very conservative," while a poll in 2014 found that 21 percent of LGBT voters stated that they "lean" Republican. In 2016 Peter Thiel, an openly gay billionaire, addressed the Republican National Convention, and Caitlyn Jenner, one of the most well-known trans women in the world, called the GOP "our best hope to get back to constitutional government."[3]

The history of the Log Cabin Republicans reveals this ideological diversity among LGBT people and a convergence between some of the ideals of the middle-class strand of the gay rights movement and the New Right. Since their initial meetings in the late 1970s, the Log Cabin Republicans have seen no contradiction between being openly gay and conservative. They have argued that Americans who believe in small government should oppose laws that restrict the freedom of people to love or sleep with others of the same sex. Americans who believe in a strong military, furthermore, should respect the right of LGBT people to serve in the armed forces. Embracing the notion that people should be honest about their sexuality, openly gay members have treated the Republican Party as a central front in the struggle for LGBT equality. Again and again, they have treated the New Right and gay rights not as contradictions but instead as mutually compatible, and even their name has suggested this belief. They have called themselves Log Cabin Republicans because they have associated Abraham Lincoln with abolitionism, staunch individualism, and a strong military.[4]

Historians have implicitly reinforced the tendency to view "gay" and "conservative" as mutually exclusive categories, describing the New Right and the gay rights movement as separate phenomena. Conservatism and LGBT history have largely remained distinct fields of study, intersecting only when the Left and Right have clashed, and this separation is understandable. The Log Cabin Republicans have attracted relatively few followers since the 1970s, and scholars have aptly focused their attention on more influential groups such as Phyllis Schlafly's Eagle Forum on the Right and the Radicalesbians and the Gay Activists Alliance (GAA) on the Left.[5] Yet recent scholarship suggests that the Log Cabin Republicans may gain more members in time. In the wake of the campaigns to legalize same-sex marriage, several historians have underscored important, long-standing, and growing rifts among LGBT people. Timothy Stewart-Winter and Christina Hanhardt, for example, have argued that as the gay rights' movement achieved important victories in the 1980s and 1990s, many white middle-class gay men and lesbians divorced themselves from larger questions of social justice related to gentrification, mass incarceration, and immigration.[6] With the legalization of same-sex marriage in all fifty states, scholars will need to pay renewed attention to the history of gay conservatives who have often found an audience among white middle-class gay and lesbian voters.

Refusing to dismiss the Log Cabin Republicans as "oxymorons" does not mean accepting their beliefs uncritically. Throughout its history, the group has struggled to make itself politically relevant and has often reinforced various kinds of racial, class, and gender inequality. Yet the Log Cabin Republicans' roots in both the gay rights movement and the New Right also indicate the durability of their project. For better or worse, gay conservatives played a consistent, if small, role in late twentieth-century politics. As long as Americans feel the effects of the New Right and gay rights movements, they will also have to deal with the complexities of gay conservatism.

Born of Two Parents

Historians have traditionally narrated the rise of the gay rights movement as a part of the larger radical upheaval of the 1960s. During the early Cold War, small groups of gay men and lesbians formed "homophile societies" that, among other things, pushed for society's acceptance of homosexuality. The antiwar movement, feminism, and the black freedom struggle later motivated a generation of LGBT people of all races to rebel and push for a more egalitarian society.[7] Several early gay Republicans drew inspiration from these social movements, associating the GOP with civil liberties and individual freedom. A high school student in the late 1960s, Tim Drake negatively associated Lyndon Johnson with the Vietnam War and the draft, both of which he opposed. The only Democrats he knew as a teenager were white Democrats who fled "the City of Gary after an African American, Richard Hatcher, was elected mayor."[8]

However, many activists who later joined the Log Cabin Republicans did not participate in these movements on the Left. Instead, they often came to politics through what historian John Andrew calls "the other side of the sixties." Even as feminism, the black freedom struggle, and the antiwar movement challenged numerous forms of social inequality, conservative activists opposed what they saw as the nation's complacency in the Cold War and an expanding welfare state.[9] A decade later these conservatives remade the GOP, pushing it farther and farther to the right on almost every political issue, and New Right strategists crafted messages designed to attract new voters to the GOP. Republican leaders, for example, promoted tax cuts as a solution to failed Keynesian economics and as a means to shrink government. These campaigns to slash taxes and federal power reinforced the GOP's outreach to white Democrats unhappy with court-ordered desegregation, welfare spending, and affirmative action. Even as Republicans promised to limit domestic spending, however, they also pledged to increase the government's role in the Cold War. Critical of détente and the Democrats' handling of the Vietnam War, conservatives in the GOP recruited voters worried about the dovishness of figures such as Jimmy Carter.[10]

This mobilization on the Right inspired many future Log Cabin Republicans. Marvin Liebman, a Cold War anticommunist, called William F. Buckley "unquestionably the most important figure" in his life in the early 1960s and worked with student groups to support Barry Goldwater.[11] Frank Ricchiazzi, who helped found a Log Cabin club in southern California, initially grew up a Democrat in Buffalo, New York. However, he defined himself as a conservative after serving in the military. Ricchiazzi pursued a college degree at several Los Angeles-area colleges after a tour of duty in Vietnam, and he grew more conservative after what he saw as the left-leaning biases of the faculty and antiwar protesters.[12]

Many future Log Cabin Republicans therefore first came to politics through activism on the Right, but many of them concealed their sexuality from other conservatives. The gay rights movement, however, motivated these conservatives to come out and inspired openly gay Republican groups. Gay organizations in places such as New York and San Francisco organized political clubs, endorsing candidates for higher office and pushing for the repeal of homophobic laws. By the 1970s this activism fell across the political spectrum, including "rights-based" assimilationists who wanted to work within the system to affect social change, liberationists who pushed for wider shifts in Americans' attitudes toward sex, and combinations of both approaches.[13] Although gay politics in this era encompassed many different attitudes and strategies, activists generally shared a common belief in the importance of speaking openly about one's sexuality, or coming-out.[14]

Many future Log Cabin Republicans joined millions of other lesbians and gay men and migrated to gay-friendly places such as San Francisco and

Los Angeles in the 1970s. Some later recalled reading left-leaning periodicals such as *The Advocate*, and they often witnessed the work of liberal and radical organizations. Stan Aten, for example, attended meetings of the Dallas Gay Alliance in the early 1980s before helping to start a Republican club.[15] Christopher Bowman followed friends to a meeting of the Stonewall Democrats not long after he moved to San Francisco in the mid-1970s.[16]

Bowman, however, like many of his conservative peers, felt out of place at meetings dominated by liberals. "I was a Cold Warrior!" he remembered, laughing at the incongruity of his presence in a room full of activists supporting nuclear freezes and left-leaning movements in Latin America. Furthermore, the reflexive association of gay rights with other liberal causes annoyed some conservatives. In the 1980s, Frank Ricchiazzi ran for an assembly district in southern California as a Republican. When he spoke to a nominally nonpartisan gay organization in Los Angeles's West Hollywood neighborhood, however, he faced hostile questions about his stance on abortion and unions. "What does abortion have to do with gay rights?" Ricchiazzi asked, surprised by what he saw as the group's liberal agenda.[17]

More often, conservatives such as Ricchiazzi participated in the burgeoning gay social life sparked by the sexual revolution in the nation's major cities. Some early club members were in long-term monogamous relationships or were so-called sweater queens who frequented high-end bars. But they also included members of local leather scenes and drag circuits. San Diego's Imperial Empress Nicole Murray-Ramirez, for example, identified as a Republican in the 1970s and 1980s, while conservative Duke Armstrong frequented the leather bars on San Francisco's Polk Street.[18] Most frequently, conservatives included adult men who only came out as gay later in life and were elated about having their first honest sexual experiences in their thirties and forties. Bowman, for example, attended some of the rowdier Halloween celebrations on San Francisco's Polk Street in the 1970s and half-jokingly described the city in that era as a place where one should "know thy limits and exceed them."[19]

Major cities such as San Francisco offered more than gay politics and social life, however. They also incubated new gay businesses, and some of the men and women who ran these enterprises formed the nuclei of later Republican clubs. *The Advocate* marveled at a "gay business boom" across the country in the late 1970s and early 1980s, profiling gay chambers of commerce in such cities as Denver, Minneapolis, Los Angeles, and Portland, Oregon.[20] In 1979, the magazine detailed the crusade of a restaurant owner near Los Angeles's Silver Lake district to lower taxes and eliminate regulation of the service industry. "They take more than half my business's gross revenues," complained Gjon Merolla. "They force businessmen to cheat in order to survive. Government has become our very real enemy."[21]

Most members of these gay chambers of commerce identified as Democrats, but early gay Republican clubs also expressed the interests of a segment of the growing business and professional class. The *Los Angeles Times* described an early meeting of a local Log Cabin chapter as "a mix of doctors, lawyers and businessmen," while Christopher Bowman remembered numerous realtors, small property owners, and "lots and lots of attorneys" in San Francisco.[22] Frank Ricchiazzi, a real estate investor himself, had a similar experience, seeing the divide between Los Angeles's gay Republicans and gay Democrats as a reflection of the social divisions between the city's east and west sides, renters and home owners. Many gay businessmen came to early meetings, which did not surprise Ricchiazzi, who saw coming out of the closet and entrepreneurship as two sides of the same coin: "A lot of gays came to California in the sixties and seventies because if you came from a small town, you knew you were trapped," he declared. "People who have to restart their life, they're a lot more entrepreneurial. You're a lot more likely to take on risk."[23]

The rise of the Religious Right, however, offered the most immediate spark for the creation of early LCRF clubs. Gay Republicans came to the GOP for many reasons, including its stance on taxes, civil rights, federal power, and the Cold War. But the ascendance of profamily conservatives in the party in the 1970s made homophobia an increasingly important part of Republican politics. Beginning in 1977, well-known antigay conservatives such as Anita Bryant and John Briggs made national headlines when they tried to roll back recently won protections for gay people in Florida and California.[24] These campaigns alarmed gay rights groups across the country but particularly concerned gay Republicans. Tim Drake described himself as a "nonpolitical" person in the mid-1970s, but after Bryant convinced voters in Miami to eliminate a gay rights ordinance, he felt "politically threatened" for the first time in his life.[25] Newly politicized, Republicans such as Drake started gay-friendly GOP groups across the country.

Many of these clubs appeared in places with vibrant gay communities, politicized conservatives, or both. Southern California simultaneously witnessed the mobilization of the New Right and gay rights movements and, consequently, produced some of the earliest and largest gay Republican groups. The first club to bear the name "Log Cabin" came together in Los Angeles's Silver Lake District in the late 1970s, and later chapters formed in Orange

County, San Diego, Riverside County, and Palm Springs. Other early organizations formed in cities with famously large gay neighborhoods, including San Francisco's Concerned Republicans for Individual Rights (CRIR) and Seattle's Gay Republicans of Washington. While many early clubs met in urban centers, some of their names also reflected the inclusion of gay suburbanites. Dallas's Metroplex Republicans, the Chicago Area Republican Gay Organization (CARGO), and the Washington, D.C., Capital Area Republicans suggested that at least some of their members lived outside traditional "gay ghettoes" in older cities.[26]

These new groups were relatively small. Two of the largest clubs, Los Angeles's Log Cabin Club and San Francisco's CRIR, only boasted approximately 120 and 188 members, respectively, in the early 1980s.[27] Their size in part reflected their inability to attract many women or people of color, and their predominantly male white membership reflected prevailing patterns in both the New Right and middle-class gay rights movements. White men defected from the GOP in growing numbers after World War II, but the Democratic Party decisively lost a majority of their vote in 1964 when President Johnson signed the Civil Rights Act into law. Later polarization over issues such as school integration, affirmative action, and abortion meant that white men increasingly voted Republican.[28] At the same time, many future Log Cabin Republicans participated in predominantly white male gay rights organizations. Although many groups on the Left, such as the GAA, often modeled themselves after the black freedom struggle, they were nevertheless, according to one historian, "blind to the whiteness in their ranks."[29] Furthermore, organizations such as the GAA often replicated the sexism of the wider society. Men dominated most positions of leadership and often refused to work with women as equals.

Consequently, early gay conservative groups were predominantly white and male. Women such as Susan Jester in San Diego and Evelyn Kotch in Philadelphia later headed Log Cabin groups, but lesbians largely avoided many of the early clubs. Ted Hoerl, who hoped to work with more women, recalled with annoyance that "no one" in CARGO "was particularly interested in lesbians because there weren't any."[30] Christopher Bowman remembered a few women at early meetings of the San Francisco chapter, but they were less than 1 percent of the total membership.[31] Black gay conservatives of either sex were even more rare. Abner Mason headed the Massachusetts chapter, and conservative columnist Leonard Greene worked with a gay Republican club in Washington, D.C.[32] However, most of the early groups' members were almost entirely white.[33]

Many of these small early gay Republican clubs nevertheless looked to the future enthusiastically. The combination of the New Right revolt in the GOP and the politicization of millions of gay and lesbian Americans gave many future LCRF clubs hope that they could make a difference. Chuck LaMoy, president of the Log Cabin Club of Los Angeles, predicted in 1982 that he would help organize approximately 200,000 lesbian and gay voters in California and "educate" the Republican Party on "gay and women's rights." In spite of their small size, many early gay conservative clubs therefore expressed hope about the future.

Dual Identities and the Two-Party Strategy

The mobilization of the New Right and gay rights movements helped create these early clubs, and both movements shaped the ideology and strategy of gay Republicans in the 1980s. Between 1979 and 1991, groups such as Los Angeles's Log Cabin Republican club and Chicago's CARGO largely worked independently, but they shared two views that bound them together. First, gay Republicans adopted language from the larger gay rights movement, using words such as "authenticity" to describe their two core identities. Early activists stressed that they were "out" as both gay people and conservatives. This emphasis on openness directly influenced a second vision common to all of the early groups: a sustained effort to make the Republican Party gay-inclusive and to make both parties compete for lesbian and gay voters. Club members in the 1980s hoped to show that gay Americans shared many of the GOP's goals, and they argued that gay people would suffer if only one party could count on their votes. Gay Republicans thus hoped to make the GOP more accepting of gay people, just as the New Right had made the party more conservative in the 1960s and 1970, and hoped to work within the Republican Party, just as liberal activists tried to make the Democrats more inclusive.

The recurring language among gay conservatives about the importance of being "out" reveals an important legacy of the gay rights movement. Gay conservatives saw authenticity as a concept that reconciled their two identities. Although they frequently saw their relationships as private matters, the reality of discrimination necessitated that they come out of the closet. Len Olds and Hugh Rouse, for example, recounted their visits to Republican conventions and meetings in the 1980s and 1990s to archivist Lisa Vecoli in 2015: "The only way in the door was to tell the truth. Never to lie. We were always an openly gay couple both to our family and friends. . . . When we went to a convention we went as a couple." Those visits to Republican events often generated controversy, and Olds and Rouse reminded Vecoli that "we were *openly* gay people."[34]

This commitment to authenticity also extended to Log Cabin members' identities as conservatives. Amid the wider left-leaning movement for gay equality, Republicans such as Olds and Rouse prided themselves as activists on the Right. In numerous statements, gay conservatives justified their loyalty to the GOP as a reflection of their dedication to their "true beliefs." Rich Tafel, for instance, attended Harvard Divinity School in the mid-1980s and expressed repeated annoyance at the left-leaning politics of his fellow students. Constantly asked how he could support the GOP, Tafel asserted that he was "'out' as a Republican" before he was "'out' as a gay person.'" His support for the free market, anticommunism, and individual rights was as fundamental to his being as his sexuality. "As I saw it," he announced, "integrity required me to be an honest Republican instead of a dishonest Democrat."[35]

Activists such as Tafel stressed being "out" about both of their identities because gay conservatism drew upon multiple, sometimes competing political traditions and spoke to several groups of supporters. On one hand, they married libertarian notions of individual liberty with some of the gay rights movement's celebration of pluralism. Gay Republicans emphasized that their lives demonstrated the diversity of the LGBT and conservative experiences in the United States. Bruce Decker told the *Washington Post* in 1984 that gay people were not "monolithic," declaring that "we have a philosophical spectrum that begins at the far left and goes to the far right."[36] At the same time, gay Republicans paired assimilationist arguments from the white middle-class wing of the gay rights movement with conservative notions of patriotism and respectability. They believed that their lives not only demonstrated the diversity of gay experiences but also disrupted stereotypes of LGBT people as abnormal or un-American. Susan Jester told the *San Diego Union Tribune* in 1985 that "most people that sit in the middle of Kansas in their living rooms and watch TV every night have no idea of the gay people around them. . . . I don't fit the image. Painted fingernails, lipstick and blonde hair is not what you see on most lesbian feminist activists."[37]

Gay Republicans therefore argued that they were simultaneously fighting for a kind of diversity and assimilation, and this duality informed a political strategy designed to make the GOP a central front in the struggle for gay equality. Activists such as Jester believed that their dual identities gave them the freedom and skills to speak to both gay people and conservatives. According to a writer in a club newsletter, when it came to dealing with "conservative issues" such as the military, "we are better situated than any Democrat to end discrimination against gay men and lesbians." At the same time, the writer hoped that their efforts to build an inclusive GOP would show "all gays and other minorities that there is a viable alternative to the liberal agenda."[38]

Gay Republicans used their two identities to pursue a two-pronged political strategy. One part of that strategy involved speaking to conservatives about gay equality. When addressing this audience, they often appealed to libertarian beliefs in small government and individual liberty. For example, Jere Real complained in the *National Review* that too much of the New Right accepted religious condemnations of homosexuality without criticism. "With ironic counterpoint," he wrote, "those who have argued so successfully against government intrusion into the lives of citizens were quite willing to let the government legislate the lives of *some* individuals—the country's homosexuals."[39]

Because many early club members were veterans, military-related concerns often dovetailed with appeals to individual liberty. Organizing amid the Cold War buildup of the 1980s, some gay Republicans addressed other conservatives with anticommunist appeals to patriotism, and no moment underscored the intersections between the gay rights movement and the New Right more than the case of Leonard Matlovich. A Republican, Vietnam War veteran, and U.S. Air Force sergeant, Matlovich challenged the military's ban on openly gay personnel by coming out to his commanding officer in 1975 and appearing in uniform on the cover of *Time* with the caption "I Am a Homosexual."[40] His protest and eventual discharge made him a martyr for the wider gay rights movement, but his efforts particularly inspired gay conservatives. Speaking about Matlovich, Jere Real asked, "Should a citizen, a homosexual citizen, be deprived of the privilege . . . of serving his country in the armed forces?" For Real, military service represented an act of individual patriotism, not a sign of big government, and bans on gay personnel such as Matlovich violated their civil liberties.[41]

The arguments that gay Republicans made in favor of civil rights laws further revealed their attempts to bridge the New Right and gay rights. During the 1970s and 1980s, gay activists across the political spectrum pushed for legal protections in housing, the workplace, and public accommodations. Like the military, many early Log Cabin members saw these laws not as government intrusions into the free market but instead as small steps by the state to create a "level playing field." Marvin Liebman, for example, argued that

"I'm not for affirmative action. But I believe that gays should have the same rights and privileges of other members of the American citizenry, and one of those rights is the right to privacy."[42] For conservatives such as Liebman, the government's minimal recognition of his "right to privacy" averted the wider enlargement of the state through "affirmative action" by allowing gay people to participate in the market on equal footing with everyone else.

This belief that antidiscrimination laws "protected privacy" and created a "level playing field" required first acknowledging the presence of publicly sanctioned homophobia. While many gay conservatives saw themselves as proponents of small government, they generally supported rules restricting the right of employers to fire them or landlords to evict them. In many cases this embrace of small government and gay rights laws amounted to hypocrisy, since the largely white male conservatives carved out an exception to an otherwise principled stance against an enlarged state that might have benefited women and people of color.

In addition to writing books and articles in conservative magazines, gay Republicans put pressure on key figures in the GOP but preferred to work within the existing party system. Len Olds recalled that "we realized that the fight—politically—wasn't going to be in just one party. . . . If we were going to get anywhere in the Republican Party, we couldn't be outside the door. We had to be inside the room."[43] Consequently, most of their efforts involved trying to make gay voters visible and relevant to the GOP. Time and time again, gay Republicans attempted to use their votes, donations, and volunteer work to leverage influence in the party. Len Olds and Hugh Rouse attended state and local Republican events in suit and ties, set up informational tables, and met with party officials: "We tried to emphasize our independence, and we'd say to our Republican Party. . . . We want *equality*. Not special rights. *Equality* for gay men and lesbians. So we would attend mayors' events, state senators' events, conventions, and then we would have a Log Cabin suite . . . and they would come in, and we'd talk with them one on one."[44]

While activists such as Olds and Rouse pitched gay rights to conservatives, they also pursued the second prong of their political strategy: selling conservatism to gay audiences. Members of CRIR dropped off copies of their newsletters in San Francisco bars and set up recruitment tables at the Castro Street Fair.[45] The Metroplex Republicans placed short announcements in *This Week in Texas*, a gay periodical.[46] Furthermore, gay Republicans sometimes collaborated with their liberal counterparts on issues of common interest. The Orange County group, for example, hosted fund-raisers with its local gay

Democratic counterpart, the Eleanor Roosevelt Club.[47] Stan Aten and Paul Rodgers both worked with Democrats in the nonpartisan Lesbian and Gay Political Coalition in Dallas.[48]

Just as activists sometimes paired gay equality with small government for the New Right, many writers praised free market conservatism in the gay press. In 1987, a columnist named "John Locke" claimed in the *Windy City Times* that gay men and lesbians should find the "libertarian" elements of the GOP attractive. While conceding that most conservatives opposed an "affirmative role for government in promoting gay rights," he argued that many of them nevertheless supported "a minimum of governmental interference in private consensual conduct."[49]

In order to make these arguments compelling, writers such as Locke paired other Republican campaign issues with what they saw as the concerns of many white middle-class gay voters. An unnamed participant in a planning session in 1988 argued that gay Republicans needed to do "missionary work" to both conservative and gay "camps," connecting "fag bashing to the need for a strong police force" and "keeping America strong with how totalitarian governments treat gays."[50] Although authorities in cities such as Chicago had long harassed gay men and lesbians, Locke similarly appealed to middle-class fears of crime by arguing that gay residents now had more to fear from "muggers, youth gangs, and other assorted misanthropes" than the police. Because "Soviet repression of homosexuality is well-known," Locke further claimed, "the hard-won freedoms of gays depend . . . upon a strong and vigilant military."[51]

Most importantly, however, many early gay Republicans argued that lesbians and gay men needed a two-party strategy to achieve equality. CARGO's Ted Hoerl worried that Democrats would take gay voters for granted and that "real" reforms "required both parties every time." Without loyal gay voters in the GOP, these activists contended, the Republican Party would inevitably see them as a lost cause and grow even more dependent on the Religious Right. Others highlighted the homophobia of their opponents, frequently expressing frustration that liberal voters excused Democrats' antigay politics while condemning those of Republicans. Rich Tafel, for instance, declared that "the question for gay voters is how to get beyond the choice between lesser evils to the day when we have a choice between two relatively friendly candidates."[52]

Gay Republican clubs therefore fielded two campaigns at once. United by a common "authentic" gay and conservative identity, they spoke to Republicans and LGBT voters. Trying to build a third way between the Religious

Right and the left-leaning gay rights movement, they argued that they embodied both the diversity of gay life in the United States and notions of patriotism and middle-class respectability. Their political strategy entailed trying to make lesbian and gay voters relevant to the GOP, and they simultaneously spoke to conservatives about the virtues of gay equality and to LGBT people about the advantages of supporting local and national Republican candidates.

Squeezed Between Two Sides

The two-party strategy gave gay Republican groups a common mission, and even many Democrats applauded their efforts. Yet the weaknesses of the strategy soon became apparent in the 1980s. While some Republicans clearly sympathized with their cause, the growing strength of the Religious Right meant that GOP candidates increasingly chose homophobic policies. Even as gay activists tried to leverage support in the party, antigay conservatives quickly foreclosed the possibility of an inclusive Republican Party. The rising homophobia of the GOP in turn pushed many LGBT voters to the left. Gay Republicans gradually felt opposition from not only other conservatives but also other gay activists. During the 1980s and early 1990s, a successful two-party strategy thus seemed increasingly unlikely.

Shortly after their creation, gay Republican groups found sympathetic ears in some parts of the GOP. Numerous early club members recalled feeling hopeful when John Anderson ran for president in 1980. A Republican congressman from Illinois, Anderson helped sponsor a federal bill that would have made discrimination in employment, housing, and public accommodations based on sexual orientation illegal.[53] Launched shortly after the Anita Bryant crusades of the late 1970s, his candidacy suggested that the GOP could support gay equality, and Drake, Huerl, and Bowman all volunteered on his ill-fated primary campaign.[54]

In 1984, Frank Ricchiazzi and Christopher Bowman worked with liberal gay activists to engineer the passage of AB-1, a landmark nondiscrimination bill in the California legislature. The two men convinced six Republicans to join a Democratic majority to pass the bill. Most dramatically, Ricchiazzi met with California senator Ed Davis, the notoriously homophobic former Los Angeles police chief. Davis once championed closing gay bars in Los Angeles, but after speaking with the Log Cabin Republicans, he saw protecting gay men and lesbians from employment discrimination as being compatible with his core conservative principles.[55] The California Log Cabin clubs scored yet another victory when U.S. senator Pete Wilson came out for gay rights during his 1988 reelection campaign. That year, he told the Orange County chapter that he believed that people with AIDS "need to be protected against discrimination" and called for the prosecution of antigay hate crimes "to the fullest extent of the law."[56] Gay Republicans met the most success in the 1980s in California, but several of them campaigned for spots in state legislatures or city councils in other parts of the country.[57] Tim Drake lost a race against a longtime Democratic legislator in Chicago, for example, but believed that his campaign nevertheless earned him the respect of other Republicans.[58]

These modest successes revived gay Republicans' faith in the two-party strategy, and they frequently noted the persistent homophobia of their political opponents. In the early 1980s the Democratic National Committee established an official gay and lesbian caucus, and liberal candidates such as Gary Hart specifically courted the gay vote.[59] Yet many Democrats also opposed gay rights either out of conviction or political expediency. Arkansas governor Bill Clinton largely avoided the issue of homosexuality in the 1980s, led an administration that spent almost nothing on AIDS-related health care, and later insisted that gay rights had "just never been issues" in his home state.[60] In 1990, liberal Republican William Weld garnered a significant share of the gay vote when he defeated Democrat John Silber for the Massachusetts governorship. During the campaign, Silber called homosexuality "not normative behavior" and refused to meet with representatives of the state's LGBT communities.[61] Looking at the Democrats' record on gay rights in 1992, David Fontaine, the director of the bipartisan Coalition for Lesbian and Gay Civil Rights, declared, "Why not gay Republicans? It's not as if either party has given us that much."[62]

Yet the 1980s represented a transitional period in which social conservatives decisively took over the Republican Party. The Religious Right fielded candidates in primaries and forced gay-friendly Republicans to change their views. California governor George Deukemajian, for example, worried about "protecting his right flank" and vetoed the nondiscrimination bill that Ricchiazzi and Bowman had championed in 1984.[63] Antigay conservatives swept into key positions in the California Republican Party in 1988, ousting more moderate members. After years of campaigning by Log Cabin Clubs to try to gain acceptance in the state's GOP, the party voted against recognizing any Republican groups "based on sexual orientation."[64] Just three years after he garnered the endorsement of the California Log Cabin Republicans for his Senate reelection, Governor Pete Wilson vetoed yet another state nondiscrimination bill to appease religious conservatives.[65]

No issue better exemplified the difficulties of a two-party strategy more than the AIDS crisis. Ronald Reagan, never a strong supporter of gay rights, limited the federal resources available to fight the epidemic and infamously neglected to even mention the word "AIDS" until 1985. By the time he gave a formal address on the topic in 1987, over 20,000 Americans had died from the disease.[66] Reagan's inaction outraged many gay Republicans. Alex Wetzel, president of the Orange County Log Cabin Republicans, spoke for many gay conservatives when he wrote a scathing response to the president's AIDS policy. "Loyalty to the Republican Party," Wetzel declared in 1987, "has to be tempered by conscience and common sense. . . . In this instance, it is all too apparent that the President's main concern is to appease the right wing."[67]

Reagan's inaction and the hostility of religious conservatives during the epidemic prompted a series of massive protests from gay rights groups such as ACT UP, including civil disobedience at the National Institutes for Health in Maryland.[68] AIDS meanwhile prompted more Democrats to speak out in favor of gay rights. As he prepared to run for president, Bill Clinton told a group of LGBT voters that he supported more AIDS funding in 1991. The gradual warming of Democrats to the AIDS issue eventually prompted the *New York Times* to mark the Clinton campaign as the moment when gay issues went "mainstream."[69]

The growing divide between the two parties on gay rights became glaringly apparent at the 1992 Republican National Convention in Houston. At the convention, former Nixon speechwriter Pat Buchanan pledged to "take back our country" from Americans who supported "radical feminism" and "homosexual rights." He condemned Bill Clinton and his running mate Al Gore as "the most pro gay and pro lesbian ticket in history" and called the 1992 election a "battle for the soul of the nation."[70] Thousands of conservatives cheered the speech, much to the discomfort of gay Republicans such as Frank Ricchiazzi, who attended the Republican National Convention that year.[71]

Some liberal gay activists welcomed their Republican counterparts in the 1980s and early 1990s and celebrated them as symbols of LGBT ideological diversity.[72] But the polarization of the era, particularly conflicts related to AIDS, also drove many on the Left to attack gay Republicans. An activist from Queer Nation in 1992 compared gay Republicans to "blacks supporting the

Ku Klux Klan" and confessed, "I don't understand why anyone who would support a party that would condemn them, shame them, and make them feel like idiots."[73]

Together, conservatives' homophobia and animosity from the Left disrupted the two-party strategy and decimated many of the country's gay Republican clubs. Christopher Bowman estimated that his chapter lost about 40 percent of its members after the Deukemajian veto in 1984 and fell to just fifty members after the 1992 Republican convention.[74] Many founders of early clubs left the GOP out of frustration with its homophobia. Paul Rodgers, an early member of the Metroplex Republicans, expressed dismay at the direction of the party. He remembered the 1980s and early 1990s as "a really frustrating time" and recalled believing that "if we just presented something decent to the Republican Party, they'd let us in the door. . . . [But] we never got our foot in the door."[75]

By the early 1990s, much of the optimism of the early years had evaporated. Defections left many gay Republican clubs largely in the hands of their most conservative members. Bowman recalled that as the San Francisco club lost supporters, its politics shifted rightward.[76] The remaining members understood the bigotry of figures such as Buchanan, but their conservative beliefs on other issues glued them to the party. Ricchiazzi acknowledged this dilemma in 1990: "We're trapped in the Republican Party. We have no place to go. We can't go to the Democratic Party. We don't believe in their philosophy."[77] The two-party strategy only worked if GOP candidates could rely on gay voters to support them, and the sheer volume of homophobic sentiment in the party meant that gay activists found fewer and fewer allies.

The Birth of the Log Cabin Republican Federation and a National Two-Party Strategy

Defections plagued gay Republican groups in the 1990s and early 2000s, but those decades also witnessed the growth of a national gay conservative movement. The hostility of the Religious Right made many LGBT people into single-issue voters, and consequently many of them who might have otherwise supported the GOP identified as Democrats. Gay conservatives who strongly identified with many other Republican policies saw little alternative to continuing their work, and in the 1990s they built a national organization that united the various local clubs. This new federation brought together numerous members who differed on a wide variety of issues and shared only a faith in gay equality and some of the Republican Party's platform. These differences forced the national leadership to employ the two-party strategy in spite of mounting evidence that fewer and fewer GOP policy makers sympathized with their cause.

Almost since the inception of the different clubs, many gay Republicans believed that clubs needed to unite in some way. The Religious Right posed too great of a threat, they argued, to remain divided, and the sprouting of new groups in the late 1980s in places such as Colorado and New York only fueled their desire to join forces.[78] The different clubs, however, could not initially agree on the details of a national organization, and the deaths from AIDS of some of their leaders made organizing more difficult. They finally succeeded in December 1990, opening an office in Washington, D.C.; choosing William Weld appointee Rich Tafel as its first national director; and uniting all of the chapters under the title "Log Cabin Republicans."

Consolidation offered greater visibility and strength in numbers but also limited clubs' autonomy. Independent gay Republican groups had offered a range of opinions. But consolidation required them to share a common message. And because conservatives with deeper ties to the wider Republican platform made up a greater share of the membership, unity frequently meant stressing gay voters' loyalty to the GOP. The California Log Cabin Clubs, for example, consolidated before the opening of the national office, and in 1990 many of the state's members believed that the group should have fought harder to keep the Republican Party from expelling groups "based on sexual orientation." In a confidential memo Marty Keller, the group's state director, tried to persuade angry members that the California Log Cabin Republicans could gain more by supporting gubernatorial candidate Pete Wilson than by protesting in public. Before consolidation, Keller argued, clubs grew accustomed "to asserting our position on issues." The newly united California groups, however, needed to show the rest of the GOP that gay voters supported the nominee. "By adopting Wilson's election as our number one goal," Keller claimed, "we voluntarily gave up a little bit of that freedom."[79]

Pete Wilson's later veto of California's antidiscrimination bill highlights the problem with this approach, but the Log Cabin office in Washington, D.C., nevertheless pursued a similar strategy to foster unity within the group in the 1990s. Little else but dedication to gay equality and the GOP united the Log Cabin Republicans. Rich Tafel started his job at a time when many

local chapters faced internal ideological divisions and the national organization tried to unite gay conservatives under one umbrella. The Orange County
club, for example, fractured in 1991 as several members left to form a new
group. The splinter faction complained in a flyer "Have you ever felt out of
place at an Orange County Republican gathering because you might be too
moderate or progressive . . . ? We Believe That: An individual has the right to
decide what being a Republican means to them; there is no wrong or right
way to be a Republican."[80]

These divisions occurred even as new recruits flooded the organization
in the wake of Pat Buchanan's 1992 speech. Although older members had
left in frustration, Tafel remembered that the homophobia at the Houston
convention inspired a wave of gay Republicans to join the movement.[81]
National polls in the 1990s and early 2000s found that roughly 15–25 percent
of self-identified gay voters also identified as committed Republicans.[82] The
nasty tenor of the convention in Houston helped drive gay support for the
Republican nominee, George H. W. Bush, down to just 14 percent in 1992.[83]
In 1996, however, 23 percent of self-identified gay voters cast their ballot for
Bob Dole.[84] In 2000 George W. Bush, a son of the former president, garnered
25 percent of the gay vote.[85] Tafel, poring over election results, concluded that
his organization found its support primarily among gay "entrepreneurs" and
those who "lived outside gay urban centers." Seven years after the creation of
the Log Cabin Federation, the organization boasted fifty-two chapters with
over 11,000 members.[86]

Tafel and other leaders opted to unite these members by tailoring their
advocacy strategy narrowly. Despite mounting evidence of the two-party
strategy's limits, they dedicated themselves to building alliances with some of
the few remaining sympathetic Republicans. In 1994, Christine Todd Whitman promised to make the GOP a "party of inclusion" and to create a New
Jersey state agency dedicated to helping gay youths.[87] New York mayor Rudy
Giuliani garnered praise from the Log Cabin Republicans for his support for
gay equality in the 1990s. Giuliani applauded the organization in 1999 for
"undermining popular stereotypes" about gay people.[88]

Yet homophobic conservatives continued to outnumber their gay opponents. In 2002, Rick Warren's Saddleback evangelical Protestant church
alone boasted thousands more members than the entire national LCRF.[89]
When Republican candidates needed to choose between gay equality and
support from the Religious Right, they often chose the latter. Many so-
called moderates within the GOP meanwhile failed to prioritize gay rights.

Just a few years after he praised the Log Cabin Republicans, Giuliani sought higher office outside of New York City and stated that although he had no problem with homosexuality "as a way of life," he agreed with the Catholic Church that homosexual acts "were sinful."[90] Whitman, by contrast, consistently supported gay equality but found herself increasingly marginalized in the GOP.[91]

The LCRF might have offset the growing power of the Religious Right by working with more liberal groups in the GOP, but the conservatism of its membership hampered those alliances. Some gay Republicans had long called for such a strategy and pushed the LCRF to take stances on issues indirectly related to the question of gay equality. In 1988, for instance, several members suggested that the LCRF "should align with feminists on issues of privacy and non-intrusion."[92] A strategy session related to the 1996 presidential race similarly included the recommendation that the LCRF should work with "other Republican groups (i.e. CRL, Republicans for Choice, Young Republicans, Congress of California Republicans, Federated Women) and 'other non-partisan groups' (i.e. PFLAG, Black Caucus, Labor, Pro-Choice, Pro-Life, NOW, minority clubs)."[93]

Tafel and other Log Cabin leaders, however, largely avoided taking stances on issues other than gay equality. They worried that their members remained divided on subjects such as abortion and health care. In an internal memo about the LCRF's strategy in 1995, Tafel declared, "Our organization itself has a wide diversity of opinions on other issues. We exist to work on this most difficult issue. . . . When we start talking about Log Cabin's position on gun control, for instance, we get off message."[94]

The LCRF's opposition or indifference to feminist and civil rights initiatives furthermore made it difficult for the organization to appeal to lesbians and gay voters of color. During the 1990s, leaders in the national office worried about the gender and racial homogeneity of the organization and suggested that the LCRF recruit more women, Latinos, and African Americans. An internal study of the different chapters found that men outnumbered women ten to one. After noting that at least four chapters lacked women altogether, the writer of the study concluded that "plans should be drawn up on the national level for plans to incorporate women into LCR ranks on the local level."[95] When JoAnn Fisher, an African American delegate from Maryland, pushed the 1994 LCRF National Convention to "reach out and increase the participation of women and women of color by at least 20%," the audience gave her a standing ovation.[96]

Yet many of the statements and actions of the Log Cabin clubs alienated the very voters they allegedly wanted to recruit. In 1994, Thomas McCormack of the Metroplex Republicans told the local newspaper that "I am one of those people who think the Democratic Party left us. . . . The Democrats started emphasizing more social things, like civil rights and welfare and economic policies that people in the suburbs just could not relate to."[97] Two years later the California Log Cabin Republican clubs endorsed Proposition 209, which amended the state constitution to prohibit governmental institutions from considering race, sex, or ethnicity in hiring or education. Although some leaders of the California branch regretted the endorsement, the national organization nevertheless invited Ward Connolly, Proposition 209's chief sponsor, to speak at its 1998 convention.[98]

Many of the Republican candidates who publicly supported gay rights also often had egregious records on issues of concern to nonwhite voters. Pete Wilson, for example, opposed affirmative action, championed several laws eliminating bilingual education in California, and supported a ballot initiative that would have denied all public services to immigrants without legal permission to work in the United States. Wilson later signed a "three strikes" bill into law, enacting legislation that disproportionately condemned African American and Latino convicts to life in prison.[99] Rudy Giuliani's policing and welfare policies in New York City in the 1990s similarly generated criticism from civil rights groups.[100]

Furthermore, some women involved in Log Cabin clubs resented what they saw as the close-mindedness of their male counterparts. Martha Maire O'Connell, cochair of Santa Clara's Log Cabin Club, offered tips to her fellow gay Republicans about how to attract more women. She advised the men to remember that lesbians "are not all alike" and not to "make the lesbian the secretary every time." She also noted that "lesbians earn 57–59 percent of what gay men make" and "are more likely than gay men to have the economic burden of child-raising."[101] Rosemary Dunn Dalton, a gay Democrat, shared her impressions of the LCRF in the *Chicago Tribune* in 1992: "Nobody among the gay Republicans has done any work to reach out to lesbians."[102]

No issue tested Tafel's narrow gay equality strategy more than the LCRF's stance on abortion. Although it might surprise some critics, numerous Log Cabin Republicans supported women's reproductive rights, at least in principle. A survey of Log Cabin Republicans in 1996 found that over two-thirds of them identified as pro-choice.[103] Orange County's Alex Wetzel believed that the Log Cabin Republicans needed to speak out in support of abortion rights for both philosophical and practical reasons: "if we sincerely believe in individual rights, then we cannot discriminate and take the position that we are entitled to our rights, but a pregnant woman is not."[104]

Others, however, worried that widening their definition of "sexual freedom" would split the group and dilute their efforts. Even though a clear majority of the group's members were pro-choice and only 20 percent called themselves "pro-life," a whopping 81 percent responded that they "do not believe that abortion is a gay or lesbian issue."[105] Scott Minos, a Republican from Palm Beach, advocated against getting involved in the fights over abortion because "expanding the definition of its purpose" would mean that "Log Cabin is in danger of losing the factor that motivates so many of its leaders—gay and lesbian equality." If individual members wanted to support other causes, he argued, they should "join organized forces that advocate their position."[106]

The abortion issue proved remarkably contentious, and the LCRF's neutral stance likely kept many women from joining the group. One unnamed lesbian Republican told the *Chicago Tribune* that few women joined the GOP because they saw the party as "antiwomen" and "strongly against pro-choice on the issue of abortion."[107] Tafel himself recognized that many lesbians saw abortion as a question of individual "power," citing the story of a Republican woman he knew in Massachusetts who became pro-choice after one of her friends was raped. He applauded his female colleague's "belief that a woman's choice is more than protecting her right to choose, it is about empowerment."[108] In practice, however, Tafel kept the Log Cabin Republicans away from abortion politics. In 1995, for example, Evelyn Kotch, vice president of the Philadelphia chapter, ignited a controversy when she called "pro-life gays" "brain dead" in a local newspaper. Tafel and other national leaders pushed her to tone down her criticism in order to maintain group unity.[109]

The 1990s therefore witnessed a shift in the organization as the LCRF, united into a single federation, garnered national recognition and grew more conservative. The group also struggled with the dilemmas of the two-party strategy that had plagued local chapters in earlier years. These problems played themselves out amid the deepening polarization of national politics in the 1990s and early 2000s. In 1992 after the Buchanan "culture war" speech, the newly minted LCRF refused to endorse George H. W. Bush for president. In subsequent national elections, however, they supported GOP leaders for the White House whom they believed might support gay equality, including Arlen Specter in 1996 and John McCain in 2000. Those candidates, however, lost the Republican nomination. In 1996 the LCRF endorsed Bob Dole for president even though he initially returned a donation from the group, and in 2000 they backed George W. Bush, applauding his calls for "compassionate conservatism." That some of these candidates seemed to avoid repeating the harshest rhetoric of the Religious Right made some Log Cabin Republicans cautiously optimistic. Tafel conceded in 1999 that he faced an uphill battle, but he believed that many in the GOP were more preoccupied with other issues and had abandoned the homophobic rhetoric of 1992. He confidently declared that "the tone has totally changed."[110]

Four years later, however, the 2004 election proved Tafel wrong. The Log Cabin Republicans hoped that their loyalty to the GOP would inspire candidates such as Dole and Bush to ignore the homophobic wing of the party. But 2004 witnessed arguably the most antigay presidential campaign in American history, and the LCRF again voted against endorsing the Republican nominee. Bush called for a constitutional ban on same-sex marriage, and delegates to the 2004 Republican National Convention condemned gay parents. Patrick Guerrero, Tafel's successor as executive director, declared that the LCRF "proudly supported" the president on many issues. His decision to support a constitutional amendment banning same-sex marriage, however, was "dramatic and disappointing." Thus, the group withheld its support for the GOP nominee for the second time in just twelve years.[111]

Conclusion: Too Divided to Win Yet Too Rooted to Fade

The vote against endorsing Bush offers one possible ending for an early history of the Log Cabin Republicans. Other events offer equally compelling conclusions. In 2004, the *Gay City News* reported that the "Log Cabin Republicans are tired of hearing the 'o word'—oxymoron that is." But the Philadelphia newspaper also included a sarcastic retort from the LCRF about the persistence of gay conservatism: "With a million gay and lesbian votes for Bush in 2000, there must be a lot of oxymorons running around."[112] In the early 2000s as moderates such as Christine Todd Whitman fled the GOP, gay conservatives tried to build an inclusive party around such leaders as California governor Arnold Schwarzenegger.[113] The LCRF expanded again in these years and founded new chapters in places such as Kentucky, South Carolina, and Oklahoma.[114] Like their predecessors, many of these new clubs were overwhelmingly white and male. Some preexisting clubs meanwhile fractured over ideology, and in 2009 a group of disaffected Log Cabin Republicans broke off to create a new more conservative organization called GOProud.[115] The LCRF also continued to approach sexual equality from the right, and in 2004 the group filed a lawsuit to overturn the armed forces' ban on openly gay personnel. "We are pro-military," the group's lawyer declared. "This will only help, not hurt, the military."[116]

These anecdotes could all provide equally fitting conclusions to the early history of the Log Cabin Republicans. Like the nonendorsement of George W. Bush, the anecdotes point to the durability and limits of the Log Cabin Republican movement. The homophobia of most GOP officials in the 1980s and 1990s prompted a mass exodus of gay voters from the party but did not end the story of gay conservatism. Too many gay voters, particularly white middle-class men, identified with other Republican causes for the LCRF to collapse entirely. This resilience has made some gay conservatives optimistic. In 2000, Tafel predicted that the LCRF would draw new members by speaking about the virtues of a strong defense, free markets, and small government and by promising them that the GOP was the "front line" in the fight for sexual inclusiveness. He declared, "Courage in gay politics today is what it always has been: the willingness to go where you need to be, not necessarily where you're welcomed."[117] For many critics, this optimism made the Log Cabin Republicans seem foolish. When David Brooks reviewed Tafel's book, he concluded that being a gay conservative must feel like "standing in the middle of a field with a hurricane hitting you from one side and a tornado slamming you from another, while you look up hopefully for blue sky."[118]

Only time will tell if the LCRF will warrant these kinds of jokes, but it is clear that the movement it represents is not epiphenomenal. Groups such as the Log Cabin Republicans will continue to push for gay equality from a conservative position and advocate for conservatism among lesbian and gay voters. This history also suggests that if the GOP shed its most homophobic policies, a significant share of gay and lesbian voters would avidly support Republican candidates. The organization's significance therefore lies not in its few victories but rather in the way it has defied most academic and popular conceptions of American politics. The evident polarization of the two major parties in the late twentieth century produced surprising outcomes, including a conservative group dedicated to gay rights. The push for gay equality meanwhile transformed Americans across the political spectrum, including people on the Right. The LCRF's history not only reveals that some gay rights activists were conservative but also that conservatism itself helped inspire some parts of the gay rights movement. Since the late 1970s, many of the group's members saw equality as fully consonant with the ideals of the New Right. If the Log Cabin Republicans are an "oxymoron," they are therefore a paradox firmly rooted in the contradictions and complexities of American politics more generally. For better or worse, their longevity suggests the surprising interplay of two of the most important social movements of the late twentieth century.

CHAPTER 8

"No Discrimination and No Special Rights"

Gay Rights, Family Values, and the Politics of Moderation
in the 1992 Election

Rachel Guberman

"There is a religious war going on in this country," Pat Buchanan thundered
to the crowds gathered in Houston's Astrodome for the 1992 Republican
National Convention. With a prime-time audience watching at home, the
conservative Christian presidential candidate warned, "It is a cultural war as
critical to the kind of nation we shall be as the Cold War itself, for this war
is for the soul of America."[1] The crowd went wild. The new GOP platform,
adopted that night, sounded the same theme, emphasizing "family values"
as central to the Republican agenda for the 1990s. Opposition to abortion,
support for school prayer, and rejection of gay rights were key planks.[2] That
November, Colorado became the first state in the nation to adopt a constitutional amendment dealing with homosexuality. Officially titled the "Colorado
No Protected Status for Sexual Orientation Amendment," the amendment
made it illegal for any government entity—city, county, or state—to offer
gays and lesbians protections from discrimination. Hotly contested right up
until election day, Amendment 2 garnered national media attention and drew
activists from across the country to the Rocky Mountain State. Its ultimate
passage, by a margin of 53–47, was heralded on the Right (and lamented on
the Left) as evidence of the Religious Right's political dominance and America's conservative turn.

In fact, the opposite was true. The campaign for Amendment 2 reveals
what pollsters consistently reported: that "family values" did not win elections. Only when they jettisoned religious and moral arguments against

homosexuality and adopted instead a racially coded language of fairness and economic access did Religious Right operatives gain traction with voters. This cuts against prevailing understandings of America's conservative turn in the 1970s and the rise of the New Right to national dominance by the mid-1990s. Using Colorado as a case study, this essay shows the success of the rights revolution in setting the terms of debate, as both Christian Right operatives and gay rights activists embraced a language of rights to press their case with voters. The essay also highlights the limits of racial progress, pointing to the ways in which playing gays and African Americans off one another has been central to the success of antigay rights strategy. At the same time, the embrace of liberal "rights talk" within LGBT communities helped to de-radicalize gay politics. Corporate support for gay rights undercut intersectional alliances with organized labor and people of color while assimilating mainstream gay politics—particularly gay white male politics—into a capitalist framework.

By "rights revolution," I mean not just the proliferation of African American civil rights activism in the mid-twentieth century and its challenge to the prevailing racial order (what Jacqueline Hall has termed the "long civil rights movement") but also the broad array of other minority groups that seized on the success of the black freedom struggle to press the case for their own expanded citizenship in the 1970s and beyond.[3] As Nancy MacLean, John Skrentny, and Serena Mayeri have shown, other ethno-racial minorities, women, and queers have all relied on the administrative and bureaucratic mechanisms, social understandings, and constitutional "rights talk" pioneered and made available by African Americans to advance their agendas. Indeed, the success of other groups in expanding their own citizenship has generally depended on the extent to which they were able to persuade policy makers and the public that they were categorically *like blacks*.[4] The reorientation of American politics generally away from New Deal and Great Society liberalism and toward a neoliberal embrace of privatization and markets undermined these efforts, co-opting the language of rights in the service of a color-blind equalitarianism just as it was beginning to gain traction.[5]

While most commentators have understood the election of a self-styled New Democrat and passage of an antigay constitutional amendment in the same election as paradoxical, they were in fact both extensions of the new political culture that had been percolating among the electorate since the late 1960s. An in-depth examination of Amendment 2 and the history of gay rights politics in Colorado more broadly raises several questions: What can be learned from the makeup of the coalitions for and against Amendment 2?

How prevalent were conservative, Christian Right ideas among the voting public, and were voters responsive to these arguments? What does the fight over Amendment 2 reveal about broader debates—within Colorado and the nation—over questions of political power, local control, individual freedom, and government transparency? Ultimately, the Amendment 2 saga reveals the failure of arguments explicitly against homosexuality to move voters. At the ostensible height of family values fervor in the United States, family values arguments in Colorado were remarkably unsuccessful at attracting votes, relying instead on coded racial messaging to prevail. Amendment 2's passage reveals the predominance of market-oriented and quality-of-life ideas—not a burgeoning cultural conservatism—in shaping American political culture.

* * *

In 1973 the Boulder City Council, led by Penfield Tate, the city's only black councilman, passed Colorado's first local ordinance banning discrimination on the basis of sexual orientation. The backlash was immediate, sparking an effort to persuade the city council to remove the new sexual orientation provision from the civil rights ordinance. Two weeks before the council vote, four hundred people crowded into the Boulder municipal building for a public hearing on the issue, filling every available inch of floor space in the council chambers and spilling over into the lobby, where they watched the three-hour proceedings via closed-circuit television. The forty-four speakers for and against reflected a range of opinion. Some, such as Hilma Skinner, a leader of the repeal effort, opposed the inclusion of sexual orientation on religious and moral grounds. By keeping sexual orientation in the ordinance, she warned, Boulder would be transformed into a "sex deviate mecca that will become as corrupt and vile as Sodom and Gommorah and Pompeii." The city's new name, she quipped, would be "Lesbian Homoville." Others quoted the Bible and pledged to go to jail before they would compromise their faith by hiring gays or lesbians.[6]

Moral and religious arguments, however, were in the distinct minority. Instead, most of the arguments revolved around the needs of local business and the status of homosexuals. Foreshadowing what would become central themes in the pro-Amendment 2 campaign two decades later, the Boulder Chamber of Commerce issued a statement in advance of the hearing distancing itself from religious arguments but nevertheless stating its opposition to the ordinance. "We do not wish to become involved in a discussion of the moral aspects of the issue," the chamber's board of directors protested, "and we base our opposition solely on the infringement of the rights of any employer to select those who work for him according to his own standards and judgments." They went on to add that "we believe that any employer has the right to hire a homosexual if he is willing to do so, but we do not feel that he should be denied the right not to hire such a person."[7] During the hearing opposition leader and local businessman Frank Cernich sounded much the same note, insisting that the ordinance threatened the free association rights of employers. Taking a different tack that would also become familiar in the later campaign, other opponents argued that homosexuals did not meet the criteria of a real minority but rather were more analogous to people suffering from alcohol or drug problems.[8]

When the vote came on March 5, 1974, a majority of Boulder council members refused to remove sexual orientation from the civil rights ordinance. In response, opponents took the matter to the people, who voted decisively to repeal the protections for gays and lesbians. That fall, citizens demanded a recall election and succeeded in removing both Councilman Tim Fuller, a supporter of the ordinance who was himself gay, and Tate.

Although the battle in Boulder ended in defeat for the nondiscrimination measure and its advocates, it was nevertheless on the leading edge of a national legal movement for gay rights. In 1972 just one year before the Boulder City Council initially passed its nondiscrimination ordinance, East Lansing, Michigan, became the first city in the nation to enact civil rights protections for gays and lesbians, followed quickly by Ann Arbor and San Francisco. When debate over the Boulder ordinance began, the American Psychiatric Association had not yet removed homosexuality as a disorder from its *Diagnostic and Statistical Manual*. That groundbreaking decision came even as Boulderites were preparing to vote on the repeal. In the years immediately following the showdown in Boulder, only one other Colorado municipality took up the question of gay rights. In 1977 as Anita Bryant waged her Save Our Children campaign to repeal the Dade County, Florida, nondiscrimination law, citizens of Aspen quietly enacted an ordinance prohibiting discrimination in employment, housing, public services, and public accommodation on the basis of, among other things, sexual orientation.[9]

For the next decade, Aspen remained the only Colorado community with an antidiscrimination ordinance that included sexual orientation. But then in the late 1980s, gay rights activists renewed their efforts to pass local ordinances. First, Boulder voters passed a law in 1987 adding sexual orientation back into the city's civil rights ordinance. By the time of that campaign, the terms of debate, along with the political climate, had shifted. Against the backdrop of the emerging AIDS crisis, the prominence of homosexuality as a topic of conversation—and the sense of urgency that permeated those discussions—had grown. Over and over, Boulder gay rights activists hammered home the importance of nondiscrimination laws in the fight against the disease. Under the headline "Discrimination Spreads A.I.D.S.," the Equality Protection Coalition, which spearheaded the initiative campaign, argued that those at risk for AIDS would be unlikely to get tested or to participate in prevention programs if they feared that coming forward would expose them to discrimination on the basis of their sexual orientation. "If you want to help stamp out A.I.D.S. and prevent the spread of this killer disease," the advertisement suggested, "You must ensure lesbian/gay rights." A vote for the ordinance, the coalition argued, was a vote for life.[10]

Other differences between the 1987 Boulder campaign and earlier conflicts pointed toward an emerging cultural shift on the issue of homosexuality and also toward the changing political economy of the area. The 1970s antigay effort had come largely from small business owners concerned about their standing in the community. For example, the owner of a local diner worried that parents would stop bringing their families to his establishment or letting their teenagers work there after school if he were forced to hire homosexuals.

By the late 1980s, however, Boulder's and the entire Front Range corridor's efforts to court major service-sector brands had borne fruit, with the result that the economy increasingly relied on multinational corporations whose business imperatives lay in attracting and retaining highly educated workers and in projecting an open and inclusive image on the national and international stage.[11] "What do Continental Airlines, AT&T, Adolph Coors and Rockwell International have in common?" one newspaper advertisement asked. The answer: "They all prohibit discrimination on the basis of *sexual orientation*."[12] Proponents of expanding the antidiscrimination law could argue that banning discrimination on the basis of sexual orientation was essential for the future of Boulder's economy and for continuing to attract major multinational corporations to the area. Whereas the earlier campaign portrayed Boulder as a leader in pioneering antidiscrimination, by 1987 proponents of the new ordinance could warn that over fifty U.S. cities already had such laws on the books, and unless the ordinance passed, Boulder would soon fall behind.

The themes that emerged in both the 1973 and 1987 Boulder ordinance campaigns—child protection, the rights of business, and the status of sexual minorities—set the terms for subsequent struggles both in Colorado and nationally. Moreover, these campaigns foreshadowed the ways in which race would be deployed by both gay rights activists and their white conservative opponents for decades to come. Gay rights arguments hinged on the proposition that gayness, like blackness, was an in-born trait and should not be discriminated against. Yet potential alliances between gay and African American communities were often troubled by tensions stemming from both the conservative religious mores of black Christianity and from the racism of the white women and, primarily, men who dominated the gay rights movement. The leading role of black politicians in supporting the Boulder ordinance (and later of black community leaders and civil rights organizations in the Denver and statewide fights) highlights the complexity and contingency of these relationships.[13]

For their part, white conservatives, who led the antigay charge, understood both the legal and rhetorical significance of the black-gay analogy and turned it to their advantage. As Gillian Frank notes in his study of Anita Bryant's 1977 Save Our Children campaign against a gay rights ordinance in Dade County, Florida, the imperative to protect children was a prominent strain in white conservative opposition to both racial and sexual minorities in the 1970s and beyond. In Colorado as in Florida, opponents of gay rights framed their objections to the equal rights provisions as a matter of parental autonomy and concern that children might be "recruited" into homosexuality.[14]

By the 1990s, these fears were layered with seemingly value-neutral arguments about economic access, using the black-gay analogy to link sexual civil rights to affirmative action and suggesting that increasing security and opportunity for sexual minorities, as with racial minorities, posed an existential threat to the heteronormative white family ideal. These scare tactics drew on long-standing tropes about racial and sexual minorities as predatory and threatening to white American families. In Colorado, these sorts of arguments with their racial and economic overtones allowed the white conservative Christians who orchestrated antigay politics in the state to cast themselves in nonreligious terms as part of a mainstream consensus on the boundaries of racial and sexual belonging.

* * *

Two events in Colorado highlight the shift from a strategic focus on morality to a focus on rights: the Religious Right's failure to block a progay Denver antidiscrimination ordinance in 1990 and its success two years later in passing an antigay constitutional amendment. In 1990, three years after Boulder's ordinance passed, Denver adopted a sweeping new law, known as the Comprehensive Anti-Discrimination Ordinance, that included protections from discrimination in housing and employment for lesbians and gays. The Equal Protection Ordinance Coalition (EPOC) marshaled a roster of over two dozen community organizations in support of the law, including church groups, professional associations, major corporations, black and Hispanic community organizations, civic associations, and the Greater Denver Chamber of Commerce.[15] As had happened before in Boulder and elsewhere, opponents, themselves mostly not Denver residents, launched an effort to remove sexual orientation from the new law by bringing the matter to a popular vote in a citywide referendum known as Initiative #1. Ultimately, however, Citizens for Sensible Rights (CSR), as the referendum's proponents called themselves, failed to persuade a majority of voters that protecting gays and lesbians from discrimination in housing and employment constituted a credible threat to Denver citizens.[16]

In the wake of the Comprehensive Anti-Discrimination Ordinance's passage, conservative activists from across the Front Range converged on Denver to push for repeal. Although the CSR described itself as a "grassroots coalition of Denver residents" that had "risen up to oppose this law," the truth was somewhat different. In fact, as EPOC and its allies were quick to point out, the CSR was a local subsidiary of the Traditional Values Coalition, an organization founded by Orange County, California, fundamentalist and family values crusader Lou Sheldon to lobby nationwide for what it called traditional Christian values. Moreover, because many of the "local" activists working for repeal were not residents of Denver, they were themselves ineligible to vote in the popular referendum for which they worked.[17] EPOC described the CSR operatives as carpetbaggers who had "singled out the gay and lesbian community as being unworthy of equal rights." In addition, EPOC characterized Initiative #1 as part of a national "Hate Campaign," pushed by people who "don't care about Denver or Colorado" but rather "seek to create fear and hysteria where none exist."[18]

The CSR was part of a national network of Christian Right groups working in concert to shape local law and elections across the nation. Sheldon himself—who was often referred to as "Son of Falwell" in a nod to Christian Right political icon Jerry Falwell—participated directly, flying to Denver to host campaign meetings and strategy sessions. The centerpiece of Sheldon's strategy was two-pronged: attacking homosexuals as a special interest group rather than a "true minority" and warning of the threat that gays and lesbians posed both to families and public health. Because analogic arguments between sexual orientation and race were fundamental to gay rights activists' claims for minority status and protection, Christian Right strategists targeted them in their campaigns, arguing that gays were categorically dissimilar from "true" minority groups such as African Americans.

Whereas gay rights advocates drew clear parallels between gay and black experience, using these as the basis for their civil rights claims, the Religious Right argued that minority status was based on inborn traits such as skin color over which individuals had no control. The Supreme Court's 1986 ruling in *Bowers v. Hardwick*, which held that sexual orientation was not a legitimate basis of minority status, became crucial to this line of argument, as advocates used the court's authority to bolster their contention that gays could not by definition be subject to discrimination. CSR's tagline, "Equal rights for all, special rights for none," neatly encapsulated this message.[19] Instead, CSR and other Religious Right groups portrayed sexual orientation as a matter of choice, anillness, or an addiction. This disagreement lay at the heart of the argument over gays and civil rights.

The CSR enthusiastically embraced this strategy. Sheldon recommended direct appeals to Hispanic and especially black Denverites in an effort to "divide and conquer." One EPOC activist who attended Sheldon's pro-Initiative #1 strategy session reported that he suggested reaching out directly to these and other racial or ethnic minority groups in Denver. "You do everything within your power to show them what is happening to the hard-earned minority status that blacks and asians and hispanics have sought to have and rightly have," the observer quoted Sheldon as saying, and tell them "now comes the aggressors (gays) who are trying to snatch and piggyback that civil right."[20] Accordingly, the CSR blanketed minority neighborhoods across the city with leaflets arguing that including sexual orientation in the city's antidiscrimination ordinance would have a direct detrimental impact on black and Hispanic Denverites.[21] "*All Americans are already guaranteed equal protection*, human rights, under the U.S. Constitution and the Bill of Rights," the CSR argued. Civil rights laws, then, were special "powerful laws which are reserved for only oppressed groups who have suffered real discrimination because of racial or ethnic traits they CANNOT change." By contrast, gays—who "have NEVER known the discrimination of sharecropping, slavery, separate schools and ghettoes which true minorities have endured, for which Civil Rights were made!"—were not truly a minority. Rather, they were a powerful special interest group demanding that "abnormal sex should have the *same privileges as skin color*" to gain access to legal protections to which they were not entitled.[22]

The CSR also gestured toward what would become the lynchpin of the following year's winning strategy to pass Amendment 2: "Homosexual 'Equal Protection,'" the group explained, "really means 'economic protection.'" By linking gays' civil rights claims to economic access, the CSR thrust the issue of discrimination against gays and lesbians onto the fraught terrain of black struggles for economic justice and also on what many white citizens perceived as the threat that claims of racial discrimination posed to their continued economic and cultural supremacy.

While most of the CSR's rhetoric emphasized secular arguments against providing legal protections for homosexuality, other CSR arguments in support of Initiative #1 made the group's ties to the Christian Right abundantly clear. Under the headline "Restore Sensible Rights to Denver," for example, accompanied by the image of a bald eagle flying across the American flag, a CSR flyer exhorted citizens to "Make a stand for traditional family values, civil rights, and religious freedom." After warning that the Denver antidiscrimination ordinance was a gateway to further licentiousness and the normalization of aberrant sexual behavior at the hands of a powerful and secretive homosexual lobby, the CSR's proposed solution began "Pray God's witness will be seen in the Church's stand against sexual perversion."[23]

The religious caste of the CSR's campaign materials and its alarmist, conspiratorial tone did not play well with Denver voters. On election day, Denverites defeated Initiative #1 by ten percentage points.[24] By the following year's Amendment 2 campaign, the CSR had learned its lesson, eliminating almost all discussion of homosexuality itself as dangerous or morally objectionable and employing more measured tones in presenting the civil rights and economic arguments that formed the bulk of its campaign.

* * *

The transit of antidiscrimination legislation from pathbreaking in the early 1970s to remarkably widespread by the early 1990s reflected not only shifting cultural mores about homosexuality but also broader social and political shifts in the way that Americans understood sexual privacy and how the public sphere should be delimited.[25] Whereas antipathy toward homosexuality drove the successful 1973 ordinance repeal effort in Boulder, by the 1990s even those who expressed personal revulsion or moral objections toward homosexuality nevertheless increasingly rejected the idea that gays should lose jobs or housing because of it. The fate of both the progay ordinances and the antigay amendment rested less on voters' attitudes about homosexuality and more on the ability of advocates on either side to be persuasive about whether gays were a minority or a special interest. Comparing the fight to protect Denver's antidiscrimination ordinance with the fight, just one year later, over Amendment 2 reveals the centrality of racialized and economic arguments to this enterprise on both the pro- and antigay sides as well as the national scope of these local legal struggles.

Following the failure of Initiative #1, the CSR and its national Religious Right allies retreated to their new base of operations just seventy miles south of Denver in Colorado Springs. Over the preceding two years, Colorado Springs had become a magnet for evangelical religious and political groups, earning the moniker "Evangelical Vatican" because of the density of Christian Right ministries and organizations headquartered there. Although the city had always been fiscally conservative, social views in the sleepy town at the southern end of the Front Range metropolitan corridor were historically varied, what many longtime residents described as "live and let live." During the 1980s, for example, residents backed both archconservative Republican U.S. senator Bill Armstrong and iconoclastic, proabortion rights Democratic governor Dick Lamm.

By the early 1990s, however, reeling from a crash in the local real estate market, city fathers were eager to attract new business to the area. Adopting a "clean growth" strategy intended to align with the city's reputation as a good place to do business and enjoy the outdoors, Colorado Springs business leaders, organized through the Economic Development Corporation, sought to lure national nonprofits by offering a variety of incentives. The effort bore fruit. In August 1991 just ahead of the Amendment 2 campaign, Focus on the Family, one of the leading national parachurch organizations involved in promoting the Christian Right's political agenda, moved its national headquarters—and four hundred employees—to the area.[26] Other like-minded groups quickly followed.

Amendment 2, which enjoyed Focus on the Family's active support, was the product of another Colorado Springs-based Religious Right organization, Colorado for Family Values (CFV). Like the CSR before it, the CFV was an offshoot of Lou Sheldon's Traditional Values Coalition. Additional support came from a host of national Christian Right organizations, many headquartered in Colorado Springs and represented on the CFV board. In drafting Amendment 2, for example, the CFV worked closely with the National Legal Foundation of Virginia Beach, Virginia, an organization whose mission was "to prayerfully create and implement innovative strategies that, through decisive action, will cause America's public policy and legal system to support and facilitate God's purpose for her."[27] In short, the push for Amendment 2 not only drew support from but was also a product of an organized strategy on the part of national right-wing religious groups to shape local law and policy across the United States.[28]

The CFV and its allies were not the only ones to make Amendment 2 a national issue. Even as opponents attacked the pro-Amendment 2 forces as out-of-towners bent on undermining local control, anti-Amendment 2 activists were themselves enmeshed in a national network of gay rights organizations. Opponents drew legal help from what was then called the National Gay Task Force, later renamed the National Gay and Lesbian Task Force, and from Lambda Legal, another gay advocacy group, as well as from the American Civil Liberties Union. What is more, the whole country, in a very real sense, was watching. Journalists from every major network, newspaper, and newsmagazine covered both the Amendment 2 campaign and the aftermath of the initiative's passage.

As the first national effort to constitutionally limit gay rights (or, for that matter, to deal with sexual orientation in any way), Amendment 2 was among the most talked about issues of the 1992 election cycle. In the wake of its passage, gay rights activists launched a national boycott of Colorado, the impact of which was keenly felt throughout the Rocky Mountain State in terms of lost revenue from tourism, conferences, and more. While the Amendment 2 fight was in one sense an intensely local and particular political struggle, in another sense it was a proxy war in a much larger national struggle over the status of gay men and women and, more broadly, over the role of religion, privacy, and rights talk in American legal and political life.[29]

The coalition arrayed against Amendment 2 represented a cross section of Denver's progressive, religious, and minority communities. Blacks, Hispanics, and organized labor in particular were crucial allies for Colorado gays and lesbians in all of their campaigns, going back to Boulder's earliest attempt to institute an antidiscrimination ordinance in 1973. During both the Denver ordinance campaign and the campaign to stop Amendment 2, Denver's black and Hispanic leaders overwhelmingly gave their support to the gay rights side, rejecting the CFV's argument that legal recognition of gay rights under-mined the cause of equality for racial and ethnic minorities. Repeal of the city's antidiscrimination ordinance became a major issue in the mayoral election, with the two front runners, District Attorney Norm Early and City Auditor Wellington Webb, both black, vying to be seen as the strongest sup-porter of gay rights. Members of the Colorado Civil Rights Commission came out against Amendment 2, as did both the local and national National Association for the Advancement of Colored People. Jesse Jackson came to march in Denver against the amendment, telling voters that "some people say unless we discriminate against gay and lesbian people, somehow our rights as African Americans or Latino Americans are lessened. *That's not true. It is immoral. Discrimination is wrong. Amendment #2 is wrong.*" Coretta Scott King lent her endorsement and that of the King Center to the gay rights cause.

The leadership of Denver's large Hispanic community was similarly to be found overwhelmingly on the progay side. Under the banner "Libertad y justicia para todos—sin excepción" (Liberty and justice for all—without exception), a full-page advertisement against the amendment signed by every major Hispanic organization and political figure in Colorado urged citizens to vote no on Amendment 2. "If the civil rights, privacy, privileges and pro-tections of citizens can be restricted because of sexual orientation," the Colo-rado Hispanic League asked, "what protects Hispanics from similar initiatives based on equally arbitrary reasons?"[30] Prominent Colorado Hispanic leaders were actively involved in EPOC, serving on the board and as cochairs of the campaign. These included among others nationally prominent Democrat Polly Baca, sitting Denver mayor Federico Pena, and, until his death shortly before the election, legendary Colorado civil rights activist Rick Castro.[31] For their part too, Colorado unions also rallied to the gay rights cause, signing on to the EPOC campaign and proclaiming forcefully to their own rank and file that "nobody should be fired just because they're black or white or brown or gray. . . . Or gay."[32]

These alliances, which were so important to the Denver ordinance and Amendment 2 fights, were the product of years of collaborative organizing on the part of blacks, gays, and Hispanics as well as organized labor. Whereas African American community leaders in many cities resisted the analogy between gay rights and black civil rights, in Colorado their embrace came early. This was no doubt in part a reflection of the small size of the local black community. Unlike large northeastern and midwestern cities such as Phila-delphia and Chicago where the black community was large and, beginning in the 1970s, politically powerful, Colorado's black population was quite small, making political alliances with other minorities, including gays, particularly important.[33] Significantly, since the mid-1970s, blacks, gays, Hispanics, and labor had been united in a local and national boycott of the Coors Brewing Company, based in Golden, Colorado, in an effort to force the brewery, known for its support of conservative political causes, to put an end to a long history of discrimination and unfair labor practices. By the early 1990s, Coors had long since adopted company-wide practices banning discrimination on the basis of sexual orientation in an effort to separate gays and lesbians from their minority allies. But the Coors family's continued support for antigay political causes prompted many in the gay community to continue shunning the brewer. The boycott experience helped to solidify relationships among gays, blacks, Hispanics, and organized labor that proved vital to the campaign against Amendment 2, as local and national unions and minority rights organizations and leaders lent their support to the gay rights cause and were in fact among the most vocal participants in anti-Amendment 2 activism.[34]

* * *

Yet even as such alliances suggested the possibility of a more radical, intersectional gay and lesbian politics, the business community's embrace of gay rights pulled in other directions. Although the CFV routinely portrayed Amendment 2 as an asset to Colorado businesses, targeting them directly throughout the campaign, Colorado business leaders were unpersuaded. Just as in the 1987 Boulder ordinance drive and the subsequent Denver struggle, many of the state's most influential businesses and business groups made the strategic choice to array themselves on the progay side. In a full-page advertisement in the *Denver Post* published just before the election, some seventy-five local businesses announced their opposition to Amendment 2. Major national corporations with offices in Colorado also joined the antiamendment chorus. Apple Computers, for example, took out an advertisement in local papers announcing the company's view that "employment discrimination wastes vitally needed talent" and urging Coloradans to vote no.[35]

After Amendment 2 passed, with gay rights activists successfully orchestrating a massive national boycott against "The Hate State," Colorado business leaders were at pains to distance themselves from the measure. The Greater Denver Chamber of Commerce quickly reiterated its opposition, recalling the group's active participation in the fight against the amendment and before that in the campaign supporting Denver's antidiscrimination ordinance. As a further show of support, the chamber acknowledged that it was in the process of developing an antidiscrimination pledge for local corporations to sign, announced plans to dedicate staff and volunteer resources to legal efforts to overturn the amendment, and touted its involvement in a statewide coalition of business, religious, and community organizations dedicated to the amendment's repeal. In explaining why the business community chose to defy the apparent will of Colorado voters, the chamber argued that "Colorado voters were duped" by a "cleverly developed 'stealth' media campaign" orchestrated by Far Right religious groups.[36]

Business's embrace of gay rights during and after the Amendment 2 campaign was significant of both a shift in national thinking about gays and lesbians and the growing dominance of "good business" arguments in American politics, over and against moral or religious ones. As gays became increasingly culturally accepted, businesses found it increasingly financially and politically expedient to be seen as supportive of gay rights. While growing acceptance bolstered the gay rights cause, it also had the effect of undermining the alliances with other minority groups that played such a crucial role in early gay rights efforts. Whereas once they had worked to show themselves categorically similar to African Americans in order to access the rights arena, cultural acceptance of gays militated against such analogies. As sexual diversity became more mainstream and especially as gays and lesbians began to receive major corporate support, a significant subset, particularly prosperous white gay men, became increasingly estranged from racial and gender minorities who might otherwise have been partners in an intersectional political coalition for minority rights.[37]

In a telling move that indicated the extent to which support for gay rights was by 1992 already becoming mainstream, even the largely conservative and Republican Colorado Springs business community worked actively against Amendment 2. Following the amendment's passage, prominent Colorado Springs attorney Greg Walta, himself an evangelical and longtime resident, went so far as to draft an alternative measure, which he and other local business leaders hoped might win enough votes to replace Amendment 2. They positioned their initiative, titled "No Special Rights or Discrimination in Employment, Housing and Public Accommodations Based on Sexual Orientation," as a compromise that would guarantee statewide protections from discrimination for gays and lesbians while simultaneously banning them from any preferred legal status, affirmative action, or quotas. The measure had the backing of Colorado Springs's most influential business leaders, notably including Bill Hybl who, as CEO of the El Pomar Foundation, had orchestrated the $4 million grant that drew Focus on the Family to the area in the first place. Backers, concerned by the boycott of Colorado and the growing national association between Colorado Springs and the Religious Right, sought to distance themselves both from Amendment 2 specifically and the Religious Right more generally.[38]

* * *

In the wake of Amendment 2's passage, observers across the country were quick to point to Colorado, in either triumph or despair, as a vanguard in a national battle over morality, "family values," and the role of religion in politics and governance. One letter to the editor of the *Rocky Mountain News*, written by a despairing former Colorado resident just days after the election, summed up the dominant understanding of the Amendment 2 victory: "I can't believe that the majority of Colorado people I lived and worked around actually voted to discriminate against a minority of fellow Coloradans," Wes Simmons lamented from his new home in Massachusetts. "I never realized how strong a hold the right-wing Christian Fundamentalists have on the state. Colorado has now become a place of hatred and bigotry instead of natural beauty and friendly people. Viewed from a distance, it looks like Colorado stands right in line behind Idaho and the Aryan Nations."[39]

But on the ground the reality was notably different. As Colorado business leaders had been quick to realize, arguments rooted in "family values" did not win elections. National public opinion polling revealed that in the run-up to the 1992 election, voters were overwhelmingly preoccupied with the economy: 43 percent listed it as their number one concern. "Family values," the rubric under which issues such as homosexuality and Amendment 2 fell, came in a distant fourth, with just 15 percent of voters listing it as their top priority. Indeed, in their postmortems following the election, many observers both inside and outside the GOP pointed to what they argued was an excessive focus on family values, both at the Republican National Convention that year and throughout the campaign, as the primary reason for Bush's defeat in the presidential race.

Colorado was no exception. Focus groups conducted in the weeks leading up to the November 3 election revealed that sizable majorities believed that discrimination against gays and lesbians in employment and housing should be illegal. Sixty-eight percent of respondents agreed with the statement "No population group should be singled out for discrimination as this amendment does." Even voters who said that they had moral or religious objections to homosexuality said that they supported basic rights for gays, believed gays and lesbians to be the subjects of discrimination, and dubbed the CFV and their supporters extremists. Among those who said that they would oppose legalized same-sex marriage or adoption by same-sex couples, a majority saw these issues as unrelated to the amendment, making any efforts by the CFV to portray Amendment 2 as a bulwark against these possibilities unfruitful.[40]

A report issued shortly before the election by the Colorado-based public opinion research firm Talmey-Drake concluded that "supporters of the Colorado for Family Values anti-gay rights initiative have assumed they were speaking for a 'silent majority' who believe homosexuality is morally wrong. The assumption is shakey [sic]." The report went on to note that were the election held at the time of the poll, the family values initiative would lose by a 52 percent to 38 percent margin. Even more significantly, the polling suggested that the amendment would lose almost as badly among voters who expressed strong moral opposition to homosexuality as among the electorate as a whole. Trying to make sense of these results, researchers surmised that voters' resistance to morality-based arguments for the amendment stemmed from a growing general belief that consenting adults had a right to privacy in their sexual conduct without interference from government, business, or their fellow citizens.[41] The failure of efforts to repeal Denver's Comprehensive Anti-Discrimination Ordinance the previous year suggested much the same conclusion. After all, the CSR, which had peppered its campaign materials with references to homosexuality as being immoral, a "perversion," and a "deviant sex practice," lost decisively.

Recognizing that family values arguments were remarkably unsuccessful at attracting a majority of voters, the proponents of Amendment 2 generally avoided moral arguments against homosexuality in making their case. The CFV insisted that "Amendment 2 doesn't hinge on religion or morality. And it *certainly* isn't about hatred. It's about fairness."[42] Or, as a CFV television advertisement in support of Amendment 2 put it, "OK, I think I've got it. *Homosexuals have equal rights; they want special rights.* That's not fair. I'm voting yes on Amendment 2."[43] The purpose of Amendment 2, the CFV argued, was to prevent an already privileged group from taking advantage of hardworking, well-meaning Coloradans.

This framing was fundamental to the entire Amendment 2 enterprise. Indeed, the very wording of the amendment reflected this careful rhetorical strategy. In a letter to the CFV offering feedback on proposed language for the amendment, Brian McCormick, a staff attorney at the conservative Virginia Beach National Legal Foundation, argued against a possible draft that referred to gay marriage, reasoning that while the public was inhospitable to "special privileges" for homosexuals, it was receptive to pleas "to be 'treated just like everyone else'":

> While homosexuals do not get far by asking the electorate for special privileges, they do get a good deal of sympathy by asking to be "treated just like everyone else." The presupposition here is that if two people love each other they ought to be able to marry, and if two men or two women "love" each other they ought to be able to marry. Since same sex marriages are not recognized in Colorado at present, I feel that the clause regarding their legal recognition hurts the initiative without really adding anything to it.[44]

Taking McCormick's advice, the CFV left any mention of same-sex marriage out of the amendment's final text and did not argue directly against homosexuality per se. This choice allowed the CFV to argue that the proposed amendment did not "remove any basic civil rights granted to homosexual individuals under the U.S. Constitution" but instead "only prohibits homosexual desires or practices . . . from being a basis for legal protected class status in the State of Colorado."[45]

The final text read

> Shall there be an amendment to Article II of the Colorado Constitution to prohibit the state of Colorado and any of its political subdivisions from adopting or enforcing any law or policy which provides that homosexual, lesbian, or bisexual orientation, conduct, or relationships constitutes or entitles a person to claim any minority or protected status, quota preferences, or discrimination.[46]

By framing the question as one of protected minority status and quotas (even though quotas had never been proposed), the CFV distanced the initiative from controversial questions about morality, relying instead on a series of racialized arguments about privilege and economic access.

Indeed, the CFV relied primarily on economic arguments in selling Amendment 2 to voters. In a climate of shrinking job opportunities and rising unemployment, CFV codirector Kevin Tebedo held up the specter of affirmative action, suggesting that without Amendment 2, "employers soon will be required to hire homosexuals by quota," with the result that someday in the not too distant future white men would have to "lie and say they are homosexual just to get a job."[47] This affirmative action argument proved especially potent for the CFV, as it spoke directly to white male voters concerned about their own employment insecurity and also provided a familiar language for dismissing charges that support for Amendment 2 was motivated by antigay bias.

Just as it became possible to say "I'm not racist. I just don't see why they should get a leg up when I've worked hard for everything I've got," so too did it become possible to say "I don't have a problem with gays. I just don't think they should have any extra advantages." In fact, none of the antidiscrimination ordinances passed or proposed in Colorado had ever suggested any sort of gay affirmative action, yet the CFV was extraordinarily effective at persuading voters that gay rights posed a serious threat to their own economic security and that "a 'yes' vote on Amendment 2 is a vote *against special rights* for *GAY SPECIAL INTERESTS*."[48] The reference to quotas in the text of the amendment was specifically intended to conjure these old, usually racialized economic fears among white and especially white male voters.

The racial undercurrents in the language surrounding Amendment 2 highlight the ways in both sides in the Amendment 2 campaign used race in making their cases about sexual orientation. The language of rights, equality, fairness, and color blindness that grew up over decades of civil rights struggle was repurposed and deployed in the early 1990s in debates over gay rights generally and Amendment 2 in particular. It was an uneasy but nevertheless effective appropriation that operated in several ways.

On the one hand, by arguing that any law protecting gays from discrimination was tantamount to affirmative action, the CFV and its allies sought to appear as sympathetic champions of the rights of "genuine" minorities. They did this overtly, as we have seen, in general press releases and media appearances as well as in campaign materials specifically targeted at black and Hispanic Coloradans. The explicit message was that "real" minorities such as blacks, Hispanics, and the disabled were entitled to the kinds of protections and benefits they received and that by demanding similar protections for a group that *was not a real minority*, gay rights advocates were harming genuine minority groups. As one black pastor and CFV supporter put it, "The freedom bus that went to Selma was never meant to go on to Sodom."[49] By repeatedly describing gays as affluent and white, the CFV and its allies sought to divide gays from the groups that they termed genuine minorities.

In one particularly stark example of this strategy, the CFV blanketed both white and African American communities across the state with leaflets purporting to reveal the dangers of allowing gay rights laws. One of the most potent anti-Amendment 2 arguments in the campaign had been that by constitutionally banning any government entity in Colorado from passing future gay rights laws, the measure effectively ran an end run around the principles of home rule and local control. In response, the CFV told a cautionary tale in the leaflet: "Remember the detestable 'Jim Crow' laws that used to oppress African Americans decades ago in the Deep South?" Those, the CFV explained, were home rule laws "designed to keep people of color 'in their place.'" Fortunately, as a result of activism and legislation during the 1960s, civil rights were no longer subject to local whims but rather were decided at the state and national levels.

By insisting on the right of local communities to pass gay rights ordinances, the CFV argued, "militant homosexuals . . . have pushed their agenda for years exactly the way the old racists did: through friendly city councils, the least democratic, least responsive of all governing bodies." Amendment 2, then, was a safeguard for civil rights, helping "all Colorado citizens make sure civil rights are never 'Jim-Crow-ised' again." Finally, the leaflet suggested, "the next time a militant gay tries to tell you Amendment 2 destroys 'home rule,' ask them: Should Colorado towns be able to vote in 'Jim Crow' laws again? NO WAY! VOTE 'YES!' ON AMENDMENT 2."[50]

In this formulation, gay rights activists were tantamount to segregationists, and voting to block future gay rights measures such as the antidiscrimination ordinances in Aspen, Boulder, and Denver was a means for African Americans to protect themselves. At the same time, the leaflet suggested, any white voter who rejected Amendment 2 was effectively supporting a return to legalized racism. This sort of rhetoric, which ostensibly demonstrated the CFV's commitment to minority rights, fell flat among African Americans. On election day Denver County, home to the vast majority of Colorado's black voters, opposed the amendment by a decisive majority.[51]

Yet the true value of the Jim Crow ad was in its implicit, far less politically correct message for white voters. Affirmative action had long been among the least understood and most reviled manifestations of the civil rights movement's legal and policy successes (indeed, even many self-professed liberals objected to it). By linking gay rights to affirmative action and quotas, however erroneously, the CFV sought to create an association between racial minorities and gays, thereby planting the suggestion for white voters that gays were yet another minority group demanding special benefits while middle-class whites were forced to struggle.

* * *

Ultimately, the CFV's framing of gay rights as a threat to white Americans overwhelmed by minority rights claims proved effective. On election day, 53 percent of voters statewide pulled the lever for the family values initiative, making Colorado the first state in the nation to put the fraught matter of sexual orientation and its legal and social standing into its constitution. Post-election polls confirmed the success of the CFV's strategy. As one voter who supported Amendment 2 explained in a letter to the *Rocky Mountain News*, "It should be reasonably clear that the passage of Amendment 2 is a message from the tax paying majority saying, 'we are tired of special interest groups and their woes.'" Indeed, after decades of mounting frustration with what many saw as the growing influence of special interests in state politics and the pressures of a struggling economy, for many Coloradans Amendment 2 offered an opportunity to make their feelings of disfranchisement heard.

Observers outside Colorado, unfamiliar with the context and background to the referendum campaign, took Amendment 2's passage as an indication of Coloradans' deep social conservatism. Certainly, homophobia was a factor. In 1992 when Amendment 2 passed, homosexuality was the subject of intense debate. Bill Clinton's apparent support for gay rights was a major issue in the presidential election that year, AIDS was a pressing national crisis, and citizens across the country were engaged at both the national and local levels in debates and electoral struggles over antigay discrimination, gay and lesbian teachers, homosexuality in school curricula, gays in the military, and more. Both in the run-up to the election and in its aftermath, the amendment and Colorado were in the national spotlight. Many viewed Amendment 2, the subsequent boycott of Colorado, and the eventual U.S. Supreme Court case as being among the opening salvos of the "culture wars" that have became the iconic representation of American politics in the 1990s.

But what happened in Colorado and indeed nationally was more interesting and subtle than homophobia alone. The ways in which the CFV, an unabashedly right-wing Christian organization with clear ties to the national

Christian Right, sought to sanitize its campaign of moral or religious content and make affirmative action or quotas the issue rather than homosexuality speaks to what at the time was a widely understood truth among religious conservatives: family values did not win elections. Outside of an admittedly sizable cadre of true believers for whom family values were the number one political issue, most voters simply did not rank it as a major factor in choosing whom to vote for. Moreover, many voters were turned off by what they perceived as the Religious Right's moralizing tone. The 43 percent of voters nationally who pulled the lever for Clinton/Gore overwhelmingly reported moderate or even center-left social views and said that the economy and jobs were their number one concern. Similarly, among the 19 percent of voters who supported independent Ross Perot for president that year—whose candidacy was often blamed for "throwing" the election to Clinton by attracting voters who would otherwise have gone Republican—an overwhelming majority articulated views that were fiscally conservative but socially well to the left of the GOP's 1992 family values platform.[52]

Colorado more or less mirrored the nation. While Bill Clinton did slightly worse in Colorado, with 39 percent of the vote, and Ross Perot did slightly better, with 23 percent, Clinton did carry the state, and their combined Colorado total of 62 percent equaled their combined national total. These results fit with the general trend of voters in Colorado since the 1970s toward self-described "moderate" or "centrist" viewpoints and a demand for greater accountability and transparency in government. Moreover, the Colorado results fit with national trends, as during the 1970s, 1980s, and 1990s and in fact up until 2010 more Americans identified as moderate than as either liberal or conservative. Private postelection polling commissioned by the GOP confirmed this assessment. In memos to leading Republicans, longtime GOP pollster Robert Teeter explained that Perot's third-party candidacy negatively affected Bush's electoral strength, particularly in the South and the Mountain West. A sizable number of voters who named Bush as their second choice, Teeter's data showed, voted for Perot because of concerns about the GOP's ability to improve economic prosperity and the party's excessive focus on social issues.[53]

In this political climate, it is no accident that a constitutional amendment billed as preventing affirmative action and "special rights" and a presidential nominee who campaigned on redefining the Democratic Party as a party of moderation and centrism, preaching "opportunity, responsibility, community," could both succeed. The story of Colorado's Amendment 2, then, is a national story in more ways than one. Exploring the Amendment 2 campaign and putting it both in a broader national context and in a much deeper context of political change in Colorado itself begins to illuminate the contours of a political realignment in the late twentieth century that challenges the simple notion of conservative ascendance and liberal decline. What emerges instead is a far more nuanced and contested politics of the center with which both parties had to grapple in their quest for continued relevance and electoral success.

CHAPTER 9

Homophobia Baiting

Queering the Trayvon Martin Archives and Challenging the AntiBlackness of Color-Blind Politics

Julio Capó Jr.

"A man was watching him," Rachel Jeantel told the court. With that, jurors heard a different perspective of what took place the night of February 26, 2012, in Sanford, Florida. Jeantel testified that in the final minutes of his life, her friend Trayvon Martin told her over the phone that a man—later identified as George Zimmerman—shadowed him as he dodged the rain on his way back to where his father was staying. According to Jeantel, Martin referred to Zimmerman as a "creepy-ass cracka." In response, she warned Martin that Zimmerman "might've been a rapist." To that, Jeantel claimed, Martin dismissively told her, "Nahhh, don't play with me like that." She disagreed and posed that if the man following you is not a rapist, *why* is he following you?[1]

Although the significance of this exchange was largely eclipsed both during and after Zimmerman's 2013 criminal trial, it carried a lot of weight in right-wing circles.[2] *The State of Florida v. George Zimmerman* charged Zimmerman with second-degree murder and manslaughter. The twenty-eight-year-old "mixed-race" Latino man patrolled his residential streets as a neighborhood watchman that evening. Zimmerman called authorities after he came across Martin, a Black hoodie-wearing seventeen-year-old. Zimmerman suspected that the teenager was a burglar suspiciously wandering the subdivision of a gated community in the Orlando suburb. Consequently, he pursued Martin on foot. According to Zimmerman, Martin soon approached and assaulted him. When the melee concluded Zimmerman had suffered minor injuries to his head and face, and Martin lay dead, face down on the grass. Zimmerman claimed that he shot and killed Martin in self-defense. A jury of six acquitted Zimmerman of all charges on July 13, 2013.[3]

Several on the right reframed Jeantel's words as "evidence" that Martin was neither a victim nor innocent and was the aggressor and a hate-mongering "gay basher." Employing a queer-of-color critique especially rooted in Black feminist thought, this essay relies on digital media sources to explore how the right sought to reconfigure Jeantel's testimony to exploit a liberal cultural politics that entails a consolidated form of LGBT activism frequently detached from the politics of racial violence, redistribution of resources, class warfare, and poverty. Influential members of the right attempted to capitalize on an entrenched "prodiversity" and anti-gay violence paradigm. Put another way, the right devised a form of homophobia baiting to hijack a critique of the state-sanctioned, privatized violence that surveilled and criminalized Martin in the first place. After all, how could the left champion Martin as a victim of such violence if he was in fact a gay basher?

Such questions sought to demarcate the liberal abandonment of marginalized groups in the pursuit of white, lesbian, gay, and bisexual decriminalization and capital. The right's homophobia baiting has parallels with statist concepts of "homonationalism" and "pinkwashing," which reiterate how both activist- and state-led discourses employ market-coherent renderings of "gay-friendliness" in ways that contribute to racist, militaristic, nationalist, and imperialist projects.[4] The "evidence" that labeled Martin a "gay basher" operated on a logic that (re)criminalized all lesbians, gays, and bisexuals; this discourse, although never absent, had increasingly receded through the politics of normativity and respectability over the past two decades with the mainstreaming of LGBT rights and politics. Despite such attempts to bait Martin as a homophobe, most mainstream single- and multi-issue LGBT organizations challenged Martin's criminalization both prior to and after the so-called revelation that he might have acted on antigay animus; that is, it seems that they did not take the bait.

Even more importantly, because statements of solidarity have limited impact, Martin's death served as an intervention, particularly helmed by three Black women, for the more explicit adoption of a queer radical politics committed to an antiracist form of social justice, especially through the establishment of the Black Lives Matter (BLM) movement that, while stressing the centrality of antiBlackness in shaping all state violence, critically linked the liberation of Black, queer, transgender, and other marginalized people. Although a rabble-rousing right sought to bait Martin as homophobic to garner support from LGBT people and, more broadly, liberals sympathetic to broader "neoliberal" trends, this essay suggests that a linear chronology that views the dominance of a single-issue and identity-based LGBT movement is both insufficient and inadequate. While diminishing radical impulses within the movement can be measured since at least the 1970s, such as with the priority to fight for same-sex marriage, the movement's and its activists' commitments to antiracist and intersectional social justice is much more nuanced and checkered than that arc makes room for.

This essay uses the term "right" to refer to a domestic politics that is largely defined by its rejection of liberalism. While discussions concerning the political economy and free market enterprise are certainly a part of this faction, particularly among the Tea Party, this essay focuses largely on the right's attacks on social and cultural issues. This includes organizational and individual contempt for public access to birth control, abortion, same-sex marriage, pornography, gun control, and affirmative Action. This contempt often takes the form of conservative populism and demagoguery but can also serve as a distraction from the vision for deregulation and free market enterprise espoused by more subdued but more powerfully situated conservative leaders.[5]

Meanwhile, this essay observes a leftist-liberal divide that is by no means bound by a partisan affiliation with a broad left associated with the Democratic Party, for instance. Although many on the right, including several sources referenced in this essay, often conflate leftists and liberals, I distinguish them here. In particular, I look to Emily K. Hobson's analysis of the radical elements of the gay movement and her argument that "the left can be broadly distinguished from 'liberal' politics by its pursuit of radical and internationalist, rather than reformist and domestic, goals and by the centrality of street protest and direct action versus electoral or legal change."[6] Certainly, while many moments of overlap and collaboration exist, leftists are more easily identifiable by their radicalism and liberals through their defense of individualism.

In its analysis of rightists and liberals alike, this essay also relies on literature that has identified a strong inclination to articulate ideas of equality and reform—whether genuine or disingenuous—through the prism of neoliberal principles and tactics. This is manifest in mainstream liberal efforts that operate *within* the status quo and corporatist models; this trend takes form under at least the pretense of color-blindness, gender neutrality, and tolerance and defense of gay, lesbian, and bisexual identities. It is not a politics of redistributive equality. In its detachment and containment of radicalism, eroticism, and queerness, this trend promotes broader notions of normalcy, mainstreaming, the pursuit of capital, and the maintenance of such processes. In this way, these efforts often utilize the language of the right to achieve reform. Certainly, the right sought to exploit both the neoliberal trend and the broader failures of postwar liberalism undergirded by false notions of liberation and equality.

The Gay Basher Fiction

Many were introduced to then nineteen-year-old Rachel Jeantel in June 2013 with the expectation that she would be the smoking gun witness in the case against the neighborhood watchman. The teenager was the prosecution's best chance to challenge Zimmerman's account of what took place that night. A year prior she was on the phone with Martin when he took his final walk from a convenience store to his father's girlfriend's home. Jeantel's testimony proved controversial, and most pundits argued that it harmed the prosecution's case. They generally read her two-day testimony as combative and disgruntled. Britney Cooper put it best when she observed that "by painting . . . Jeantel as the aggressor, as the one prone to telling lies and spreading untruths, it became easy for the white male defense attorney to treat this . . . working-class black girl . . . as hostile, as a threat, as the one who needed to be regulated and contained."[7]

Jeantel's Blackness and her Afro-Caribbean ancestry further implicated her testimony as suspicious and not credible before the criminal system. Attorneys, the court reporter, the judge, and even a juror interrupted her throughout her grueling testimony. They could not decipher her soft-spoken and informal speech, best understood as a particular socioeconomic idiom distinct to her background.[8] Jeantel was born and raised in Miami to parents of Haitian and Dominican heritage and grew up in a multilingual home speaking Haitian Creole, Spanish, and English. At one point, state attorney Bernie de la Rionda tried to explain his witness's incoherent speech. He told her, "I know you grew up in a Haitian family so make sure everyone can hear you. Try to speak as clear . . ."[9] Surely, Cuban-born de la Rionda understood that Jeantel's speech and demeanor likely left a sour taste in the jury's mouth. In his closing argument, he showed the jurors—who were all white except one—a slide that urged them not to dismiss Jeantel's testimony. He did so by posing the question "do you just disregard what she said because" Jeantel's "family [is] from Haiti," she "isn't sophisticated," or she "can't read cursive?" According to her courtroom audience, Jeantel did not speak eloquently.[10] Jeantel's Blackness helped give shape to the court's treatment of her as an untrustworthy subject.[11]

Moreover, the trial attorneys and the general public's use of social media delegated Jeantel to the role of spokeswoman for her "culture," even suggesting that her testimony revealed an innate homophobia in Black communities. As Black radical lesbian-feminist Audre Lorde argued, "it is the members of oppressed, objectified groups who are expected to stretch out and bridge the gap between the actualities of . . . [their] lives and the consciousness of . . . [their] oppressor."[12] The "cultural" question that Jeantel was asked to answer before the court played out most directly in response to her testimony that she had warned Martin that the man following him could be a "rapist." This revelation sparked new attacks aimed at both Jeantel and the deceased Martin. In his cross-examination, West asked Jeantel to clarify. "What culture is that where people describe other people as creepy-ass crackers?" Confused, Jeantel simply responded "a pervert." West backtracked: "Do you understand what I mean by the culture? The culture you were raised in." Her testimony seemed to be lost in cultural translation. West sought to discredit the witness and her testimony by attempting to portray Jeantel and Martin as Black people who vilified whiteness and used hateful language to articulate their disdain. West reworded his question. "I'll say it this way: do people you live around and with call white people creepy-ass crackers?" She responded, "Not creepy, but cracka, yeah." West clarified: "So the creepy is the pervert part that you were talking about? . . . Forget that for a second." Her clarification was in fact soon forgotten.[13]

While Jeantel had clarified that the adjective "creepy" was what made her believe that Martin read Zimmerman as a potential sexual predator, many argued that Jeantel inadvertently revealed that her deceased friend may have been a "gay basher." Twitter and other social media platforms criticized Jeantel's testimony; many in the general public wondered why she referenced a "pervert" culture. It seems likely that after hours of testimony, Jeantel lost pace with West's questions. According to Jeantel, both she and Martin suspected that Zimmerman might have been "creepy" or a "pervert."[14] Jeantel had another opportunity to publicly clarify her position when she appeared on CNN's *Piers Morgan Live*. She elaborated:

Definitely after I say he might be a rapist. For every boy or every man every . . . who's not that kind of way, see a grown man following them, will they be creep out? So you gotta take as a parent when you tell your child, "when you see a grown person follow you, run away!" and all that. What, you gonna stand there? . . . If you tell your child, "stand there," we gonna see your child in the news for missing person.[15]

Jeantel also suggested that Martin might have believed that Zimmerman was a sexual predator when she discussed their anxieties over the safety of Martin's soon-to-be stepbrother, who remained in the house. "People need to understand, he didn't want that creepy-ass cracka going to his father girlfriend's house to go get . . . mind you, his little brother is there. . . . Mind you, I told you, I told Trayvon it might've been a rapist."[16] It is important to note how the state's historical repudiation of Black masculinity and families has heavily dictated Black heteropatriarchy. These state-led discourses have helped breed homophobia in marginalized communities—historical processes that made it seem "natural" that even in the absence of evidence, Jeantel and Martin fostered some sort of antigay animus.[17]

To many on the right, Jeantel's interview was further proof that Martin's distrust and physical response to Zimmerman was the product of his homophobia. One major transformation in the U.S. conservative movement today is the expansion and pervasiveness of affiliated or sympathetic news stations and programs.[18] In April 2018, the right-leaning Fox News celebrated its sixty-fifth consecutive quarter as the most watched news network in total viewers. Fox counts among its shows the nation's highest-rated shows too, with personalities such as Sean Hannity, Laura Ingraham, Glenn Beck, and Rush Limbaugh reaching millions of people daily through several media.[19] While all of the aforementioned media personalities served as apologists for Zimmerman and pushed for a so-called color-blind reading of the case, Limbaugh made one of the most incendiary claims. Shortly after Jeantel's interview with Piers Morgan, Limbaugh told his radio audience that "when Trayvon described Zimmerman to her [Jeantel] . . . she began to fear that Zimmerman was gay. A rapist. She then told Trayvon to run, run, run." Limbaugh used Jeantel's interview as evidence of Martin's and Jeantel's homophobia. "That means she says to Trayvon: 'This guy could be gay. He could be a rapist. He might want to rape you. You run, Trayvon, run, run. For every boy, every man, who's not that kind of way'—meaning everybody who's straight—'see a grown man following them, would you be creep out?'" Limbaugh told his audience that Martin, whom Limbaugh believed "the media has made practically an angel," was "actually a gay basher."[20] In this formulation, homophobia helped define Martin's "criminality," which in turn helped justify his death.

As several on the right quickly labeled Martin a "gay basher," Zimmerman's older brother Robert became a spokesperson for his family and vigorously defended his brother in several media outlets—even suggesting that George's acceptance of Robert's gay identity was evidence that Martin's death was not racially motivated. The right-leaning *Washington Times* profiled this side of George Zimmerman. Robert Zimmerman discussed coming out as a gay man a decade before the trial: "George was the first person who reached out. He came to my house, he reached out to my partner at the time, who I was actually with for eleven years, and tried to make me and him feel very comfortable and was very supportive because I had been true to myself."[21] So while Martin became a de facto "gay basher," George Zimmerman extended his hand to his gay brother and became his "staunchest advocate."[22] Just as homophobia became a measuring stick for criminality, the acceptance of homosexuality similarly served as a sort of requisite for innocence. It is also hard to ignore the role that the respectable gay man—who had been coupled for eleven years—played in achieving this.

Meanwhile, some conservative blogs and social media posts argued that Jeantel was responsible for Martin's death. In suggesting that Zimmerman could be a "rapist" seeking out her friend, some maintained that she had provoked Martin by challenging his manhood. These accusations called into question Jeantel's own ideas of masculinity—Black or otherwise. Feminist scholar bell hooks notes how white patriarchy has historically diminished, violated, and attacked Black masculinity. This has helped create a form of Black hypermasculinity that reifies patriarchal modes of oppression and violence.[23] It can also manifest in overt homophobia as a defensive against any attack on Black masculinity.[24] The right found opportunity to exploit this even as it ignored the structural forces that helped create the Black hypermasculine defensive. During her interview with Piers Morgan, Jeantel challenged Zimmerman's masculinity when he did not take the stand in his own defense: "If you were a real man, you would stand on that stage and tell what happened."[25] Her assumptions of masculinity helped fuel the accusations that she was responsible for Martin's death. In the online forum A Voice for Men, contributor August Løvenskiolds rationalized that "Martin freaked out over the idea that Zimmerman might have sexual designs on him or his family, and this seems to have precipitated the attack on Zimmerman." According to him, this revealed "the degree of Martin's revulsion that he went from flight to fight mode in so short a time."[26] His perspective was by no means anomalous, as similar observations were made throughout social media.[27] Limbaugh suggested this too: "The reason Trayvon Martin descended on Zimmerman and started pummeling him was because he was offended. He thought because of what she said to him that Zimmerman was gay. . . . What other interpretation is there?"[28]

What got left out of this so-called logic is revealing. The rhetoric that labeled Martin a "gay basher" failed to include that an anonymous woman known as "witness #9" had accused Zimmerman of sexual assault. Investigators interviewed her, whom the defense team identified as Zimmerman's cousin, nearly a month after the shooting. She told authorities that he repeatedly sexually violated her and other young women over a period of ten years.[29] Her testimony was ruled inadmissible in court.[30] The accusations shed light on the animus that led right-wing commentators to twist Jeantel's words in an effort to unveil Martin's "innate" homophobia. This by no means suggests that Zimmerman pursued Martin with sex on his mind. Rather, it observes the facility in which Martin became a "gay basher" but the absurdity in reading Zimmerman as a "rapist."

At its core, the rhetoric that labeled both Jeantel and Martin homophobic also helped isolate Blackness from queerness. This became clear when Limbaugh noted that the left would have to champion one over the other following Jeantel's "revelation": "So I thought, boy, the left is going to have a real problem here. They're going to have to balance which group are they going to favor? Gays or blacks?"[31] He also noted that Jeantel's statement "throws this thing 180 degrees out of phase. So now Trayvon Martin, who is the recipient of full-fledged, 100 percent victim status. . . . It turns out could well be a gay basher, and the left has been defending him! So what do they do? They have two interest groups here that they represent and champion: African Americans and homosexuals. . . . I figured they'd be very conflicted today."[32] The website Tea Party Nation featured a post that argued that this made "Trayvon a deeply flawed leftist idol and it puts every leftist in a complex dilemma."[33] An article in the *American Spectator* argued that Martin's perceived homophobia was "unmentionable" to "liberals" and that "the black leftist establishment and Attorney General Eric Holder" were hell-bent "to play the race card."[34]

Meanwhile, several on the right fostered a particular so-called race-neutral stance—particularly in stressing Zimmerman's "mixed-race" identity—to argue that any discussions of race were confined within a liberal imaginary. Zimmerman's brother stated, "Our family very deliberately left the injection of another racial element off the table."[35] He claimed that his family downplayed their mother's Afro-Peruvian heritage to further remove race from this heated conversation. This pretense of color-blindness served as a means in which to deflect racist accusations. Zimmerman's father similarly issued a statement defending his son from racist accusations: "George is a Spanish speaking minority with many black family members and friends. He would be the last to discriminate for any reasons whatsoever."[36] At least two major news outlets generally derided by the right, CNN and the *New York Times*, referred to Zimmerman as a "white Hispanic."[37] The conservative website Breitbart suggested that labeling Zimmerman a "white Hispanic" was an attempt to garner "lefty political cred[entials] by injecting a hostile racial narrative into every report on the Zimmerman murder trial."[38] In a somewhat different strategy—although still within the pretense of race neutrality—several other conservative voices chimed in, even blaming Latinx organizations and outlets such as the National Council of La Raza and Univision for remaining silent on the matter. They argued that Latinx organizations and community representatives could have diffused this racial narrative by reminding viewers that Zimmerman was a man of color. Conservative pundit Laura Ingraham expressed frustration over this silence in light of Latinx attacks on "voter ID laws" and their "push for amnesty."[39] Media representatives on the right pushed a particular narrative: Zimmerman's Afro-Latino heritage precluded factoring in the role that race played in Martin's death.

Several problems arise from this perspective. First introduced in the 1980 census as an identity category, "Hispanic" represents "a free-floating ethnic category of any race." The term designates a minority group that can also be white. This amorphous category influenced the creation of another ethno-racial designation, "non-Hispanic white," which distances itself from both ethnic and racial Otherness.[40] It is also important, as the cofounders of the BLM movement have demonstrated, that we do not dismiss the key role of antiBlackness writ large, including within Latinx communities.[41]

Just the same, because this essay is not interested in assessing Zimmerman's own ideas on race, it is important to factor how so-called color-blind politics allow, according to Eduardo Bonilla-Silva, for racism to exist without "racists."[42] That is, "racial stories associated with colorblind racism assist whites in making sense of their world in ways that reinforce the racial order."[43] Zimmerman's ethnic and racial ambiguity afforded him the role of the "honorary white" whose experiences and circumstances—or perhaps passability—permitted him at least a slice of white privilege.[44] Color-blind racism has a long and textured history. By the late 1960s and early 1970s, a coalition of Black rights movements had changed the political landscape and the ways that people spoke about race and racism in the United States. As Keeanga-Yamahtta Taylor notes, this coalition had "demonstrated, some fifty years before the slogan would appear, that Black lives mattered."[45] On both sides of the political aisle, outward articulations of antiBlack sentiment and anxieties found release in more subtle discursive forms. Fears of "welfare queens" and the criminality associated with "inner cities" were indeed "racist baits for the white conservative electorate" who became literate in this antiBlack code. As Taylor argues, "the political framework of colorblindness allowed portions of the political establishment to separate Black hardship from the material conditions that activists had worked so hard to expose. It was as if the signing of civil rights legislations had wiped the slate clean and African Americans had been given a new start."[46] At its core, questioning whether Zimmerman was a "racist" ignores how racism operates structurally through social, political, and economic institutions dictated by hierarchies of power. That is where we now turn.

The Burdens of History

In light of the many ways that racism exists without racists, this case also sheds light on how homophobia exists in the absence of homophobes and how those two configurations have historically shaped one another. The case exposes how the right's at best tenuous solidarity with gender and sexual non-conformists hoped to serve as a political module in which to shore up support from an LGBT base at the expense of Black lives.

While the discursive logic that labeled Martin a "gay basher" was a misrepresentation of the presented facts, the ease and decisiveness in which the "rapist" became synonymous with gay men in the right's popular rhetoric is the product of a rich history. Surely, had Martin and Jeantel been correct about Zimmerman being a "rapist" or "pervert"—to use her terms—keen on the teenage boy, the perpetrator may have espoused same-sex sexual desires. A dominant paradigm in the social sciences maintains, however, that rape is more frequently motivated by a number of other nonsexual factors such as domination and power. Even scholars who maintain that rape *is* sexually motivated and that the social construction perspective is a feminist machination seem to agree that it most often occurs in concurrence with other factors outside the pleasures of the flesh.[47] The presumption of homosexuality in male-male rape cases involves a more complex evaluation of the perpetrator's psyche independent of sexual identity.

This phenomenon is further complicated by the long history that has constructed and stigmatized the "homosexual" as a sexual deviant akin to a rapist, a pedophile, and other sexual offenders. The social upheaval caused by World War II ushered in the Cold War era's "sex crime panic," which ultimately helped regulate nonnormative gender and sexual representations. Lesbians and gays were often conflated with violent deviations from the norm, including murderers and child molesters. They became measuring sticks for what would be defined as normal in society.[48]

The mid-twentieth century also witnessed the consolidation of homosexuality as white and crime and violence as Black. In documenting responses to the "sexual psychopath" in the post-World War II era, Estelle Freedman has argued that "white men who committed sexual crimes had to be mentally ill; black men who committed sexual crimes were believed to be guilty of willful violence."[49] Roger N. Lancaster argues that the mid-twentieth century gradually "de-raced" the "predatory bogeyman." Then, according to Lancaster, the "racial double standard" that Freedman documented "coded crime and generic violence as 'black' and homosexuality or specialized sexual perversion as 'white.'"[50]

As Limbaugh's statements suggest, the social and political discourse that associated homosexuality as a dangerous sexual deviancy had not disappeared. Both the social sciences and the medical profession historically solidified this logic by pathologizing same-sex behaviors and eroticism. The American Psychological Association did not remove homosexuality from its list of mental disorders until 1973. Four years later, Florida Orange Juice spokeswoman Anita Bryant launched her influential Save Our Children campaign. Bryant and others argued that a Metro Dade County ordinance that shielded gays, lesbians, and bisexuals from discrimination in housing, public accommodations, and employment granted special privileges to a group of immoral citizens who would attempt to recruit or convert children to homosexuality. In seeking to exploit the tensions of a rights-based liberalism that pitted lesbian, gay, and bisexual rights against the rights of mothers to defend their children from harm, Bryant and her followers argued that there was a very real need to "Save Our Children."[51] This message, which had deep-seated roots, proved massively influential across the United States and beyond.

Quantitative research has demonstrated that many self-identified heterosexuals still regard gay men as likely child molesters, admittedly in smaller numbers than in previous decades.[52] Clear vestiges of this sentiment are present in debates over the Catholic Church sex abuse scandals and the Boy Scouts' May 2013 decision to permit gay scouts into the organization while still prohibiting gay adults from leadership roles.[53]

For decades, lesbian, gay, bisexual, and transgender activists fought to dismantle these criminal and deviant associations. A small but visible and influential homophile movement emerged in the 1950s and "rupture[d] the consensus that shaped social attitudes toward homosexuality and society's treatment of gay people."[54] By the late 1960s, many radical liberationists modeled the social and political machinations of the New Left to dismantle homophobia. Working on the foundation of the homophiles and inspired by the radical politics of their era—including Black civil rights, second-wave feminism, and the antiwar and counterculture movements—liberationists fought larger sociopolitical inequalities. This included state violence, racism, capitalism, poverty, misogyny, imperialism, militarism, and class warfare. Homophobia (and to a smaller extent transphobia) was *one* of the evils that many gay liberationists sought to eradicate. It was often understood as but a cog in a much larger statist wheel that produced injustice in the United States and abroad.[55]

As the movement grew and gradually became less radical, a more resourced liberal faction focused more on rights-based organizing that largely substituted former multi-issue group politics with the single issue of lesbian, gay, and bisexual rights. Many LGBT activists and sympathizers grew skeptical about any affiliation with the more radical impulses of the left especially among Black nationalists, such as socialism and the work of the Black Panther Party. In some instances, this stemmed from the vitriolic rhetoric employed by some on the left. Activists criticized members of Students for a Democratic Society and the Black Panther Party who asserted their own power and place by employing homophobic and sexist language, such as calling police officers and other state actors "cocksuckers" or "faggots." Many lesbian, gay, and bisexual activists started to wonder how they would fare under socialism, largely disillusioned by the 1959 Cuban Revolution.[56] Dubious commitments to radical Black Panthers further strained relationships, and by December 1969 former members of the Gay Liberation Front broke off to create the Gay Activists Alliance (GAA).[57] The GAA's founders sought to safeguard their organization and movement by noting that it would "not endorse, ally with, or otherwise support any political party, candidate for public office, and/or any organization not directly related to the homosexual cause."[58] In abandoning the multi-issue approach that had fueled the era's radicals, the GAA and many subsequent organizations demonstrated for the most part that they were less interested in transforming the United States through revolution and helped orient a movement that looked more favorably toward integration and assimilation. Radical activism did not altogether disappear; it was, however, largely achieved at the individual level.[59] By the early 1970s, a new movement had crystallized that privileged gay identity. As Elizabeth Armstrong observed, the "proliferation and diversification of gay organizations" did not "reflect redistributive politics, as few of the new organizations focused on the political or economic transformation of society."[60]

As the movement increasingly focused on a single-issue gay identity agenda, a white, moneyed, and cisgender male constituency took control of the more powerful and well-funded organizations that increasingly combined social change with the marketability of an emerging gay consumer at the expense of more radical politics that maintained its commitment to anti-racism, anticolonialism, and redistributive politics.[61] The discernible attention to identity politics based on race, gender, and sexuality—and especially the power specifically wielded by white cisgender men—also helped fracture the left. For instance, often disillusioned by both the homophobia of feminist organizations and the sexism of gay organizations, many lesbians separated from past affiliations and formed new alliances.[62] Similarly ostracized and ignored, transgender activists increasingly created separate groups during this period.[63] Among all of these and other groups, for many queers of color, assuming a lesbian, gay, bisexual, or transgender identity meant risking isolation from racial or ethnic communities.[64]

Black feminist thought offered solutions. As many Black women had done in the past, the Black radical feminists behind the groundbreaking 1977 Combahee River Collective Statement articulated the politics of what was termed "intersectionality" over a decade later: "The most general statement of our politics at the present time would be that we are actively committed to struggling against racial, sexual, heterosexual, and class oppression, and see as our particular task the development of integrated analysis and practice based upon the fact that the major systems of oppression are interlocking."[65] To say the very least, there were formidable radical alternatives that challenged single-issue white gay politics; these never dissipated.[66]

Through it all a more visible leftist-liberal divide emerged, even though it did not occur in a linear fashion and was a far more checkered and nuanced process with deep historical roots. The 1981 "discovery" of what later became known as HIV/AIDS and its devastating effects on queer and people of color communities represents just one historical opportunity to reexamine what has largely been understood as the diminishing radical nature of the movement by the mid-1970s.[67] As Jennifer Brier has demonstrated, in the wake of state apathy and violence, queer activists applied feminist and gay liberationist models to combat systemic multiple forms of oppression.[68] While this suggests a greater continuation of gay liberation well into the 1980s, several developments—including the desexualization of the movement, growing sympathy from members outside of the community, and successes such as the 1996 release of protease inhibitors—ushered in a new era of LGBT rights-based politic that was more entrenched with the mainstream and consumerism.[69]

It is important to remember that campaigns such as Bryant's that helped mobilize LGBT rank-and-file activists were mere episodes in a much larger conservative movement known as the New Right that became entrenched in U.S. culture by the 1980s and helped blur the lines between liberals and leftists. The New Right largely emerged out of the culture wars that married the Religious Right with the Republican Party beginning in the late 1970s. Busing, gay rights, feminism, abortion, pornography, affirmative action, prohibiting prayer at schools, and attacks on gun ownership were among the issues that the so-called silent majority challenged.[70] While this helped shore up a conservative base, these efforts were connected to corporate America's push for state deregulation, free market enterprise, privatization, reduced taxes for businesses, and the suppression of labor unions.[71] The rise of the New Right also proved to be a moment of urgency that found new modes of collaboration between liberals and leftists in the gay movement; after all, the New Right sought to destroy their visions in equal measure. As Hobson notes, however, although the liberal faction in the gay movement gained greater traction and influence in the end, we should not discount the critiques that radicals made during this period that shaped and often found their way into gay electoral and legislative victories.[72]

Other pressures, particularly those connected to surmounting social, economic, and political anxieties, found many LGBT activists seduced by a neoliberal impulse gaining traction among liberal circles of instrumentalizing the state in pursuit of individual protections. In the midst of oppressive state-led policies—particularly the slow and ineffective response to HIV/AIDS, increased physical violence, and the U.S. Supreme Court's 1986 decision in *Bowers v. Hardwick* that upheld sodomy laws in the United States and thus the criminalization of those who engaged in same-sex acts—many LGBT activists turned even more forcefully to a rights-based platform as a means of gaining greater acceptance from the state. Many others adopted a politics of "homonormativity" that reproduced hegemonic white, middle-class, and traditional family ideals. The pursuit of capital and assimilation became central to this vision.[73] Perhaps one of the best examples remains the push for same-sex marriage by mainstream LGBT organizations, especially by the 1990s.[74] This radical shift among many of viewing marriage as an oppressive hetero-patriarchal institution to the main objective of the most powerful gay organizations was not just an assimilationist strategy; it was also a product of a neoliberal turn. As the welfare state continued to contract, lesbians, gays, and bisexuals sought new avenues to secure protections and benefits for their families and dependents. For some, marriage became a retort to the neutered welfare state and offered more tangible solutions to combating issues such as illness, underemployment and unemployment, poverty, and the privatization of reproductive politics.[75]

Connected to this, the protection and fortification of particular "defensible spaces" for predominantly white middle-class residents was one of the more critical modes of seduction for many liberals, including LGBT people. Lest we forget, Zimmerman's vigilante role with Sanford's neighborhood watch program positions him as a by-product of the fortification of suburbia, the surveillance state, the privatization of "crime prevention," and the criminalization, incarceration, and state-sanctioned violence of Black bodies. Founded in 1972 by the National Sheriffs' Association, the National Neighborhood Watch Program at least partly delegates the task of crime prevention to civilians such as Zimmerman. The program operates at the local level, frequently in collaboration with a community police department, and has received grants from the U.S. Department of Justice.[76] In sharing the responsibility for "law and order" with residents independent of the police, the program arms—both literally and figuratively—residents with the power to police others deemed suspicious. This voluntary monitoring is carried out, according to the Neighborhood Watch manual, to create "a greater sense of security, responsibility, and personal control."[77] The individualizing grammar of taking charge of one's "responsibility" and maintaining "personal control" of perceived threats is indeed (neo)liberal in its ciphering of the state's own duties to *all* of its people—especially those whose bodies are inherently read as suspicious and dangerous in state-sanctioned defensible spaces. Instead, members of the neighborhood are implored to be on constant alert.[78]

In 1987, Florida's legislature passed a series of laws that allowed armed people such as Zimmerman to surveil the streets. These laws helped pave the way for Florida's "Stand Your Ground" law, which many claim helped decriminalize Zimmerman's killing of Martin that night. One of the laws the state passed in 1987 allowed qualifying citizens to carry a concealed weapon. In a clear convergence of liberal and neoliberal thought, this massively expanded "gun rights" in Florida, a phrase that distinctly operationalizes the state in its rights-based dialectic.[79] The Florida legislature also passed the Safe Neighborhood Act that year. It was part of the legislature's Crime Prevention and Control Act that governed "the use, regulation, distribution, and prohibition of controlled substances," much like other acts passed during the "war on drugs."[80] Among other things, the law allowed the creation of special districts that formed committees to study and combat crime. The law also provided the possibility for state-matched grants with eligible municipalities to incorporate new modes of crime prevention. Some critics believed that the law would be used "by wealthier developments to control who gets to use public roads." If a neighborhood received that particular designation, it could restrict access to a public road by posting a guard or barrier. One commissioner from Florida's Orange County believed that the law would be better described as the "Elitist Neighborhoods Act." He expressed concern that it served the "rich neighborhood where the poor aren't welcome."[81] In his study of the act, Stephan McCrea noted that it was the "first state-level program based on crime prevention through environmental design." It had the power to privatize and surveil spaces that were once public and designate them—largely through constructions of race and class—according to their so-called need for "revitalization," employing the language of liberalism's failed exercise in urban clearance programs. This time, however, it would do so through incentives such as installing larger windows in homes, organizing neighborhood watches, increasing lighting, and setting up cameras.[82]

Such initiatives held sway for many liberal gender and sexual nonconformists who sought protection and approval from the state as well as the trappings of middle-class consumerism. Since the 1940s, federal and state policies helped consolidate suburbs such as Sanford as white, middle class, and heterosexual writ large. Suburbia's tax benefits, deregulation, segregation, and exclusivity represent "neoliberalism's back yard."[83] Clayton Howard has similarly demonstrated how federal housing programs and policies "reinforced both racial segregation and sexual homogeneity."[84]

This too was reflective of the diminishing radical orientation of the gay movement. Some lesbians, gays, and bisexuals quickly fled to the suburbs and further embraced middle-class consumer culture. According to Tim Retzloff, "Moderate and conservative gay suburbanites rejected the in-the-streets militant activism of the city in favor of a muted challenge to the not-in-my-back-yard [sic] culture of suburbs."[85] Hanhardt argues that some lesbians, gays, and bisexuals articulated such rhetoric in their pursuit and construction of "safe spaces" since the 1970s. In what she calls "militant gay liberalism," they espoused a new cultural politics that voiced a neoliberal vocabulary that sought the protection of the state against perceived threats of violence and in their pursuit of capital. This body politic, which privileged decriminalization and normalization of same-sex sexualities, often came at the expense of racial and ethnic minorities, the urban poor, and other marginalized groups criminalized by the state.[86] As they increasingly found comfort in middle-class consumerism and state-sanctioned safety, many of the gay activists' political tenets were effectively decoupled from the struggle for racial and class justice.

More generally, gay identity politics' dominance has stifled the politics of racial and class justice, which has been rendered secondary to the cause of "gay rights." For instance, while earlier gay leftist politics had taken up the issue of prison activism, it too declined in the 1980s and 1990s. Regina Kunzel traced the shifting "position that 'we are all prisoners' to a feeling of distance and disidentification, especially on the part of the predominantly white, middle-class readers of gay magazines, from those behind bars."[87] This desertion occurred just as the United States, as Michelle Alexander and others have documented, redesigned Jim Crow racial discrimination in the form of mass incarceration of Black and Brown men. Since the 1970s, the war on drugs coded and profiled men of color as criminal. While this was orchestrated in "color-blind" or race-neutral discourses, by the mid-1990s "ninety percent of those admitted to prison for drug offenses in many states were black or Latino."[88]

Several scholars have pointed to the marketability of an "equality" paradigm espoused by mainstream LGBT organizations that is a manifestation of neoliberal cultural politics. Lisa Duggan points to the 1990s as the period in which new identity-based alliances created mechanisms that undermined racial and gender equality. In this process, "organizations, activists, and writers promote 'color-blind' anti-affirmative action racial politics, conservative-libertarian 'equality feminism,' and gay 'normality.'" The neoliberal turn witnessed the departure of "progressive-left affiliations" in exchange for the cultural politics of the right. This includes same-sex marriage, respectability, privatization, open markets, and corporatism.[89] In her 1995 impassioned critique of the movement, activist Urvashi Vaid noted how the movement had only managed to achieve a form of "virtual equality" by choosing legal reform and civil rights over liberation. This often includes half-gestures and tokenist responses from liberals and at times some on the right, which often articulated a commoditized version of multiculturalism and diversity—what Vaid calls the "economy of queerness" and Duggan calls the "Benetton-ad style of 'diversity.'"[90] This is exactly at the heart of the right's tenuous and imaginary defense of "gay rights" in Martin's case. At its core, in the name of higher profits, free markets avoided openly discriminating or isolating LGBT consumers.

It is important to emphasize how the new stigma attached to Martin as a "gay basher" was distinctly framed in "hate crime" language employed by gay rights groups, suggesting how the right sought to provoke a particular impulse within liberal circles. Conservative commentator Pat Dollard published a post on his website titled "Did Widespread Homophobia in the Black Community Lead Trayvon Martin to Attack George Zimmerman?"[91] Similarly, a post in the *Gay Patriot*, branded the "Internet home for the American gay conservative," posed "Trayvon the Gay Basher?"[92] Author Jack Cashill maintained that "in looking closely at the trial transcripts and post-trial comments . . . it seems likely that if anyone committed a hate crime it was Trayvon Martin. Evidence strongly suggests that he attacked Zimmerman because he believed him to be gay."[93] This legal protectionist language worked to further criminalize Martin by pitting him against members of the LGBT community. In 2009 several LGBT groups celebrated the passage of the Hate Crime Prevention Act, also known as the Matthew Shepard and James Byrd Jr. Hate Crimes Prevention Act. This federal legislation assists and provides funds to "state, local, or tribal law enforcement agencies" to investigate and prosecute crimes "in which the defendant intentionally selects a victim . . . because of the actual or perceived race, color, religion, national origin, ethnicity, gender, disability, or sexual orientation of any person."[94] It was this broader reformist impulse that the right sought to capitalize on.

Some contend that a "progay" and multicultural narrative also reified the state's ability to disproportionately criminalize and surveil Black bodies while strengthening the tenets of the American "punitive turn."[95] Not all LGBT organizations were on board with such hate crime legislation. Some organizations that were more radical, such as Queers for Economic Justice and the Sylvia Rivera Law Project, fought against such hate crime laws as being inimical to social justice. Among the critiques, one argued "that the push for hate crimes laws as the solution to antiqueer and antitrans violence will never actually address why we are vulnerable to violence in the first place or why homophobia and transphobia are encouraged in our cultures."[96] Such steps fuel the punitive state's criminalization narrative by attacking perceived "bigoted" individuals through a system that particularly targets the poor and people of color. Critics argue that such laws provide a false sense of safety while ignoring the systemic structures that lead to violence and oppression in the first place. The right's framing of Martin's perceived criminality through hate crime language was a discursive liberal trap that distracted from the broader appeal—among conservatives and certainly many liberals as well—to defend white property rights and capital.

By 2012, the year Zimmerman killed Martin, the United States had traded George W. Bush, who suggested amending the U.S. Constitution to define marriage as being between a woman and a man, with Barack Obama, who since 2009 helped usher in an unprecedented level of social and political credibility for LGBT people in the presidential office. This is evident in the repeal of "Don't Ask, Don't Tell," Obama's "evolution" on same-sex marriage, and his placement of Stonewall alongside Seneca Falls and Selma in his 2013 inauguration speech. In a 2012 cover story for *Newsweek*, conservative gay writer Andrew Sullivan even posed whether this effectively qualified Obama, the first African American U.S. president, also as the "first gay president."[97] Radicals maintained, however, that this new phase often distracted and silenced critiques of Obama's dismal relationship with U.S. imperialism and interventionism, violent immigration policies, militarization, and the privatization and profit of Black incarceration and death, among many other issues.

As the LGBT movement increasingly entered mainstream politics, homosexuality has been not only decriminalized but also institutionally normalized and manicured for consumption under the umbrella of "multiculturalism." This paradigm has learned a great deal from corporatist models.[98] LGBT acceptance has become a near-requisite for legitimacy in many political and social circles. In this vein, Martin's credibility was measured, at least partially, by his perceived stance on homosexuality. Whereas an accusation that Martin operated on some sort of antigay animus would have been tolerable—perhaps even reasonable—or altogether irrelevant even in the late twentieth century, a new paradigm—certainly familiar within the right but not entirely foreign to liberals either—practically implicated that Martin's imagined homophobia be understood as indicative of his "criminality."

Both during and after the Zimmerman criminal trial, several news pundits and social media users questioned why Jeantel did not alert the police that her friend was being pursued by a "creepy-ass cracka." Had she really believed that the unknown man pursuing Martin was a possible rapist, why hadn't she called the authorities following their phone conversation? This question failed to comprehend how the fortressing of spaces deemed white and middle class and a shift toward surveillance and punitive retribution are structured to disproportionately criminalize Black people. This case serves, then, as a reminder of the state's powerful arm and not so color-blind eyes. In this context, Jeantel and her deceased friend became "gay bashing" homophobes rather than casualties of a state that hyperpoliced and criminalized them. The framing of "normalized" lesbians, gays, and bisexuals, however, largely required that Martin's perceived criminality be understood vis-à-vis an imagined contempt for LGBT people—even as this logic erased the trauma of rape. The credibility of both Jeantel and Martin—as both witness and moral character—was tarnished by the stigma of a perceived homophobia. In this way, discourses surrounding the acceptance or disdain for homosexuality served as another backdrop to discredit and criminalize the Black body.

Jeantel and Martin were ensnared at the intersection of these aforementioned histories. Although Jeantel never specifically referenced homosexuality in her testimony, many followed and made sense of this narrative-fantasy and even sought to criminalize her in the process. Martin's Blackness simultaneously rendered him an outsider in the suburbs, a suspected criminal linked to drugs and prime for prison and now a violent homophobe. To entertain the unfounded idea that Martin acted on some sort of antigay animus ultimately serves to erase the impetus that deemed the unarmed Black teenager a suspicious character worth pursuing in the first place. The leap from "rapist" or "pervert" to "gay" is a product of a long history that hinged on the continued criminalization of the homosexual amid new but historically familiar modes of criminalizing Blackness. Surely, we could easily dismiss Limbaugh's rhetoric as reactionary and sensational; that, however, only serves to trivialize the beliefs of many who followed, reproduced, and promoted his logic. In light of this image, who would take up Martin's cause?

Conclusion: Toward an Antiracist Queer Politics

Black and queer liberationists gave Martin new life and Jeantel renewed dignity in sparking a new movement with the power to radically transform our landscape. Among the more encouraging outcomes of this political moment was that the right did not succeed in its attempt to seduce liberal support through its homophobia baiting of Martin. Twenty-three national LGBT organizations issued a joint open letter that called Martin's death "a national call to action" before Zimmerman's trial and Limbaugh's "revelation." Issued on April 2, 2012, a few weeks after Martin died, the letter stated that "many in our community have been targets of bigotry and bias. We have a great deal of experience grappling with the role bias plays in violent crimes against our communities." It then expanded on how racial violence was part of what they seek to dismantle. "Trayvon's killing is a wakeup call to the enduring cancer of racism and racial profiling. The pain his family continues to endure transcends communities and unites us all. Every person, regardless of race, religion, sexual orientation or gender identity, must be able to walk the streets without fear for their safety." Signers included the largest LGBT rights organization, the Human Rights Campaign, as well as GLAAD, Lambda Legal, UNID@S, and the National Gay and Lesbian Task Force.[99] That they made this stance over a year *before* Limbaugh's revelations that baited Martin with homophobia is most encouraging. That Martin appeared "suspicious" before the general public, the media, jurors, the court, law enforcement, and even Zimmerman had always been a "queer issue" insofar it concerned state violence, racism, surveillance, and uneven power structures.

The LGBT organizations' response to Martin's death—prior to his being baited as homophobic and more immediately because it served the tenets of queer radical politics—was not universally lauded, however. Kevin Naff, an editor and co-owner of the *Washington Blade*, one of the most influential gay news outlets, responded to the call to action. Although he lamented Martin's death and criticized the "nation's lax gun laws," he believed that such solidarity statements "stoked racial tensions while ignoring the problem of gun proliferation. . . . Not to be left out of all the bandwagon posturing, the nation's leading LGBT advocacy groups belatedly leapt into the fray . . . to draw parallels between black and LGBT crime victims and express solidarity with Martin's family."[100] Maya Rupert, the policy director for the National Center for Lesbian Rights, criticized Naff's piece, noting that it "misunderstands the role that racial bias played in this situation and the way systemic racism operates in this country. . . . Racial justice is an LGBT issue."[101]

We saw further gestures in this direction from LGBT organizations following Zimmerman's acquittal. Several noted the similarities between Martin and antigay crimes of the past, particularly that of Matthew Shepard. In an op-ed piece in *The Advocate* titled "Where Trayvon Martin and Matthew

Shepard Collide," journalist Michelle Garcia explored the continued use of both the "Black panic" and "gay panic" defenses in the U.S. legal system.[102] In Chicago's *Windy City Times*, Tracy Baim argued that "just as homophobia and sexism are things we just 'know' when we experience them, racism is something some people just understand permeates the mindset of huge numbers of Americans."[103] If official statements and positions of solidarity were any indication, most mainstream LGBT organizations agreed. A blog post on behalf of Equality Matters, a watchdog organization monitoring LGBT issues in the media, questioned why the right-wing media was portraying Trayvon Martin as a gay basher. Contributor Luke Brinker sought to expose how right-wing commentators had tried to appropriate a language of gay protectionism in order to vilify Martin. "Given that their ostensible solidarity with gays is so obviously disingenuous, what explains the right-wing media's attempt to portray Martin as a vicious homophobe?"[104] Following Zimmerman's acquittal, several dozen LGBT organizations issued another statement calling for justice: "Our community has been targets of bigotry, bias, profiling and violence." In noting that "every person, regardless of race, religion, sexual orientation or gender identity, must be able to walk the streets without fear for their safety," these organizations sought to disassociate Martin from accusations of homophobia.[105] They also clarified that this was their fight too. Activists Darnell L. Moore and Charles Stephens rightfully argued, however, that "it is insufficient for LGBT organizations to merely acknowledge" systemic forms of violence against Black people. "We can no longer sit idly by as you, mainstream LGBT organizations, center your movements and advocacy work on some within our varied communities but not others."[106] As several antiracist queer activists and organizations—and many liberals—observed, Limbaugh's accusation that Martin was a gay basher should not be the LGBT movement's entry point to his cause. Rather, many articulated that Martin lost his life due to the systemic violence that criminalized Blackness and that they must challenge the state that orchestrated the young man's death and designated his life worthless. That Limbaugh baited Martin with homophobia only added insult to injury.

These antiracist queer activists and organizations took the lead from a long history of Black feminist thought, as Zimmerman's 2013 acquittal catapulted a movement that has far more effectively reenergized a grassroots revolutionary politics that shared but also pushed many of the radical tenets of Black and gay liberationists of decades past. When the jury found Zimmerman not guilty, three Black women, Alicia Garza, Patrisse Khan-Cullors, and Opal Tometi, helped take a protest hashtag—which organizes metadata on social media sites—from the digital world to the streets; they created, in their own words, a "political project."[107] At its core, as Garza has noted, "Black Lives Matter is an ideological and political intervention in a world where Black lives are systematically and intentionally targeted for demise. It is an affirmation of Black folks' contributions to this society, our humanity, and our resilience in the face of deadly oppression."[108] BLM gained even more momentum and support after August 9, 2014, when a police officer fatally shot an eighteen-year-old Black man named Michael Brown in Ferguson, Missouri; this recalled many of the systemic forms of state violence seen in the deaths of Martin and several others. Activists from throughout the country created local BLM chapters and flocked to Ferguson, where they took to the streets demanding racial and social justice.[109]

At its core, BLM has centered the eradication of antiBlack violence while maintaining a firm commitment to "fostering a Trans- and Queer-affirming network" as a means to liberate all "from the tight grip of heteronormative thinking."[110] Two of the three cofounders, Garza and Khan-Cullors, identify as queer. As Garza noted in her herstory of the movement, "Black Lives Matter affirms the lives of Black queer and trans folks, disabled folks, Black-undocumented folks, folks with records, women and all Black lives along the gender spectrum. It centers those that have been marginalized within Black liberation movements." While BLM serves as "a tactic to (re)build the Black liberation movement," it also has the power to reenergize some of the more radical impulses and vestiges of gay liberation and lesbian feminism.[111] Garza refers to the infusion of Black feminist and queer thought in BLM as "intentional."[112] Note how Khan-Cullors recalled being inspired by the grassroots work of the Black Youth Project 100 (BYP100), founded in 2013 to train and mobilize young organizers using a Black feminist and queer lens. According to Khan-Cullors, "After Ferguson, when we speak of ourselves, we always lead with this, that not only are we unapologetically Black, a term coined by BYP100, but we are also Queer- and Trans-led and non-patriarchal."[113]

Despite this revolutionary vision that has the power to liberate everyone, it is important to remember, as BLM reminds its members, that Black women cannot and must not do this work alone. In recalling the womanist-of-color critique, such labor is at the heart of what constitutes "this bridge called my back."[114] Although a decentralized organization that is member-led and nonhierarchical, BLM's Black and queer liberationist vision has found many LGBT activists embracing a multi-issue approach to their activism.

A December 24, 2014, solidarity march called "Queers Come Out for #BlackLivesMatter" took place in San Francisco's Castro District, a long-established gay neighborhood. That Christmas Eve, queer and trans activists sought to "create a visible, united front speaking out against the racist forces of police and vigilante violence against Black and Brown people, many of whom are queer or trans."[115] Multiracial LGBTQ protestors and allies carried a banner that read "BLACK LIVES MATTER" alongside the pink triangle, a historically significant iconography that pays homage to the state-sanctioned murder of queers originally in Nazi Germany and in later years in the United States for its murder—largely through its willful inaction and neglect—of queers, people of color, and others who died of AIDS. That rally ended with a die-in where protestors held placards noting "SILENCE = VIOLENCE" and "WHITE SILENCE = VIOLENCE."[116] That phraseology supplemented "SILENCE = DEATH," the radical axiom of queer activists connected to ACT UP, or the AIDS Coalition to Unleash Power. Beginning in 1987 and through the group's waning influence after 1992, ACT UP activists employed direct action and civil disobedience to demand not just more AIDS funding and an end to homophobia but also universal health care and the dismantling of racist, classist, and sexist power structures that contributed to the spread of the disease.[117]

Recent antiracist and intersectional grassroots movements that challenge state oppression and violence, particularly BLM, are where the greatest queer radical momentum can be seen today. Rather than interpret the LGBT movements' historical trajectory through its diminishing radical returns, it is important to highlight the organizations and activists who remain committed to dismantling power structures that systemically oppress those most vulnerable and susceptible to state violence. The Audre Lorde Project and the Sylvia Rivera Law Project have also proven successful in affecting community-driven change while maintaining the multi-issue approach to social justice. The UndocuQueer movement of the early 2010s came together because of the U.S. Congress's failure to pass the DREAM Act, or the proposed Development, Relief, and Education for Alien Minors Act, to provide legal immigration relief for thousands of undocumented minors living in the United States. In borrowing tactics from gay and feminist liberation, UndocuQueers come out as both undocumented and queer despite the debilitating fears and dangers lurking through both of those identities that have long forced them to remain "closeted." These activists joined other undocumented DREAMers in applying pressure for immigration reform, including Obama's 2012 directive

"Deferred Action for Childhood Arrivals," or DACA, which provided a discretionary and provisional reprieve from deportation.[118]

This queer politics, outlined so beautifully by activists and scholars such as Cathy J. Cohen, seeks to "challenge and bring together all those deemed marginal and all those committed to liberatory politics."[119] Such change is both possible and necessary. Queer commitment to combating state oppression and empowering people of color and those who are economically disadvantaged—LGBT or otherwise—has certainly lagged at certain points in history even if it has never fully ceased. Since Obama left office in 2017 and surprise Republican candidate Donald J. Trump took office, perhaps we are primed to see a new reunification—if not radical reorientation—of a leftist-liberal divide. Perhaps we will witness a new popular front. As Garza outlines in her hope for the next phase of the BLM movement, through a shared commitment to combating antiBlackness and state violence and centering Blackness and Black-led visions for the future, it is only with solidarity that liberation is possible.[120] If the resurgence of new grassroots and direct-action movements is any indication, and this essay optimistically believes that it may be, many queer activists have taken note and responded to such calls with renewed spirit and fervor.

NOTES

Introduction

1. Leaflet, "Questions and Answers about the NYC Union of Lesbians and Gay Men," Men of All Colors Together Papers, Cornell University Special Collections, box 1, folder 46.

2. Allan Bérubé, "How Gay Stays White and What Kind of White It Stays," in Bérubé, *My Desire for History: Essays in Gay, Community, and Labor History* (Chapel Hill: University of North Carolina Press, 2011), 202–30.

3. Elizabeth A. Armstrong, *Forging Gay Identities: Organizing Sexuality in San Francisco, 1950–1994* (Chicago: University of Chicago Press, 2002), 135.

4. The classic trailblazing text remains John D'Emilio, *Sexual Politics, Sexual Communities: The Making of a Homosexual Minority in the United States, 1940–1970* (Chicago: University of Chicago Press, 1983, 1998). Numerous local studies followed, including George Chauncey, *Gay New York: Gender, Urban Culture, and the Making of the Gay Male World, 1890–1940* (New York: Basic Books, 1994); Nan Alamilla Boyd, *Wide-Open Town: A Queer History of San Francisco to 1965* (Berkeley: University of California Press, 2003); Marc Stein, *City of Sisterly and Brotherly Loves: Lesbian and Gay Philadelphia, 1945–72* (Chicago: University of Chicago Press, 2000). See also Martin Meeker, *Contacts Desired: Gay and Lesbian Communications and Community, 1940s–1970s* (Chicago: University of Chicago Press, 2006).

5. Margot Canaday, *The Straight State: Sexuality and Citizenship in Twentieth-Century America* (Princeton, NJ: Princeton University Press, 2009); Marc Stein, *Sexual Injustice: Supreme Court Decisions from Griswold to Roe* (Chapel Hill: University of North Carolina Press, 2013).

6. See Bruce Miroff, *The Liberals' Moment: The McGovern Insurgency and the Identity Crisis of the Democratic Party* (Lawrence: University Press of Kansas, 2007); Timothy Stanley, *Kennedy vs Carter: The 1980 Battle for the Democratic Party's Soul* (Lawrence: University Press of Kansas, 2010). The existence of gay politics in the GOP has yet to receive significant treatment, the essay in the present volume excepted.

7. See Emily K. Hobson, *Lavender and Red: Liberation and Solidarity in the Gay and Lesbian Left* (Berkeley: University of California Press, 2016).

8. Jennifer Brier, *Infectious Ideas: US Political Responses to the AIDS Crisis* (Chapel Hill: University of North Carolina Press, 2009); Patricia Siplon, *AIDS and the Policy Struggle in the United States* (Washington, DC: Georgetown University Press, 2002).

9. For critiques of the de-radicalization of sexual politics, see Michael Warner, *The Trouble with Normal: Sex, Politics, and the Ethics of Queer Life* (Cambridge, MA: Harvard University Press, 1999); Urvashi Vaid, *Virtual Equality: The Mainstreaming of Gay and Lesbian Liberation* (New York: Anchor, 1995).

10. Joanne Meyerowitz, *How Sex Changed: A History of Transsexuality in the United States* (Cambridge, MA: Harvard University Press, 2002); Susan Stryker, *Transgender History* (Berkeley, CA: Seal, 2008); Lillian Faderman, *Odd Girls and Twilight Lovers: A History of Lesbian Life in Twentieth-Century America* (New York: Columbia University Press, 1991); Dean Spade, *Normal Life: Administrative Violence, Critical Trans Politics, and the Limits of Law* (Durham, NC: Duke University Press, 2015); Aaron Devor and Nicholas Matte, "ONE Inc., and Reed Erickson: The Uneasy Collaboration of Gay and Trans Activism, 1964–2003," in *The Transgender Studies Reader* (New York: Routledge, 2006); David Valentine, *Imagining Transgender: An Ethnography of a Category* (Durham, NC: Duke University Press, 2007).

11. Cathy J. Cohen, *The Boundaries of Blackness: AIDS and the Breakdown of Black Politics* (Chicago: University of Chicago Press, 1999); Martin F. Manalansan IV, *Global Divas: Filipino Gay Men in the Diaspora* (Durham, NC: Duke University Press, 2003); José Esteban Muñoz, *Disidentifications: Queers of Color and the Performance of Politics* (Minneapolis: University of Minnesota Press, 1999); Lawrence LaFountain-Stokes, *Queer Ricans: Cultures and Sexualities in the Diaspora* (Minneapolis: University of Minnesota Press, 2009); Gayatri Gopinath, *Impossible Desires: Queer Diasporas and South Asian Public Cultures* (Durham, NC: Duke University Press, 2005); Kathryn Bond Stockton, *Beautiful Bottom, Beautiful Shame: Where "Black" Meets "Queer"* (Durham, NC: Duke University Press, 2006); Patricia Hill Collins, *Black Sexual Politics: African Americans, Gender, and the New Racism* (New York: Routledge, 2005); Eithne Luibheid and Lionel Cantú, eds., *Queer Migrations: Sexuality, U.S. Citizenship, and Border Crossings* (Minneapolis: University of Minnesota Press, 2005); Horacio N. Roque Ramírez, "'That's My Place!': Negotiating Racial, Sexual, and Gender Politics in San Francisco's Gay Latino Alliance, 1975–1983," *Journal of the History of Sexuality* 12, no. 2 (2003): 224–58.

12. Timothy Stewart-Winter, *Queer Clout: Chicago and the Rise of Gay Politics* (Philadelphia: University of Pennsylvania Press, 2016).

13. Much of the rightward-bound historical literature ignores LGBT politics altogether, and historical overviews of the 1980s tend to relegate the subject to a story of Reagan administration indifference toward the AIDS crisis and the struggle of activists in ACT UP to push for drug treatments. See in particular Jefferson Cowie, *Stayin' Alive: The 1970s and the Last Days of the Working Class* (New York: New Press, 2011); Judith Stein, *Pivotal Decade: How the United States Traded Factories for Finance in the 1970s* (New Haven, CT: Yale University Press, 2011); Bruce Schulman and Julian Zelizer, eds., *Rightward Bound: Making America Conservative in the 1970s* (Cambridge, MA: Harvard University Press, 2008); Robert M. Collins, *Transforming America: Politics and Culture During the Reagan Years* (New York: Columbia University Press, 2009), 133–44; Doug Rossinow, *The Reagan Era: A History of the 1980s* (New York: Columbia University Press, 2015), 130–34, 212–15; Iwan Morgan, *Reagan: American Icon* (London: I. B. Tauris, 2016). There are larger portraits of LGBT politics in the 1980s but in books specifically about LGBT activism or about the American Left, including Hobson, *Lavender and Red*; Howard Brick and Christopher Phelps, *Radicals in America: The U.S. Left Since the Second World War* (Cambridge: Cambridge University Press, 2015), chap. 6; Bradford Martin, *The Other Eighties: A Secret History of America in the Age of Reagan* (New York: Hill and Wang, 2011), chap. 8.

14. One of the most critically important interventions of Canaday's *The Straight State* was placing the power of the state during and after the New Deal to police sexuality at the heart of her analysis. An important recent critique of political attempts to hark back to the New Deal-era solutions to problems of economic inequality that erase the realities of contemporary social

diversity is Namara Smith, "The Woman's Party: On Hillary Clinton and Welfare," *n+1*, no. 26, https://nplusonemag.com/issue-26/the-intellectual-situation/the-womans-party/.

15. Jeffrey Escoffier, "The Political Economy of the Closet: Toward an Economic History of Gay and Lesbian Life before Stonewall," in *American Homo: Community and Perversity*, 65–98 (Berkeley: University of California Press, 1998); Meeker, *Contacts Desired*. A crucial early intervention in the debate over capitalism as an engine of sexual identity formation is John D'Emilio, "Capitalism and Gay Identity," in *Powers of Desire: The Politics of Sexuality*, ed Ann Snitow, Christine Stansell, and Sharan Thompson, 100–113 (New York: Monthly Review Press, 1983).

16. *How to Survive a Plague* (dir. David France, 2013); David France, *How to Survive a Plague: The Inside Story of How Citizens and Science Tamed AIDS* (New York: Picador, 2016).

17. Randy Shilts, *And the Band Played On: Politics, People, and the AIDS Epidemic* (New York: St. Martin's, 1987).

18. Cohen, *The Boundaries of Blackness*; Martin Duberman, *Hold Tight Gently: Michael Callen, Essex Hemphill, and the Battlefield of AIDS* (New York: New Press, 2014); Kevin Mumford, *Not Straight, Not White: Black Gay Men from the March on Washington to the AIDS Crisis* (Chapel Hill: University of North Carolina Press, 2016); Irene Vernon, *Killing Us Quietly: Native Americans and HIV/AIDS* (Lincoln: University of Nebraska Press, 2001); William Hawkeswood, *One of the Children: Black Gay Men in Harlem* (Berkeley: University of California Press, 1997).

19. Canaday, *The Straight State*.

20. France, *How to Survive a Plague*; Brier, *Infectious Ideas*; Tamar Carroll, *Mobilizing New York: AIDS, Antipoverty, and Feminist Activism* (Chapel Hill: University of North Carolina Press, 2015).

21. See "Here Are 17 Major Companies Protesting States' New Anti-Gay Laws," Huffington Post, 30 March 2015, http://www.huffingtonpost.com/2015/03/30/businesses-protest-gay-laws _n_6969854.html; "Corporations No Longer Sit Idly by on Discrimination," *New York Times*, 31 March 2016.

Chapter 1

1. David Scondras, interview by the author, January 6, 2001.

2. The project was eventually scrapped after a large and sustained community protest of which the Black Panther Clinic was a part. See Alan Lupo, Frank Colcord, and Edmund P. Fowler, *Rites of Way: The Politics of Transportation in Boston and the U.S. City* (Boston: Little, Brown, 1971).

3. Scondras interview.

4. The Massachusetts General Laws, chapter 121B, section 4, in 1957, and Chapter 652, section 12, in 1960, granted the BRA authority. For more overview information on the BRA, see http://www.bostonplans.org/about-us/bra-history.

5. Fenway Community Health Center, *Opening New Doors . . . 20 Years of Making a Difference: An Oral History of the Fenway Community Health Center* [booklet], ed. Kirk Kinder (Boston: Fenway Community Health Center, 1991).

6. "Our History," Fenway Community Development Corporation, http://www.fenwaycdc .org/our-history/; *Benjamin Jones v. James T. Lynn*, no. 73-1057, United States Court of Appeals, First Circuit, 1973.

7. Karla Rideout, interview by the author, July 12, 2007.

8. Ibid.

9. Both Looker and Osman have demonstrated similar tactics in other locations in the 1970s, where neighborhoods politicized the notion of local community or neighborhood as a way to both gain political power within and resist power from outside their local context. However, this political model failed to be as effective in the 1980s for a wide array of reasons, including those outlined here in the Fenway clinic's case. For more, see Benjamin Looker, *A Nation of Neighborhood: Imagining Cities, Communities, and Democracy in Postwar America* (Chicago: University of Chicago Press, 2015); Suleiman Osman, "The Decade of the Neighborhood," in *Rightward Bound: Making America Conservative in the 1970s*, ed. Bruce J. Schulman and Julian E. Zelizer (Cambridge, MA: Harvard University Press, 2008).

10. Scondras interview; Fenway Community Health Center, *Opening New Doors*.

11. Fenway Community Health Center, *Opening New Doors*; Scondras interview.

12. Rideout interview; Fenway Community Health Center, *Opening New Doors*.

13. Rideout interview.

14. Ibid.

15. Fenway Community Health Center, *Opening New Doors*.

16. Lenny Alberts, interview by the author, July 11, 2007.

17. Bureau of the Census, *1970 Census of Population and Housing: Census Tracts Boston, Massachusetts Standard Metropolitan Statistical Area* (Washington, DC: U.S. Government Printing Office, 1972). This number is significantly higher when focused solely on children or the elderly. The actual numbers fluctuate slightly depending on how "poverty" is defined and calculated. For a more in-depth explanation, see Jonathan Engel, *Poor People's Medicine: Medicaid and American Charity Care Since 1965* (Durham, NC: Duke University Press, 2006), 5–7; Michael Harrington, *The Other America; Poverty in the United States* (New York: Macmillan, 1962), 180–91.

18. Ira Wyman, "Boston's Symphony Rd. A Medley of Fires, Drugs, Decay, and Fear," *New York Times*, October 25, 1977, 18. In fact, according to the 1970 census, over 55 percent of those living in the Fenway neighborhood were between the ages of eighteen and twenty-four, while that age range made up only 12 percent of the larger Boston population. Over 40 percent of area residents were college students.

19. Alberts interview.

20. Ibid.

21. Scondras interview.

22. There was also a women's health night on Thursdays. The clinic location also served as home to the cooperative day care center and on Saturday mornings provided a venue for the showing of movies for the children of the neighborhood, reflecting the closeness of the community and the centrality of this location in nurturing the strong identity of the community.

23. Theresa Tobin and Stephen Brophy, interview by the author, September 17, 2007.

24. Ibid.

25. Michael Vance, interview by the author, December 13, 2007.

26. Fenway Community Health Center, *Opening New Doors*.

27. Scondras interview.

28. Ibid. This comment, which speaks to a sort of color-blindness within the clinic, comes from a white person. The clinic's focus on serving residents of the immediate neighborhood proved effective, as records show that there was a racially and economically diverse group of clients and volunteers working at the clinic that matched the neighborhood demographics. However, as the clinic changed to become more focused on the gay and lesbian community in the

early 1980s, its outreach to gay and lesbian communities of color was not strong or intentional. This outreach improved dramatically over the late 1980s and the 1990s. I was unable to find any sources that gave specific voice to the perspectives of people of color associated with the clinic during its first decade.

29. Fenway Community Health Center, *Proposal to Otherfund, Inc.*, December 15, 1974, 3–4, Laura McMurry Collection, #17, box 1, series II, folder 16, History Project Archives, Boston.

30. Alberts interview.

31. Fenway Community Health Center, *Opening New Doors*.

32. Alberts interview; Tobin and Brophy interview.

33. Also to a lesser extent, the Fenway clinic offered services for lesbians. Given the limited understanding of the specific needs of the lesbian community, all of the services for lesbians were offered under the auspices of women's health. Tobin and Brophy interview.

34. At the time employers had access to employee medical insurance claims; thus, VD testing and treatment could lead employers to uncover closeted employees.

35. Alberts interview.

36. Vance interview.

37. Scondras interview.

38. Rosemary Stevens, Charles E. Rosenberg, and Lawton R. Burns, *History and Health Policy in the United States: Putting the Past Back In* (New Brunswick, NJ: Rutgers University Press, 2006); Irwin Miller, *American Health Care Blues: Blue Cross, HMOs, and Pragmatic Reform Since 1960* (New Brunswick, NJ: Transaction Publishers, 1996); Bonnie Lefkowitz, *Community Health Centers: A Movement and the People Who Made It Happen* (New Brunswick, NJ: Rutgers University Press, 2007); Alice Sardell, *The U.S. Experiment in Social Medicine: The Community Health Center Program, 1965–1986* (Pittsburgh, PA: University of Pittsburgh Press, 1988); Rosemary Stevens, *The Public-Private Health Care State: Essays on the History of American Health Care Policy* (New Brunswick, NJ: Transaction Publishers, 2007); Marie Gottschalk, *The Shadow Welfare State: Labor, Business, and the Politics of Health-Care in the United States* (Ithaca, NY: ILR Press, 2000).

39. Alberts interview.

40. Fenway Community Health Center, *Opening New Doors*.

41. Tobin and Brophy interview. These hospitals also regularly encouraged students and residents to volunteer their time at the Fenway clinic, as state matching grants rewarded hospitals' service to underserved communities. David Smith and Judith Moore, *Medicaid Politics and Policy, 1965–2007* (New Brunswick, NJ: Transaction Publishers, 2008); Engel, *Poor People's Medicine*; Ken Mayer, interview by the author, July 11, 2007; Alberts interview.

42. Fenway Community Health Center, *Opening New Doors*, 4.

43. Sally Deane, interview by the author, August 2, 2007.

44. Ibid.; Tobin and Brophy interview.

45. Scondras interview.

46. Ibid.

47. Tilo Schabert, *Boston Politics: The Creativity of Power*, De Gruyter Studies on North America 4 (New York: W. de Gruyter, 1989), 118–30. Tobin and Brophy interview; Scondras interview.

48. Scondras interview.

49. Ibid.

50. Ibid.; Deane interview.

51. Alberts interview; Deane interview; Scondras interview; Tobin and Brophy interview.

52. Deane interview; Tobin and Brophy interview.

53. Scondras interview.

54. Fenway Community Health Center, *Opening New Doors*; Vance interview; Deane interview; Rideout interview; Alberts interview; Scondras interview.

55. Scondras interview.

56. Fenway Community Health Center, *Opening New Doors*.

57. Discrepancies exist among those interviewed on just how long the debate over this lasted, ranging from days to nearly a year. A majority of sources claim that the debate took twenty-four hours spaced out over several days. Tobin and Brophy interview; Rideout interview; Scondras interview.

58. Fenway Community Health Center, *Opening New Doors*.

59. Scondras interview; Tobin and Brophy interview; Fenway Community Health Center, *Opening New Doors*.

60. Tobin and Brophy interview.

61. Fenway Community Health Center, *Opening New Doors*.

62. Ibid.

63. Tobin and Brophy interview.

64. "Every Week Events," *Gay Community News*, October 9, 1976.

65. Fenway Community Health Center, *Opening New Doors*.

66. Deane interview; Ron Vachon, "Letter to Walter Lear, August 16, 1978," Walter Lear Personal Collection, Philadelphia.

67. John Graczak, "Investigation of Disease Will Begin in Co-Operative Effort," *Gay Community News*, October 28, 1978.

68. Ibid.

69. Deane interview.

70. Tobin and Brophy interview.

71. Deane interview.

72. Ibid.

73. Fenway Community Health Center, *Opening New Doors*.

74. Tobin and Brophy interview.

75. The extensive "services listing" in *Gay Community News* throughout the 1970s occasionally included gay health clinic information for a clinic in Vermont and another in western Massachusetts, but these listing were very inconsistent. Additionally, mental health services, including rap sessions, were plentiful for both gays and lesbians in Boston, yet physical health services within the city and generally in the region were limited to those offered by the Fenway clinic. Meanwhile, the Gay Health Collective grew to two nights per week starting in late 1976. See "Every Week Events"; Graczak, "Investigation of Disease Will Begin in Co-Operative Effort."

76. Deane interview.

77. Alberts interview.

78. The emergence of gay health services in the absence of gay health activism was not unique to the Fenway clinic, though the Boston clinic appears to be the only one that was not a public health clinic that evolved this way. Public health clinics in San Francisco, New York City, Denver, and Seattle went to great lengths to attract and cater to a gay clientele, gaining reputations locally and nationally as gay health clinics even though they were actually public health

clinics intended for the general population. Michael Brown and Larry Knopp, "The Birth of the (Gay) Clinic," *Health & Place* 28 (2014): 99–108.

79. See Bruce Schulman, *The Seventies: The Great Shift in American Culture, Society, and Politics* (New York: Free Press, 2001); Edward D. Berkowitz, *Something Happened: A Political and Cultural Overview of the Seventies* (New York: Columbia University Press, 2006); Stephanie A. Slocum-Schaffer, *America in the Seventies* (Syracuse, NY: Syracuse University Press, 2003); Sam Binkley, *Getting Loose: Lifestyle Consumption in the 1970s* (Durham, NC: Duke University Press, 2007); David Frum, *How We Got Here: The 70's, the Decade That Brought You Modern Life (for Better or Worse)* (New York, NY: Basic Books, 2000); Andreas Killen, *1973 Nervous Breakdown: Watergate, Warhol, and the Birth of Post-Sixties America* (New York: Bloomsbury, 2006).

80. "The Cambridge Women's Center Newsletter, September/October, 1980," Boston Women's Health Book Collective Collection, box 94, folder 5, Schlesinger Library, Radcliffe Institute, Harvard University, Boston.

81. The incidence of highly resistant strains of VD grew steadily in the waning years of the decade, resulting in new clients and more visits from some existing clients. While doctors at the time were unsure of the spike in these cases, we now know that they were the early stages of what would become the AIDS crisis. Alberts interview.

82. Deane interview.

83. Tom Reeves, "Boston's Boring Whiteness," *Gay Community News*, November 11, 1978.

84. "Violence Against Gays Continues in Boston," *Gay Community News*, October 7, 1978.

85. "Fenway Mugging," *Gay Community News*, July 12, 1973; "Boston Man Paralyzed in Shooting," *Gay Community News*, October 28, 1978.

86. Deane interview.

87. Ibid.; Fenway Community Health Center, *Opening New Doors*.

88. Tobin and Brophy interview. The AIDS crisis that appeared in Boston in the fall of 1981 seems to have either eclipsed or undercut outreach efforts specifically for racial minorities and low-income people as the clinic struggled to meet the needs of a clientele that was both growing and facing much more extreme health issues than the clinic previously managed. However, by the middle of the decade the clinic implemented outreach programs for these communities, many of which continue today.

89. Alberts interview.

90. Jerry Feuer, interview by the author, January 30, 2014.

91. Deane interview; Susan Robinson, interview by the author, August 1, 2007.

92. Catherine Batza, "From Sperm Runners to Sperm Banks: Lesbians, Assisted Conception, and the Fertility Industry, 1971–1983," *Journal of Women's History* 28, no. 2, (Summer 2016).

93. Gay Public Health Workers, "Membership Analysis," in Walter Lear personal collection, Philadelphia, 1978.

Chapter 2

1. Don Kilhefner oral history, interviewed by Ian M. Baldwin, West Hollywood, California, 2 February 2014.

2. See Margot Canaday, *The Straight State: Sexuality and Citizenship in Twentieth-Century America* (Princeton, NJ: Princeton University Press, 2009); Marisa Chappell, *The War on Welfare: Family, Poverty, and Politics in Modern America* (Philadelphia: University of Pennsylvania Press, 2010); Robert Self, *All in the Family: The Realignment of American Democracy Since the 1960s* (New York: Hill and Wang, 2012).

3. For a good overview, see Annelise Orleck and Lisa Gayle Hazirjian, eds., *The War on Poverty: A New Grassroots History, 1964–1980* (Athens: University of Georgia Press, 2011). In Los Angeles, these trends were especially strong. See Robert Bauman, *Race and the War on Poverty: From Watts to East L.A.* (Norman: University of Oklahoma Press, 2008).

4. See Timothy Stewart-Winter, *Queer Clout: Chicago and the Rise of Gay Politics* (Philadelphia: University of Pennsylvania Press, 2016).

5. See Martin Meeker, *Contacts Desired: Gay and Lesbian Communications and Community, 1940s–1970s* (Chicago: University of Chicago Press, 2006).

6. Gail Radford, *Modern Housing for America: Policy Struggles in the New Deal Era* (Chicago: University of Chicago Press, 1996), 166.

7. Clayton Howard, "Building a 'Family Friendly' Metropolis: Sexuality, the State, and Postwar Housing Policy," *Journal of Urban History* 39, no. (2013): 933.

8. Lillian Faderman and Stuart Timmons, *Gay L.A.: A History of Sexual Outlaws, Power Politics, and Lipstick Lesbians* (New York: Basic Books, 2006), 112; C. Todd White, *Pre-Gay L.A.: A Social History of the Movement for Homosexual Rights* (Chicago: University of Illinois Press, 2009), 30.

9. Josh Sides and Douglas Flamming detail the pervasive use of covenants in Los Angeles. See Josh Sides, *City Limits: African American Los Angeles from the Great Depression to the Present* (Berkeley: University of California Press, 2006); Douglas Flamming, *Bound for Freedom: Black Los Angeles in Jim Crow America* (Berkeley: University of California Press, 2006).

10. Knights of the Clock journal, undated, W. Dorr Legg Papers, box 6, folder 26, ONE National Gay and Lesbian Archives, Los Angeles, California.

11. *ONE*, August 1956, Southern California ACLU Collection, box 17, folder 14, Young Research Library, UCLA; *ONE*, December 1956, Southern California ACLU Collection, box 18, folder 1, Young Research Library, UCLA.

12. United States Mission fliers, undated, United States Mission Collection, box 1, folder 3, ONE National Gay and Lesbian Archives, Los Angeles, California.

13. For additional information on homophiles and the War on Poverty in the 1960s, see Martin Meeker, "The Queerly Disadvantaged and the Making of San Francisco's War on Poverty," *Pacific Historical Review* 81, no. 1 (2012): 21–59.

14. R. Fryman to David Glascock and Ed Edelman, 19 August 1977, box 910; J. Johnston to Ed Edelman, 13 January 1975, box 823; R. Greene to Ed Edelman, 8 September 1976, box 822; D. Allen to Ed Edelman, 29 September 1976, box 821; P. Bernerian to Ed Edelman, 9 April 1981, box 821; J. Terrell to Ed Edelman, 4 June 1976, box 826; and J. Sutorius to Ed Edelman, 25 March, 1981, box 825. All in Ed Edelman Collection, Huntington Library, San Marino, California.

15. John D'Emilio, *Sexual Politics, Sexual Communities: The Making of a Homosexual Minority in the United States, 1940–1970* (Chicago: University of Chicago Press, 1983), 141.

16. Kilhefner oral history.

17. Jon Platania oral history, interviewed by Ian M. Baldwin, 3 March 2014, Berkeley, California.

18. I am borrowing the term from Robert Self, who applies it to the Black Power movement in Oakland. Robert Self, *American Babylon: Race and the Struggle for Postwar Oakland* (Princeton, NJ: Princeton University Press, 2003), 218.

19. Don Kilhefner, "Creating a Gay Community: The Hoover Street Commune," *Frontiers*, 1 November 2009, 38.

20. Kilhefner oral history.

21. Los Angeles Women's Liberation Newsletter, September 1970, Joan Arial Collection, box 1, folder 2, University of California–Irvine.

22. Faderman and Timmons, *Gay L.A.*, 185.

23. Dan Berger, ed., *The Hidden 1970s: Histories of Radicalism* (New Brunswick, NJ: Rutgers University Press, 2010), 5.

24. See Donna Murch, *Living for the City: Migration, Education, and the Rise of the Black Panther Party in Oakland, California* (Chapel Hill: University of North Carolina Press, 2010); see Bauman, *Race and the War on Poverty*.

25. For two examples, see Marc Stein, *Rethinking the Gay and Lesbian Movement* (New York: Routledge, 2012); Christina B. Hanhardt, *Safe Space: Gay Neighborhood History and the Politics of Violence* (Durham, NC: Duke University Press, 2013).

26. Kilhefner, "Creating a Gay Community," 38.

27. Platania oral history.

28. Kilhefner oral history.

29. Gay Community Services Center Liberation House intake form, 1973, GCSC Records, box 11, folder 37, ONE National Gay and Lesbian Archives, Los Angeles, California.

30. See Meeker, *Contacts Desired.*

31. Gay Community Services Center general revenue sharing grant, 3 March 1975, GCSC Records, box 11, folder 37, ONE National Gay and Lesbian Archives, Los Angeles, California.

32. Gay Community Services Center Liberation House proposal, January 1972, GCSC Records, box 7, folder 53, ONE National Gay and Lesbian Archives, Los Angeles, California.

33. See especially Natasha Zaretsky, *No Direction Home: The American Family and the Fear of National Decline* (Chapel Hill: University of North Carolina Press, 2007); Heather Murray, *Not in This Family: Gays and the Meaning of Kinship in Postwar North America* (Philadelphia: University of Pennsylvania Press, 2012); J. Brooks Flippen, *Jimmy Carter, the Politics of Family, and the Rise of the Religious Right* (Athens: University of Georgia Press, 2011); Self, *All in the Family*; Daniel Rivers, *Radical Relations: Lesbian Mothers, Gay Fathers, and Their Children* (Chapel Hill: University of North Carolina Press, 2013).

34. Platania oral history.

35. Gay Community Services Center Liberation House intake form, 1973, GCSC Records, box 11, folder 37, ONE National Gay and Lesbian Archives, Los Angeles, California.

36. Platania oral history.

37. Gay Community Services Center Liberation House intake form, 1973, GCSC Records, box 11, folder 37, ONE National Gay and Lesbian Archives, Los Angeles, California.

38. Gay Community Services Center general revenue sharing grant, 14 March 1975, GCSC Records, box 11, folder 34, ONE National Gay and Lesbian Archives, Los Angeles, California.

39. Kilhefner oral history.

40. Annelise Orleck, in Annelise Orleck and Lisa Gayle Hazirjian, eds., *The War on Poverty: A New Grassroots History, 1964–1980* (Athens: University of Georgia Press, 2011), 7–9.

41. See Annelise Orleck, *Storming Caesar's Palace: How Black Mothers Fought Their Own War on Poverty* (Boston: Beacon, 2005); Donna Murch, *Living for the City: Migration, Education, and the Rise of the Black Panther Party in Oakland, California* (Chapel Hill: University of North Carolina Press, 2010).

42. See Jonathan Bell, "'To Strive for Economic and Social Justice': Welfare, Sexuality, and Liberal Politics in San Francisco in the 1960s," *Journal of Policy History* 22, no. 2 (2010); Martin

Meeker, "The Queerly Disadvantaged and the Making of San Francisco's War on Poverty," *Pacific Historical Review* 81, no. 1 (2012); Hanhardt, *Safe Space*.

43. See Alice O'Connor, *Poverty Knowledge: Social Science, Social Policy, and the Poor in Twentieth-Century U.S. History* (Princeton, NJ: Princeton University Press, 2002).

44. Meeker, "The Queerly Disadvantaged," 27.

45. Gay Community Services Center founding document, July 1971, courtesy of Jon Platania.

46. Timothy Stewart-Winter, *Queer Clout: Chicago and the Rise of Gay Politics* (Philadelphia: University of Pennsylvania Press, 2016), 1.

47. Jim Gilson oral history, interviewed by Ian M. Baldwin, Los Angeles, California, 20 December 2013.

48. Jonathan Bell, *California Crucible: The Forging of Modern American Liberalism* (Philadelphia: University of Pennsylvania Press, 2012), 264.

49. Ed Edelman campaign brochures, 1974, Ed Edelman Subject File, folder 2, ONE National Gay and Lesbian Archives, Los Angeles, California.

50. "L.A. Gays Win the EDE," *The Advocate*, 4 December 1974, Ed Edelman Subject File, folder 2, ONE National Gay and Lesbian Archives, Los Angeles, California.

51. Ed Edelman to David Glascock, 1976, Ed Edelman Collection, box 909, folder 7, Huntington Library, San Marino, California.

52. David Glascock to Bill C., 2 December 1977, Ed Edelman Collection, box 909, folder 2, Huntington Library, San Marino, California.

53. Don Kilhefner to David Glascock, 12 July 1976, GCSC Records, box 15, folder 91, ONE National Gay and Lesbian Archives, Los Angeles, California.

54. See Tom Sitton, *The Courthouse Crowd: Los Angeles County Government, 1850–1950* (Los Angeles: Historical Society of Southern California, 2013).

55. Edward D. Berkowitz, *Something Happened: A Political and Cultural Overview of the Seventies* (New York: Columbia University Press, 2006), 123. See also Judith Stein, *Pivotal Decade: How the United States Traded Factories for Finance in the Seventies* (New Haven, CT: Yale University Press, 2010), 179.

56. Bauman, *Race and the War on Poverty*, 124–25.

57. Kilhefner oral history.

58. Bauman, *Race and the War on Poverty*, 66–67.

59. Clayton Wells to Los Angeles City Council, 29 August 1977, Stonewall Democratic Club Records, box 1, folder 25, ONE National Lesbian and Gay Archives, University of Southern California.

60. Kilhefner oral history.

61. Gay Community Services Center general revenue sharing grant, 14 March 1975, GCSC Records, box 11, folder 34, ONE National Gay and Lesbian Archives, Los Angeles, California.

62. Gay Community Services Center to Ed Edelman, 28 October 1976, GCSC Records, box 15, folder 91, ONE National Gay and Lesbian Archives, Los Angeles, California; aide to Ed Edelman, 7 June 1977, GCSC Records, box 248, folder 1, ONE National Gay and Lesbian Archives, Los Angeles, California.

63. Don Kilhefner to Ed Edelman, 10 August 1976, GCSC Records, box 15, folder 91, ONE National Gay and Lesbian Archives, Los Angeles, California.

64. L. Reh to Sheldon Andelson, 20 October 1975, box 10, folder 24; Ed Edelman to Gay Community Services Center, 19 November 1975, box 10, folder 24; Don Kilhefner to Peggy Stevenson, 24 November 1975, box 10, folder 24; Peggy Stevenson to Arthur Dvorin, 11 December

1975, box 10, folder 24. All in GCSC Records, ONE National Gay and Lesbian Archives, Los Angeles, California.

65. Don Kilhefner to Tom Bradley, 30 July 1976, GCSC Records, box 6, folder 6, ONE National Gay and Lesbian Archives, Los Angeles, California.

66. Don Kilhefner to Arthur Snyder, 19 October 1976, GCSC Records, box 6, folder 6, ONE National Gay and Lesbian Archives, Los Angeles, California.

67. David Glascock to Ed Edelman, 26 September 1976, Ed Edelman Collection, box 909, folder 3, Huntington Library, San Marino, California.

68. Richard Llewellyn oral history, interviewed by Ian M. Baldwin, Los Angeles, California, 25 April 2014.

69. David Glascock to Ed Edelman, 15 June 1976, Ed Edelman Collection, box 248, folder 1, Huntington Library, San Marino, California.

70. Aide to Ed Edelman, 28 June 1977, Ed Edelman Collection, box 909, folder 2, Huntington Library, San Marino, California.

71. Kilhefner oral history; Faderman and Timmons, *Gay L.A.*, 203.

72. See Susan Hartmann, "Feminism, Public Policy, and the Carter Administration," in *The Carter Presidency: Policy Choices in the Post-New Deal Era*, ed. Gary Fink and Hugh Graham (Lawrence: University Press of Kansas, 1998); Chappell, *The War on Welfare*.

73. Art Seidenbaum to Gay Community Services Center, 18 July 1973, box 7, folder 59; J. L. Rowe to Morris Kight, 17 July 1973, box 7, folder 57; L. Westley to Morris Kight, 20 July 1973, box 7, folder 57; Burt Pines to the Gay Community Services Center, 18 July 1973, box 7, folder 59; East-Los Chicano Education Training and Research Organization to Gay Community Services Center, 22 February 1974, box 7, folder 59; C. Makins to the Gay Community Services Center, 27 February 1974, box 7, folder 59; Asian Women's Center to Gay Community Services Center, 25 February 1974, box 7, folder 59. All in GCSC Records, ONE National Gay and Lesbian Archives, Los Angeles, California.

74. Cartoon, *The Advocate*, 22 January 1976, Stonewall Democratic Club Records, box 1, folder 3, ONE National Lesbian and Gay Archives, University of Southern California.

75. Stonewall Democratic Club bylaws, March 1976, Stonewall Democratic Club Records, box 1, folder 1, ONE National Lesbian and Gay Archives, University of Southern California.

76. Stonewall Democratic Club Gay Rights Plank, 1975, California Democratic Council Records, box 24, folder 37, Southern California Library for Social Research.

77. Sabrina Schiller campaign brochure, 1976, Stonewall Democratic Club Records, box 1, folder 8, ONE National Lesbian and Gay Archives, University of Southern California; Tom Hayden for U.S. Senate brochure, 1976, Stonewall Democratic Club Records, box 1, folder 20, ONE National Lesbian and Gay Archives, University of Southern California.

78. Clayton Wells to Ed Edelman, 21 March 1978, Stonewall Democratic Club Records, box 2, folder 1, ONE National Lesbian and Gay Archives, University of Southern California.

79. See Bell, *California Crucible*.

80. Stonewall Democratic Club memo, 1976, Stonewall Democratic Club Records, box 1, folder 20, ONE National Lesbian and Gay Archives, University of Southern California.

81. California Democratic Caucus pamphlet, 1976, California Democratic Council Records, box 17, folder 2, Southern California Library for Social Research.

82. Stonewall Democratic Club Tenth Anniversary letter, 1 May 1985, Stonewall Democratic Club Records, box 2, folder 9, ONE National Lesbian and Gay Archives, University of Southern California.

83. "Gay Rights Movement Gains Political Momentum in L.A.," *Los Angeles Times*, 19 March 1978, C1.

84. Letters urging adoption of Gay Rights Plank, 1976, Stonewall Democratic Club Records, box 1, folder 20, ONE National Lesbian and Gay Archives, University of Southern California.

85. See Stein, *Pivotal Decade*.

86. See Randall Balmer, *Redeemer: The Life of Jimmy* Carter (New York: Basic Books, 2014).

87. Flippen, *Jimmy Carter*, 83–84; Dudley Clendinen and Adam Nagourney, *Out for Good: The Struggle to Build a Gay Rights Movement in America* (New York: Simon and Schuster, 1999), 272–73.

88. Robert Rygor, "A Message to the Gay Community," 1976, Stonewall Democratic Club Records, box 1, folder 21, ONE National Lesbian and Gay Archives, University of Southern California.

89. David Moran to Morris Kight, 4 March 1976, Stonewall Democratic Club Records, box 1, folder 20, ONE National Lesbian and Gay Archives, University of Southern California.

90. Robert S. Havely to Clayton Wells and Morris Kight, 31 October 1976, Stonewall Democratic Club Records, box 1, folder 21, ONE National Lesbian and Gay Archives, University of Southern California.

91. Stonewall Democratic Club Gay Rights Plank, 1975, California Democratic Council Records, box 24, folder 37, Southern California Library for Social Research.

92. Lonnie Bunch, "A Page from Our American Story: A Higher Standard; Patricia Roberts Harris," Smithsonian Institution, http://go.si.edu/site/MessageViewer?em_id=17367.0.

93. Hartmann, "Feminism, Public Policy, and the Carter Administration," 235.

94. Flippen, *Jimmy Carter*, 119, 301.

95. Barbara Katz, "Rules Say Gay Couple Can Be a Public-Housing Family," *New Hampshire Observer*, 20 June 1977, Housing subject file, folder 1, ONE National Lesbian and Gay Archives, University of Southern California.

96. See especially Natasha Zaretsky, *No Direction Home: The American Family and the Fear of National Decline* (Chapel Hill: University of North Carolina Press, 2007); Murray, *Not in This Family*; Flippen, *Jimmy Carter*; Self, *All in the Family*.

97. "H.U.D. Will Accept Unmarried Couples for Public Housing," *New York Times*, 29 May 1977, 22.

98. Flippen, *Jimmy Carter*, 144–45.

99. Katz, "Rules Say Gay Couple Can Be a Public-Housing Family"; "Public Housing for Gay Couples," *The Advocate*, 27 July 1977; "House Bans Housing Aid for Unmarrieds," *San Francisco Examiner*, 16 June 1977; "Senate Bill on Housing Skips the Gay Issue," *San Francisco Chronicle*, 25 June 1977; "No Gay-Rights Debate—$67 Billion Okd for Housing," *Chicago Tribune*, 25 June 1977. All in Housing subject file, folder 1, ONE National Lesbian and Gay Archives, University of Southern California.

100. See Thomas Sugrue, "Carter's Urban Policy Crisis," in *The Carter Presidency: Policy Choices*, ed. Gary M. Fink and Hugh Davis Graham (Lawrence: University of Kansas Press, 1998).

101. Flippen, *Jimmy Carter*, 103, 163; Chappell, *The War on Welfare*, 164.

102. Self, *All in the Family*, 336.

103. "Carter Opens Conference on Families," *Washington Post*, 6 June 1980, A2.

104. "Conference on Families Produces a 57-Point Plan," *New York Times*, 9 June 1980, C16.

105. Flippen, *Jimmy Carter*, 270–71.

106. "Conference on Families Endorses ERA," *Los Angeles Times*, 13 July 1980, A3.

107. Flippen, *Jimmy Carter*, 172, 220.

108. See Elizabeth Hinton, *From the War on Poverty to the War on Crime: The Making of Mass Incarceration in America* (Cambridge, MA: Harvard University Press, 2016); Julilly Kohler-Hausmann, *Getting Tough: Welfare and Imprisonment in 1970s America* (Princeton, NJ: Princeton University Press, 2017); Max Felker-Kantor, "Liberal Law-and-Order: Tom Bradley, the LAPD, and the Politics of Police Reform in Los Angeles," *Journal of Urban History* (forthcoming).

Chapter 3

1. Jeffrey Levi to Michele Wilson, 8 April 1986, National Gay and Lesbian Task Force Records, box 10, folder 24, Cornell University Special Collections.

2. Justin Raimondo, "In Praise of Outlaws: Rebuilding Gay Liberation," Students for a Libertarian Society pamphlet, Sean Little Papers, box 1, Electoral Politics folder, GLBT Historical Society, San Francisco.

3. See Emily K. Hobson, *Lavender and Red: Liberation and Solidarity on the Gay and Lesbian Left* (Berkeley: University of California Press, 2016). Much of the Radical Left press in the United States in the 1970s was highly critical of the state as currently constituted. See Socialist Newspapers Collection, Stonewall Library, Fort Lauderdale.

4. Margot Canaday, *The Straight State: Sexuality and Citizenship in Twentieth-Century America* (Princeton, NJ: Princeton University Press, 2009); Marc Stein, *Sexual Injustice: Supreme Court Decisions from Griswold to Roe* (Chapel Hill: University of North Carolina Press, 2010); Siobhan Somerville, "Queer *Loving*," *GLQ: A Journal of Lesbian and Gay Studies* 11, no. 3 (2005): 335–70; David K. Johnson, *The Lavender Scare: The Cold War Persecution of Gays and Lesbians in the Federal Government* (Chicago: University of Chicago Press, 2004).

5. In this essay I use a historical methodology and time frame to engage with the arguments of Cathy Cohen in her groundbreaking "Punks, Bulldaggers, and Welfare Queens: The Radical Potential of Queer Politics?," *GLQ* 3 (1997): 437–65.

6. Claire Bond Potter, "Paths to Political Citizenship: Gay Rights, Feminism, and the Carter Presidency," *Journal of Policy History* 24, no. 1 (2012): 95–114; William B. Turner, "Lesbian/Gay Rights and Immigration Policy: Lobbying to End the Medical Model," *Journal of Policy History* 7, no. 2 (1995): 208–25; Steven Epstein, "Gay Politics, Ethnic Identity: The Limits of Social Constructionism," *Socialist Review* 17, no. 2 (1987): 9–54.

7. See Elizabeth Armstrong, *Forging Gay Identities: Organizing Sexuality in San Francisco, 1950–1994* (Chicago: University of Chicago Press, 2002); Joshua Gamson, "Must Identity Movements Self-Destruct? A Queer Dilemma," *Social Problems* 42, no. 3 (August 1995): 390–407; Terrence Kissack, "Freaking Fag Revolutionaries: New York's Gay Liberation Front, 1969–1971," *Radical History Review* 62 (1995): 104–34. Martin Meeker argues that earlier homophile activism in the 1950s and 1960s also manipulated a politics of respectability in order to gain far more political traction than it otherwise would have achieved. See Martin Meeker, "Behind the Mask of Respectability: Reconsidering the Mattachine Society and Male Homophile Practice, 1950s and 1960s," *Journal of the History of Sexuality* 10, no. 1 (2001): 78–116.

8. See John D'Emilio, "Organizational Tales: Interpreting the NGLTF Story," in *Creating Change: Sexuality, Public Policy, and Civil Rights*, ed. John D'Emilio, William B. Turner, and Urvashi Vaid, 469–86 (New York: St. Martin's, 2000).

9. See Nan Alamilla Boyd, *Wide Open Town: A History of Queer San Francisco to 1965* (Berkeley: University of California Press, 2003).

10. SIR summary of activity, May 1970, Phyllis Lyon and Del Martin Papers, box 19, folder 7, GLBT Historical Society, San Francisco.

11. Outline of powers of responsibilities of SIR board committees, Don Lucas Papers, box 11, folder 2, GLBT Historical Society, San Francisco.

12. SIR Statement of Purpose, 1965, Don Lucas Papers, box 11, folder 2, GLBT Historical Society, San Francisco.

13. A significant community of mostly white preoperative male-to-female transsexuals had made the Tenderloin their home by the mid-1960s, forming a group called COG (Conversion Our Goal or Change Our Goal). See Joanne Meyerowitz, *How Sex Changed: A History of Transsexuality in the United States* (Cambridge, MA: Harvard University Press, 2002), 230–32.

14. Edward Hansen et al., "The White Ghetto: Youth and Young Adults in the Tenderloin Area of Downtown San Francisco," Don Lucas Papers, box 15, folder 5, GLBT Historical Society, San Francisco.

15. Mattachine SF proposal for confronting the Tenderloin problem, 1966, Don Lucas Papers, box 15, folder 1, GLBT Historical Society, San Francisco.

16. Gay Health Project document, n.d., Gay Health Project (1975) information packet, GLBT Historical Society, San Francisco.

17. San Francisco Department of Health Weekly Bulletin, 4 August 1975, Gay Health Project packet.

18. NY State Dept of Health, "Gay Men and STDs," Stonewall Center of the University of Massachusetts at Amherst Papers, box 6, folder 55, UMass Amherst Special Collections.

19. FAN Free Clinic leaflet, National Lesbian and Gay Health Foundation Papers, box 13, folder 10, Cornell University Special Collections.

20. Grant bid by Gay Health Collective of Boston to Medical Foundation Inc, 1 April 1977, box 2, folder 60, National Lesbian and Gay Health Foundation Records, Cornell University.

21. Gay Health Inc. grant bid for Christopher Street Multiservices Center, National Lesbian and Gay Health Foundation Records, box 2, folder 60, Cornell University.

22. Sherron Mills form letter, n.d. (late 1970s), Phyllis Lyon and Del Martin Papers, box 91, folder 5, GLBT Historical Society, San Francisco.

23. "A History of Women's Alternative Health Services Inc.," Phyllis Lyon and Del Martin Papers, box 91, folder 5, GLBT Historical Society.

24. "Women and Health Care," statement of Women's Health Abortion Project, New York, September 1969, Lesbians and AIDS/HIV file, Sexual Minorities Archive.

25. "FTM 101—The Invisible Transsexual," Transgender Subject files, FTM and Health folder, Sexual Minorities Archive.

26. Erickson Educational Foundation list of clinics and private surgeons, 26 April 1972, David Kessler—Community United Against Violence Records, Transsexualism folder, GLBT Historical Society, San Francisco. For more information on the EEF, see Meyerowitz, *How Sex Changed*, chap. 4.

27. EEF booklet "Guidelines for transsexuals," July 1974, Kessler Records, Transsexualism folder, GLBT Historical Society, San Francisco.

28. "US May Let Medicare Pay for Sex Changes," *Fort Lauderdale News*, 12 April 1978; "Healthy People 2020—Transgender Health Fact Sheet," Trans and Health file, Sexual Minorities Archive.

29. See Potter, "Paths to Political Citizenship."

30. Bruce Voeller and Jean O'Leary to Jimmy Carter, 18 August 1976, Margaret Constanza Subject Files, box 4, folder 14, Jimmy Carter Library, Atlanta.

31. Voeller and O'Leary to Margaret Constanza, 3 May 1976, Margaret Constanza Subject Files, box 4, folder 14, Jimmy Carter Library.

32. "As the Hot Air Trial Balloons Soar, Let's Look at Where the Prexy Hopefuls Stand on Gay Rights," *The Advocate*, 10 March 1976; Jimmy Carter to Mark Segal of GAA Philadelphia, 3 September 1975, Records of the 1976 Campaign Committee to Elect Jimmy Carter, box 18, Gay Rights 1976 file, Jimmy Carter Library. The six presidential hopefuls who expressed some support for gay rights to *The Advocate* were Birch Bayh, Jimmy Carter, Morris Udall, Fred Harris, Milton Shapp, and Sargent Shriver. George Wallace did not respond to the request for a statement, and Henry Jackson had gone on record in a 1975 interview as being strongly opposed to homosexuality.

33. "It's Time," special issue newsletter of the NGTF, 1976, Constanza files, box 4, folder 18, Jimmy Carter Library.

34. Randy Shilts, "The Gay Presence at the Democratic Convention," *The Advocate*, 12 August 1976, Robert Malson files, box 7, folder 7, Jimmy Carter Library.

35. Draft advert "Carter-Mondale-Moynihan—They'll Help You Make Ends Meet Again," Moynihan Papers, box 490, folder 3, Library of Congress.

36. "Jobs, Not Welfare," campaign leaflet for Carter-Mondale-Moynihan, Moynihan Papers, box 490, folder 18, Library of Congress.

37. Moynihan for Senate labor speech, 12 August 1976, Moynihan Papers, box 491, folder 3, Library of Congress. The speech was not in the end delivered.

38. Moynihan's campaign launch quoted in a memorandum from Bill Kristol to Bill Hannay, 23 July 1976, "a summary refutation of the most common charges against Daniel P. Moynihan," Moynihan Papers, box 490, folder 5, Library of Congress.

39. See Robert O. Self, *All in the Family: The Realignment of American Democracy Since the 1960s* (New York: Hill and Wang, 2012). See also Molly Michelmore, *Tax and Spend: The Welfare State, Tax Politics, and the Limits of American Liberalism* (Philadelphia: University of Pennsylvania Press, 2012).

40. Moynihan to Livingston, 12 October 1976, Moynihan Papers, box 820, folder 12, Library of Congress.

41. Goodstein quoted in Robert Chesley, "Goodstein Faces 'Unkempt, Unemployable, Neurotics,'" *Gay Community News* 4, no. 36 (3 March 1977), Constanza files, box 4, folder 17, Jimmy Carter Library.

42. Nancy Friedman, "Gay Power: From Closet to Voting Booth," *California Journal*, October 1975, 341–44; Goodstein quoted in Robert Chesley, "Goodstein Faces 'Unkempt, Unemployable, Neurotics," *Gay Community News* 4, no. 36 (3 March 1977), Constanza files, box 4, folder 17, Jimmy Carter Library.

43. Randy Shilts, *The Mayor of Castro Street: The Life and Times of Harvey Milk* (New York: Griffin, 2008), 156.

44. Voeller note to Constanza with *Gay Community News* clipping, 3 March 1977, Constanza files, box 4, folder 17, Jimmy Carter Library.

45. Potter, "Paths to Political Citizenship," 98.

46. Constanza memo, undated, on 1976 Democratic platform, Constanza files, box 4, folder 14, Jimmy Carter Library.

47. "1976 Democratic Party Platform," American Presidency Project, July 12, 1976, http://www.presidency.ucsb.edu/ws/index.php?pid=29606.

48. Jimmy Carter, *White House Diary* (New York: Farrar, Straus & Giroux, 2010), 127.

49. Memorandum, Marilyn Haft to Margaret Constanza, 25 March 1977, "Meeting with the National Gay Task Force 26 March 1977," Constanza files, box 5, folder 16, Jimmy Carter Library.

50. Profile of George Raya—"Not the typical lobbyist"—in Nancy Friedman, "From Closet to Voting Booth," *California Journal*, October 1975, 344.

51. Paul Gebhard of Institute of Sex Research to NGTF, 18 March 1977; Clark Taylor of UC Berkeley to George Raya, 14 March 1977; Dorrwin Jones of Meals on Wheels to Raya, 10 March 1977; Robert Hewes, Director GMVDC to NGTF, 4 March 1977; statement from Mark Weisman of Gay Health Project, San Francisco, Constanza files, box 28, folder 8, Jimmy Carter Library.

52. Mark Weisman statement, Constanza files, box 28, folder 8, Jimmy Carter Library.

53. Robert Hewes to NGTF, 4 March 1977, Constanza files, box 28, folder 8, Jimmy Carter Library.

54. George Raya report on Health, Education, and Welfare for the 26 March 1977 White House meeting, Constanza files, box 28, folder 8, Jimmy Carter Library.

55. Bob Malson notes of the NGTF meeting, 26 March 1977, Domestic Policy Staff, Bob Malson files, box 7, folder 6, Jimmy Carter Library.

56. Constanza to Carter, 8 April 1977, "Report on the March 26 1977 Meeting with the National Gay Task Force," Constanza files, box 7, folder 6, Jimmy Carter Library.

57. "Carter on National Health Insurance," Domestic Policy Staff, Jim Morgan and Joseph Onek subject files, box 31, Health Services Administration file, Jimmy Carter Library; Jim McIntyre to Carter, 6 April 1978 re meeting with Senator Kennedy and organized labor, Morgan/Onek files, box 46, National Health Insurance—agency memorandums [2] folder, Jimmy Carter Library.

58. Charlie Schultze of the Council of Economic Advisers to Health Secretary Joseph Califano, 2 May 1978, Morgan/Onek files, box 46 NHI agency memorandums [1] folder, Jimmy Carter Library. The different federal departments under Carter had widely divergent views of National Health Insurance, with the Department of Labor and HEW pushing the idea and the Office of Management and Budget, the Department of Commerce, and the Council of Economic Advisers strongly against. See letters from these departments in the same folder.

59. Califano speech to Consumer Federation of America, 9 February 1979, Landon Butler Subject files, box 101, Hospital cost containment task force 1979 folder, Jimmy Carter Library.

60. Larry Gage to Dick Moe, "Recruiting business support for hospital cost containment," 27 February 1979, Office of Chief of Staff files, box 175, folder 11, Jimmy Carter Library.

61. Bruce Mansdorf to Bob Berenson, "Presidential decisions to promote more vigorous market forces and expanded individual choice," 29 January 1980, Domestic Policy Staff, Robert Berenson files, box 12, folder 1, Jimmy Carter Library.

62. For an example of NGTF lobbying, see Jean O'Leary and Bruce Voeller to Carter, 26 December 1978, annoyed at not being invited to a White House conference on human rights, Office of Anne Wexler files, box 200, gay rights file, Jimmy Carter Library; Allison Thomas to Mike Chanin, 11 February 1980: "Gays across the country are also feeling neglected. . . . This feeling of neglect extends into the area of White House social events." Anne Wexler subject files, box 34, NGTF folder, Jimmy Carter Library.

63. Allison Thomas to Mike Chanin, 11 February 1980, Anne Wexler subject files, box 34, NGTF folder, Jimmy Carter Library; Marilyn Haft to Constanza, 14 October 1977 re US Commission on Civil Rights meeting with National Gay Task Force, October 12 1977, Constanza files, box 22, folder 16, Jimmy Carter Library; Allison Thomas to Anne Wexler, 18 December 1979, re meeting with NGTF 19 December, Robert Malson files, box 8, folder 2, Jimmy Carter Library.

64. Bob Malson to Administration staff, 20 May 1980, re talking points on gay issues, Assistant to the President on Women's Affairs files, box 68, gay issues folder, Jimmy Carter Library.

65. NGTF press release, 21 December 1979, "White House receives gay rights petition, discusses Presidential Executive Order," Bob Malson files, box 8, folder 2, Jimmy Carter Library.

66. Notes of White House staff meeting with Allison Thomas, Bob Malson, Diana Rock, Mike Chanin, 10 December 1979, Malson files, box 7, folder 1, Jimmy Carter Library. The final State of the Union address made no mention of civil rights beyond the single sentence "We will never abandon our struggle for a just and decent society here at home." See "The State of the Union Address Delivered Before a Joint Session of the Congress, January 23, 1980," The American Presidency Project, https://www.presidency.ucsb.edu/documents/the-state-the-union-address -delivered-before-joint-session-the-congress.

67. "Gay rights issues at the federal level," National Convention Project, Malson files, box 7, folder 4, Jimmy Carter Library.

68. Allison Thomas to Anne Wexler, 13 May 1980, re meetings in California with leaders of the gay community, Office of Congressional Liaison files, box 177, gay rights California folder, Jimmy Carter Library.

69. Anne Wexler to Chip Bishop, re VP drop-by at ACLU dinner, 15 May 1980, Office of Congressional Liaison files, box 177, gay rights California folder, Jimmy Carter Library.

70. Toklas and Milk Clubs mailer, 1980, Office of Congressional liaison files, box 177, Gay Rights California folder, Jimmy Carter Library.

71. NGTF press release, 6 March 1980, "Carter appeals for gay support," Bob Malson files, box 7, folder 9, Jimmy Carter Library.

72. Thomas Bastow to Martin Franks, 14 April 1980, Bob Malson files, box 7, folder 10, Jimmy Carter Library; "Reagan for President?," Gay News, 21 March–3 April 1980, Bob Malson files, box 7, folder 10, Jimmy Carter Library.

73. Tom Bastow to Martin Franks, n.d., "Impact of the gay vote on the Presidential election in November," Malson files, box 7, folder 4, Jimmy Carter Library.

74. Overview of NGTF AIDS Program, NGLTF Records, box 117, folder 5, Jimmy Carter Library.

75. Walter Lear form letter, n.d., Gay Health Project information packet, GLBT Historical Society, San Francisco.

76. ACT UP Treatment and Data meeting, 18 March 1991, ACT UP Boston Records, box 4, folder 34, Northeastern University, Boston.

77. Robert Maddox, Carter's Assistant for Religious Liaison, to Mark Paul Pierpoint, 2 September 1980, Anne Wexler files, box 105, folder 12, Jimmy Carter Library.

Chapter 4

1. "Chicago Police Chief Names Liaison to Gay Community," The Advocate, March 6, 1984; Raymond Risley to William Schneider, June 10, 1987, in Police-Community folder, Illinois Lesbian/Gay Task Force Records, Gerber/Hart Library and Archives; CPD Department Special Order on Acquired Immune Deficiency Syndrome, January 11, 1984, and David G. Ostrow, MD, to Fred Rice, January 17, 1984, in Police/Rice folder, both in box 4, Illinois Lesbian/Gay Task Force Records, Gerber/Hart Library and Archives.

2. Mary Patten, "The Thrill Is Gone: An ACT UP Post-Mortem (Confessions of a Former AIDS Activist)," in The Passionate Camera: Photography and Bodies of Desire, ed. Deborah Bright, (New York: Routledge, 1998), 392; Charles Mount, "AIDS Ward Is Opened to Women," Chicago Tribune, April 27, 1990.

3. Guenter B. Risse, *Mending Bodies, Saving Souls: A History of Hospitals* (New York: Oxford University Press, 1999), 660.

4. Randy Shilts, *And the Band Played On: Politics, People, and the AIDS Epidemic* (New York: St. Martin's, 1987).

5. Jennifer Brier, *Infectious Ideas: U.S. Political Responses to the AIDS Crisis* (Chapel Hill: University of North Carolina Press, 2009).

6. Cathy J. Cohen, *The Boundaries of Blackness: AIDS and the Breakdown of Black Politics* (Chicago: University of Chicago Press, 1999); Deborah B. Gould, *Moving Politics: Emotion and ACT UP's Fight Against AIDS* (Chicago: University of Chicago Press, 2009). Important books by nonhistorians also include Anthony M. Petro, *After the Wrath of God: AIDS, Sexuality, and American Religion* (New York: Oxford University Press, 2015); Dagmawi Woubshet, *The Calendar of Loss: Race, Sexuality, and Mourning in the Early Era of AIDS* (Baltimore: Johns Hopkins University Press, 2015).

7. Phil Tiemeyer, *Plane Queer: Labor, Sexuality, and AIDS in the History of Male Flight Attendants* (Berkeley: University of California Press, 2013). See also Richard A. McKay, *Patient Zero and the Making of the AIDS Epidemic* (Chicago: University of Chicago Press, 2017).

8. Kevin J. Mumford, *Not Straight, Not White: Black Gay Men from the March on Washington to the AIDS Crisis* (Chapel Hill: University of North Carolina Press, 2016); see also Martin Duberman, *Hold Tight Gently: Michael Callen, Essex Hemphill, and the Battlefield of AIDS* (New York: New Press, 2014).

9. Katie Batza, *Before AIDS: Gay Health Politics in the 1970s* (Philadelphia: University of Pennsylvania Press, 2018).

10. See Brier, *Infectious Ideas*.

11. There is strikingly little scholarship on the state and local policy response, but see Ronald Bayer, *Private Acts, Social Consequences: AIDS and the Politics of Public Health* (New York: Free Press, 1989); Daniel M. Fox, "The Politics of HIV Infection: 1989–1990 as Years of Change," in *AIDS: The Making of a Chronic Disease*, ed. Elizabeth Fee and Daniel M. Fox, 125–43 (Berkeley: University of California Press, 1992); Jennifer Brier, "'Save Our Kids, Keep AIDS Out': Anti-AIDS Activism and the Legacy of Community Control in Queens, New York," *Journal of Social History* 39, no. 4 (Summer 2006): 965–87.

12. Tracy Baim, "Cook County Hospital's Sable/Sherer Clinic Offers Treatment, Support for AIDS Patients," *GayLife*, August 30, 1984; John J. Accrocco, "Sable and Sherer: Two Doctors That Changed AIDS in Chicago," *Windy City Times*, February 15, 2012.

13. Wes Smith, "Underclass Falling Victim to AIDS Siege," *Chicago Tribune*, February 17, 1987. See also Allan Bérubé, "How Gay Stays White and What Kind of White It Stays," in *Privilege: A Reader*, ed. Michael Kimmel and Abby L. Ferber (Boulder, CO: Westview, 2003): 253–83.

14. Rex Wockner, "C-FAR Disrupts LyphoMed Annual Meeting," *New York Native*, June 6, 1988. In October 1988, C-FAR changed its name to ACT UP/Chicago, adopting the name coined by New York activists the previous year—AIDS Coalition to Unleash Power—and joining what was becoming a nationwide movement that had gained momentum from the second March on Washington for Lesbian and Gay Rights in the fall of 1987. Gould, *Moving Politics*, 129, 221–22.

15. Jack Houston, "Suit Challenges CTA for Barring AIDS Ad," *Chicago Tribune*, September 14, 1989; Rex Wockner, "'Significant' Victories in Daley Battle," *Outlines*, December 1989.

16. Last will and testament of Roland Pena, May 13, 1992, box 1, Roland Pena Papers, Gerber/Hart Library and Archives, Chicago, Illinois.

17. "Statistics 'AIDS' Cases Chicago," Community Services Series, Central Office Records, box 24, folder 8, Harold Washington Archives and Collections, Chicago Public Library.

18. Sydney Lewis, *Hospital: An Oral History of Cook County Hospital* (New York: New Press, 1994), 28–29. As the anthropologist Carol Stack observed in her landmark ethnography of a poor urban black community, "The ways in which the poor die reflect the conditions of their lives." Carol B. Stack, *All Our Kin: Strategies for Survival in a Black Community* (New York: Harper & Row, 1974), 4.

19. Lewis, *Hospital*, 28–29.

20. Clarence Page, "Gays, Stupidity and Political Clout," *Chicago Tribune*, July 27, 1986.

21. Dirk Johnson, "Fear of AIDS Stirs New Attacks on Homosexuals," *New York Times*, April 24, 1987; Jean Latz Griffin, "Reports of Gay Harassment Soaring," *Chicago Tribune*, May 11, 1987.

22. Ms. Aurellio Garza to Pope John Paul II, March 11, 1987, copy, Community Services Series, Mayoral Records, box 28, folder 1, Harold Washington Archives and Collections, Chicago Public Library.

23. "Doctor with AIDS Back at Hospital," *New York Times*, February 5, 1987; "Chicago Patients Gain Curb on AIDS Carriers," *New York Times*, September 22, 1988; Peter Freiberg, "Chicago Doctor with AIDS Allowed to Treat Patients," *The Advocate*, September 1, 1987; Peter Freiberg, "Gay Doctor with AIDS Fights to Continue Seeing Patients," *The Advocate*, March 31, 1987; William Burks, "Politicos Oust PWA Doctor," *New York Native*, March 16, 1987.

24. Travelers and Immigrants Aid of Chicago, untitled document on AIDS in Chicago, n.d., Community Services Series, Mayoral Records, folder 20, box 28, Harold Washington Archives and Collections, Chicago Public Library. Paralleling the Chicago Housing Authority security director's remark above, this document states that "Shelters are also inappropriate centers for people at risk of opportunistic infection."

25. Urvashi Vaid, *Virtual Equality: The Mainstreaming of Gay and Lesbian Liberation* (New York: Anchor, 1995), 74–78.

26. "AIDS Cases Reported to Chicago Department of Health by Risk Behavior Within Racial/Ethnic Group," Community Services Series, Mayoral Records, box 28, folder 4, Harold Washington Archives and Collections, Chicago Public Library.

27. Jenny Robles, "Health Department Reneges on AIDS Funding," *Windy City Times*, December 8, 1988.

28. Frank E. James, "AIDS Bills in Illinois Reflect a Backlash Against Moderate Public-Health Policies," *Wall Street Journal*, July 3, 1987; Dirk Johnson, "Broad AIDS Laws Signed in Illinois," *New York Times*, September 22, 1987. Ron Sable charged that "the Illinois Legislature has enacted the worst AIDS related legislation anywhere in the U.S." Sable, et al. to March on Washington Executive Committee, n.d., Lesbian and Gay Voter Impact '88 folder, box 1, Ron Sable Papers, Gerber/Hart Library and Archives.

29. Memo from Kit Duffy to Jacky Grimshaw (Intergovernmental Affairs), April 9, 1986, Community Services Series, Mayoral Records, box 28, folder 9, Harold Washington Archives and Collections, Chicago Public Library.

30. Dirk Johnson, "Broad AIDS Laws Signed in Illinois," *New York Times*, September 22, 1987; Peter Freiberg, "Illinois Governor Limits Coercive Action in Statewide AIDS Bills," *The Advocate*, October 27, 1987; Susy Schultz, "Gay Protestors Ask Governor to Veto AIDS Bills," *Chicago Sun-Times*, August 17, 1987; Flyer asking Gov. James R. Thompson to veto four bills, Community Services Series, Mayoral Records, folder 10, box 29, and Illinois AIDS

Interdisciplinary Advisory Council minutes, August 15, 1986, Community Services Series, Mayoral Records, folder 18, box 28, Harold Washington Archives and Collections, Chicago Public Library; Tom Brune and Howard Wolinsky, "New Jab at AIDS Testing," *Chicago Sun-Times*, June 22, 1987; Albert Williams, "'Veto!' Cries Ring as 70,000 Gather for Pride Parade," *Windy City Times*, July 2, 1987; Dirk Johnson, "Veto of AIDS Testing Bills Is Urged in Illinois," *New York Times*, July 7, 1987; Susy Schultz, "Prenuptial AIDS Tests Criticized by Scientists," *Chicago Sun-Times*, n.d. [fall 1987], clipping in Municipal Reference Library, Chicago Public Library. On AIDS criminalization and antiblack racism, see Steven Thrasher, "How College Wrestling Star 'Tiger Mandingo' Became an AIDS Scapegoat," BuzzFeed, July 7, 2014, https://www.buzzfeed.com/steventhrasher/how-college-wrestling-star-tiger-mandingo-became-an-hiv-scap.

31. Gould, *Moving Politics*, 155, 162–63, 317.

32. "Illinois May End Premarital AIDS Testing," *New York Times*, January 5, 1989.

33. Rex Wockner, "HIV Testing in Illinois: The Worst Bill Yet," *New York Native*, September 12, 1988.

34. "Other States Show Interest in Illinois 'AIDS' Law," *New York Native*, November 5, 1990.

35. Risse, *Mending Bodies, Saving Souls*, 661.

36. "AIDS and Insurance Companies," *Chicago Tribune*, June 16, 1987.

37. Paul Starr, "The Health Care Legacy of the Great Society," in *LBJ's Neglected Legacy: How Lyndon Johnson Reshaped Domestic Policy and Government*, ed. Robert H. Wilson, Norman J. Glickman, and Laurence E. Lynn Jr. (Austin: University of Texas Press, 2015), 242.

38. Arnold R. Hirsch, *Making the Second Ghetto: Race and Housing in Chicago, 1940–1960* (Chicago: University of Chicago Press, 1983); Thomas J. Sugrue, *The Origins of the Urban Crisis: Race and Inequality in Postwar Detroit* (Princeton, NJ: Princeton University Press, 1996).

39. Paul Starr, *The Social Transformation of American Medicine: The Rise of a Sovereign Profession and the Making of a Vast Industry* (New York: Basic Books, 1984), 426.

40. Gunnar Almgren and Miguel Ferguson, "The Urban Ecology of Hospital Failure: Hospital Closures in the City of Chicago, 1970–1991," *Journal of Sociology and Social Welfare* 26, no. 4 (December 1999): 5–25.

41. Lonnie C. Edwards, opening statement to AIDS roundtable, April 11, 1986, Community Services Series, Mayoral Records, box 29, folder 8, Harold Washington Archives and Collections, Chicago Public Library.

42. Kit Duffy to Jacky Grimshaw, March 19, 1987, Community Services Series, Mayoral Records, box 28, folder 19, Harold Washington Archives and Collections, Chicago Public Library. On the Reagan cuts to Community Development Block Grants, see Roger Biles, *The Fate of Cities: Urban America and the Federal Government, 1945–2000* (Lawrence: University Press of Kansas, 2011), 250–86, esp. 265–67.

43. Kit Duffy to Jacky Grimshaw, March 19, 1987, Community Services Series, Mayoral Records, box 28, folder 19, Harold Washington Archives and Collections, Chicago Public Library.

44. Ronald Bayer and Gerald M. Oppenheimer, *AIDS Doctors: Voices from the Epidemic* (New York: Oxford University Press, 2000), 97.

45. Lewis, *Hospital*, 25.

46. Jean Latz Griffin, "AIDS Activists Beg for Funding," *Chicago Tribune*, March 10, 1992.

47. COGLI minutes, May 27, 1987, Community Services Series, Mayoral Records, box 4, folder 40, Harold Washington Archives and Collections, Chicago Public Library.

48. Eric Zorn, "Home Open for Victims of AIDS," *Chicago Tribune*, March 12, 1986.

49. Kate Sosin, "Open Hand Chicago Starts Rolling Out Meals," *Windy City Times*, November 23, 2011.

50. See, among other works, Dennis Altman, "Legitimation Through Disaster: AIDS and the Gay Movement," in *AIDS: The Burdens of History*, ed. Elizabeth Fee and Daniel M. Fox (Berkeley: University of California Press, 1988): 301–15; Robert A. Padgug and Gerald M. Oppenheimer, "Riding the Tiger: AIDS and the Gay Community," in *AIDS: The Making of a Chronic Disease*, 245–78; Gould, *Moving Politics*, esp. 67, 156, 258.

51. Sid Smith, "Stars Hit Chicago for AIDS Benefit," *Boston Globe*, September 23, 1987; Tracy Baim, "$1 Million Raised at AIDS Benefit," *Outlines*, October 1, 1987.

52. Chinta Strausberg, "Batter Plan for Victims of AIDS," *Chicago Defender*, July 17, 1987.

53. Shilts, *And the Band Played On*, 188.

54. Max Smith, interview with the author, January 16, 2007.

55. Jo A. Moore, "Kupona Rift Revealed at COGLI Session," *Windy City Times*, February 2, 1986.

56. Timothy Stewart-Winter, *Queer Clout: Chicago and the Rise of Gay Politics* (Philadelphia: University of Pennsylvania Press, 2016), 186–206.

57. Howard Brown Memorial Clinic, "PWA Client Population Data," July 31, 1987, Community Services Series, Mayoral Records, box 28, folder 22, Harold Washington Archives and Collections, Chicago Public Library.

58. Tom Brune, "15 Hospitals Diagnose Most Area AIDS Cases," *Chicago Sun-Times*, November 8, 1987.

59. Howard Brown Memorial Clinic, "PWA Client Population Data," July 31, 1987, Community Services Series, Mayoral Records, box 28, folder 22, Harold Washington Archives and Collections, Chicago Public Library. On poverty and early AIDS cases, see Michelle Cochrane, *When AIDS Began: San Francisco and the Making of an Epidemic* (New York: Routledge, 2004).

60. Tom Brune, "In Gay Bars, Reminders Abound," *Chicago Sun-Times*, April 28, 1987.

61. "City Has Failed Black and Hispanic AIDS Victims, Researcher Says," *Chicago Tribune*, November 17, 1988.

62. Howard Brown Memorial Clinic, "PWA Client Population Data."

63. For a devastating critique of Shilts, see Tiemeyer, *Plane Queer*.

64. Jesse Green and Peter S. Arno, "The 'Medicaidization' of AIDS: Trends in the Financing of HIV-Related Medical Care," *Journal of the American Medical Association* 264, no. 10 (September 12, 1990): 1261–66; Jonathan Engel, *The Epidemic: A Global History of AIDS* (New York: Smithsonian Books, 2006), 177.

65. Shelton Watson, interview with the author, January 15, 2007.

66. Often a language of "lag" was used to describe the relationship: "No one knows how fast AIDS infections are spreading in Chicago," wrote a reporter in late 1985 two months after the death of movie star Rock Hudson drew the nation's attention to the crisis, "but the city appears to be about two to three years behind New York and San Francisco." Ronald Kotulak, "State Mapping Plan for AIDS Epidemic," *Chicago Tribune*, December 8, 1985.

67. COGLI to Harold Washington, January 14, 1986 [erroneously labeled 1985], Community Services Series, Mayoral Records, box 29, folder 9, Harold Washington Archives and Collections, Chicago Public Library; Jennifer Kapuscik, "Commissioner on Prostitutes and AIDS," *GayLife*, January 9, 1986; John A. Fall, "Midwest Health Official Denies Quarantine Plans," *New York Native*, February 10, 1986. See also Bayer, *Private Acts, Social Consequences*, 173–86.

68. Tom Brune, "AIDS Groups Hit City on Long-Overdue Funds," *Chicago Sun-Times*, March 27, 1987.

69. "2 more Gay Groups Ask City Health Chief Firing," *Chicago Sun-Times*, March 26, 1987; Tom Brune, "AIDS Groups Hit City on Long-Overdue Funds," *Chicago Sun-Times*, March 27, 1987; Tracy Baim, "City Announces AIDS Response, Pays Groups," *Windy City Times*, April 2, 1987.

70. COGLI minutes, May 27, 1987, and Paul Varnell, "Health Dept. Needs to Fix Flaws in its AIDS Program," Community Services Series, Mayoral Records, box 4, folder 40, Harold Washington Archives and Collections, Chicago Public Library; "Lonnie Edwards Should Resign or Be Fired," *Windy City Times*, August 6, 1987.

71. Richard Gray to Lonnie Edwards, June 16, 1987, Community Services Series, Mayoral Records, box 28, "Gay and Lesbian Book 4 of 4" folder, Harold Washington Archives and Collections, Chicago Public Library. A somewhat similar and even higher-profile conflict developed in New York in 1989–1990 over the appointment by Mayor David Dinkins of Woodrow Myers, an African American man, to lead that city's health department. See Vaid, *Virtual Equality*, 101, 350.

72. John Kass, "City Health Chief Asked to Stay," *Chicago Tribune*, January 7, 1988; Deborah Nelson, "Fund Cuts, Staff Loss Cripple City AIDS Work," *Chicago Sun-Times*, September 11, 1988; Albert Williams, Paul Handler, and Paul Tarini, "Abetting the AIDS Crisis," *Chicago Reader*, December 22, 1988.

73. Mark Schoofs, "Politics: Gays and Daley," *Chicago Reader*, November 17, 1989.

74. Quotations from both the Ann Sather's forum and the Daley Plaza protest were transcribed by the author from *The 10% Show*, episode 10, video recording in 10% Show Collection, Gerber/Hart Library and Archives.

75. G. Stephen Bowen, Katherine Marconi, Sally Kohn, Dorothy M. Bailey, Eric P. Goosby, Sonya Shorter and Steve Niemcryk, "First Year of AIDS Services Delivery Under Title I of the Ryan White CARE Act," *Public Health Reports* 107, no. 5 (September–October 1992), 494.

76. John-Manuel Andriote, *Victory Deferred: How AIDS Changed Gay Life in America* (Chicago: University of Chicago Press, 1999), 232.

77. Tracy Baim, "Chicago HIV/AIDS Cases Pass 36,000," *Windy City Times*, April 20, 2011.

78. Jane Lowers, "The Funding Crunch: AIDS, Gay and Lesbian Organizations Compete for Limited Resources," *Outlines*, June 1995, 16; see also Vaid, *Virtual Equality*, 75.

79. Terry Wilson, "Blacks Worry Funds Won't Reach Hard-Hit Group," *Chicago Tribune*, May 16, 1997.

80. Curtis Winkle and Andrea Carr, with the assistance of Shyamala Parameswaran, "Evaluation of Ryan White CARE Act Title I as Implemented in Chicago, Illinois," August 12, 1994, 46, box 4, folder 4, ACT UP/Chicago Records, Special Collections Research Center, University of Chicago Library.

81. Girma Woldemichael, Demian Christiansen, Sandra Thomas, and Nanette Benbow, "Demographic Characteristics and Survival with AIDS: Health Disparities in Chicago, 1993–2001," *American Journal of Public Health* 99, Supplement 1 (March 2009), S118–S123.

Chapter 5

1. Lawrence Altman, "Rare Cancer Seen in 41 Homosexuals," *New York Times*, July 3, 1981; Pat McKeown, "No AIDS Cure, So 'Buddies' Offer Comfort," *Philadelphia Daily News*, August 10, 1983; Philadelphia Department of Public Health, "Acquired Immune Deficiency Syndrome (AIDS) Cases in Philadelphia and Philadelphia Primary Metropolitan Statistical Area (PMSA)

Monthly Report," December 7, 1984, Scott Wilds Papers, box 4, "Lavender Health," Temple University Manuscripts and Special Collections.

2. Randy Shilts's classic account of the early AIDS epidemic focused on California, New York, and the Centers for Disease Control in Atlanta. Randy Shilts, *And the Band Played On: Politics, People, and the AIDS Epidemic* (New York: St. Martin's, 1987). Historical works on AIDS in the United States that focus in whole or in part on New York or San Francisco include Michelle Cochrane, *When AIDS Began: San Francisco and the Making of an Epidemic* (New York: Routledge, 2003); Susan M. Chambré, *Fighting for Our Lives: New York's AIDS Community and the Politics of Disease* (New Brunswick, NJ: Rutgers University Press, 2006); Jennifer Brier, *Infectious Ideas: U.S. Political Responses to the AIDS Crisis* (Chapel Hill: University of North Carolina Press, 2009); Deborah B. Gould, *Moving Politics: Emotion and ACT UP's Fight Against AIDS* (Chicago: University of Chicago Press, 2009); Tamar W. Carroll, *Mobilizing New York: AIDS, Antipoverty, and Feminist Activism* (Chapel Hill: University of North Carolina Press, 2015).

3. For the history of Philadelphia's political economy over the course of the twentieth century, see James Wolfinger, *Philadelphia Divided: Race and Politics in the City of Brotherly Love* (Chapel Hill: University of North Carolina Press, 2011); Matthew Countryman, *Up South: Civil Rights and Black Power in Philadelphia* (Philadelphia: University of Pennsylvania Press, 2006); Lisa Levenstein, *A Movement Without Marches: African American Women and the Politics of Poverty in Postwar Philadelphia* (Chapel Hill: University of North Carolina Press, 2009).

4. Marc Stein, *City of Sisterly and Brotherly Loves: Lesbian and Gay Philadelphia, 1945–1972* (Philadelphia: Temple University Press, 2004); Kevin J. Mumford, "The Trouble with Gay Rights: Race and the Politics of Sexual Orientation in Philadelphia, 1969–1982," *Journal of American History* 98, no. 1 (June 2011): 49–72; Christopher Hepp, "Gays Take Clout Out of the Closet," *Philadelphia Daily News*, April 23, 1984; Jessica Ann Levy, "Selling Atlanta Black Mayoral Politics from Protest to Entrepreneurism, 1973 to 1990," *Journal of Urban History* 41, no. 3 (May 2015): 420–43; Timothy Stewart-Winter, *Queer Clout: Chicago and the Rise of Gay Politics* (Philadelphia: University of Pennsylvania Press, 2016).

5. Stein, *City of Sisterly and Brotherly Loves*; Kevin J. Mumford tells the story of black gay author Joseph Beam in *Not Straight, Not White: Black Gay Men from the March on Washington to the AIDS Crisis* (Chapel Hill: University of North Carolina Press, 2016); Beam also recounts his experience working at Giovanni's Room in his edited collection of black gay men's writing, *In the Life: A Black Gay Anthology* (Boston: Alyson Books, 1986); Jose de Marco, interview with the author, September 4, 2012, Philadelphia, Pennsylvania; Arnold Jackson, "On the Outside Looking In," *Au Courant*, March 10, 1986. All articles from *Au Courant* and *Philadelphia Gay News* found in the William Way Community Center Archive's collection of gay newspapers.

6. In *City of Sisterly and Brotherly Loves*, Marc Stein states that gay men reported playing a significant role in gentrifying parts of Center City and the surrounding area. For local newspaper coverage of gentrification, see Barbara Kantrowitz, "Money Pours In, Forcing Some People Out," *Philadelphia Inquirer*, April 26, 1979; Howard Spodek, "Gentrification: Don't Forget the Poor," *Philadelphia Inquirer*, July 19, 1979. Andrew Maykuth mentions "quiche-and-fern bars" in "Challenge to Popular Thinking on Cities," *Philadelphia Inquirer*, June 18, 1984. For more on gentrification, see Paul R. Levy, *Queen Village, the Eclipse of Community: A Case Study of Gentrification and Displacement in a South Philadelphia Neighborhood* (Philadelphia: Institute for the Study of Civic Values, 1978); Carolyn Adams et al., *Philadelphia: Neighborhoods, Division, and Conflict in a Postindustrial City* (Philadelphia: Temple University Press, 1991). Available census data show that the proportion of white residents in the area just below South

Street, including Queen Village, rose significantly between 1970 and 1990. Between 1970 and 1980 the number of white residents in census tracts 15 and 16, which run along the south side of South Street from Broad Street to the Delaware River, increased by 14.4 and 25.4 percentage points, respectively. The wave of gentrification continued moving west between 1980 and 1990, when the proportion of white residents in census tract 15 rose another 12.1 points and the proportion of white residents in the adjacent tract 14 rose by 19.4 points. In each case the loss in proportion of the tract's black population was equivalent or greater. While these neighborhoods still experienced population loss between 1970 and 1980, the effect of gentrification along the South Street corridor in the late 1970s can be better captured by the increase in residents that the area experienced over the following decade. U.S. Census Bureau, "1970 Census of Population and Housing: Census Tracts, Philadelphia, P.A.-N.J. Standard Metropolitan Statistical Area," General Characteristics of the Population Table P-1, https://www2.census.gov/library/publications/decennial/1970/phc-1/39204513p16ch05.pdf; "1980 Census of Population and Housing: Census Tracts Philadelphia, PA.-N.J. Standard Metropolitan Statistical Area," Race and Spanish Origin Table P-7, Internet Archive, https://archive.org/stream/1980censusofpo8022831unse; "1990 Census of Population and Housing: Population and Housing Characteristics for Census Tracts and Block Numbering Areas, Philadelphia, PA-NJ PMSA, Section 1," Race and Hispanic Origin Table 8, Internet Archive, https://archive.org/stream/1990censusofpopu32591unse.

7. Center City is here defined as bounded by I-676, South Street, and the Schuylkill and Delaware Rivers, which included census tracts 1 through 12. By this definition, Center City was around 90 percent white in 1970 and 1980 and 85 percent white in 1990.

8. Philadelphia Department of Public Health, "Acquired Immune Deficiency Syndrome (AIDS) Cases in Philadelphia and Philadelphia Primary Metropolitan Statistical Area (PMSA) Monthly Report," August 3, 1984, Scott Wilds Papers, box 4, "AIDS in Phila" folder, Temple University Manuscripts and Special Collections. Racial discrimination was not unique to Philadelphia's gay community and hampered AIDS outreach efforts in other cities as well. See Darius Bost, "At the Club: Locating Early Black Gay AIDS Activism in Washington, D.C.," *Occasion* 8 (August 31, 2015), http://arcade.stanford.edu/occasion/club-locating-early-black-gay-aids-activism-washington-dc; Brier, *Infectious Ideas*; Stephen J. Inrig, *North Carolina and the Problem of AIDS: Advocacy, Politics, and Race in the South* (Chapel Hill: University of North Carolina Press, 2011).

9. "Lavender Health," n.d., Scott Wilds Papers, box 4, "Lavender Health," Temple University Manuscripts and Special Collections; "News and Views of the Institute for Social Medicine and Community Health" (Institute for Social Medicine and Community Health, September 1982), Scott Wilds Papers, box 4, "Lavender Health," Temple University Manuscripts and Special Collections; McKeown, "No Aids Cure."

10. James Roberts, "Black Gays Need More PATF Outreach, Says Activist," *Au Courant*, March 31, 1986.

11. Many chapters of the group Black and White Men Together became involved in local campaigns against discrimination in gay bars. See, for example, Howard Erickson, "Bias Practice Noted," *BWMT LA Newsletter*, January 1982, Periodicals, BWMT Newsletters, BWMT–Los Angeles 1980–1982, ONE National Gay and Lesbian Archives. Allan Bérubé also discusses racist carding practices at gay bars in his essay "How Gay Stays White and What Kind of White It Stays," in *The Making and Unmaking of Whiteness*, ed. Birgit Rasmussen, Eric Klineberg, Irene Nexica, and Matt Wray, 234–65 (Durham, NC: Duke University Press, 2001).

12. Tommi Avicolli, "Uniform Carding Policy Urged," *Philadelphia Gay News*, June 20–26, 1986; Jackson, "On the Outside Looking In."

13. Mumford describes the racism that Joseph Beam encountered in the Philadelphia gay scene as well as his literary legacy in *Not Straight, Not White*; James Roberts, "Black Gays Speaking for Themselves," *Au Courant*, June 9, 1986; Joseph Beam, "Domestic Terrorism: No Cheek Left to Turn to Racism," *Au Courant*, October 27, 1986. At the time Beam was living near the intersection of 21st and Spruce, two blocks away from Rittenhouse Square in downtown Philadelphia. See Mark Thompson, "Letter to Joseph Beam," July 8, 1987, Joseph Beam Papers, box 4, folder 3, Schomburg Center.

14. Don Ransom, "Taking the Forces to Task for Excluding Racial Minorities" [letter to the editor], *Au Courant*, October 13, 1986.

15. By August 1984, just over 51 percent of reported AIDS cases in the city were among African Americans, who made up only about 38 percent of the city's total population. Philadelphia Department of Public Health, "AIDS Monthly Report," August 3, 1984.

16. Evelyn Dickerson, "Blacks Fall Victim to AIDS, Too," *Philadelphia Tribune*, July 31, 1984; "Apathy Slows AIDS Fight," *Philadelphia Tribune*, July 31, 1984.

17. Tyrone Smith, interview with the author, May 7, 2012, Philadelphia.

18. de Marco interview.

19. Ibid. Mia Bay describes a similar inversion of racial stereotypes by black intellectuals in *The White Image in the Black Mind: African-American Ideas About White People, 1830–1925* (Oxford University Press, 2000).

20. Dickerson, "Blacks Fall Victim to AIDS, Too"; Smith interview; de Marco interview; Linda Burnette, interview with the author, May 15, 2012, Philadelphia.

21. Fawn Vrazo, "From Philly, a Rap Record About Aids, for Black Men," *Chicago Tribune*, July 18, 1985; Vanessa Williams, "Among Black People, AIDS Is Taking a Heavier Toll," *Philadelphia Inquirer*, March 11, 1986; "Respect Yourself Rap Record Now on Sale," *Au Courant*, May 26, 1986; "Respect Yourself!" lyrics quoted in Gregg Bordowitz, *The AIDS Crisis Is Ridiculous and Other Writings, 1986–2003* (Cambridge, MA: MIT Press, 2004), 36. The song was later used by the New York AIDS activist video collective Testing the Limits in its work.

22. David Fair, Letter to Thomas Livers, November 24, 1986, Scptt Wilds Papers, box 4, "David Fair—various controversies" folder, Temple University Manuscripts and Special Collections.

23. Cei Bell, "Racism Charges at Phila. AIDS Task Force Unfounded," *Philadelphia Gay News*, April 4, 1986.

24. Darlene Garner, IMPACT letter, July 1, 1986, Scott Wilds Papers, box 4, "David Fair—various controversies," Temple University Manuscripts and Special Collections; "PCHA Elects New Board," *Au Courant*, May 19, 1986, 15. During the 1980s some news sources referred to Hassan as "Rashidah," her Muslim name, and others as "Lorraine," her given name. Since she sometimes signed her correspondence "Rashidah Lorraine Hassan," I use the first of the two names. Although she has since divorced and remarried, taking Abdul-Khabeer as her last name, for the sake of coherence I use "Hassan" when referring in the text to the oral history I conducted with her in 2012. In citing the interview I use her current name, Rashidah Abdul-Khabeer. When referring to oral histories, I use the present tense to differentiate between recent recollections and information gleaned from past sources. Rashidah Abdul-Khabeer, interview with the author, April 11, 2012, Philadelphia, African American AIDS History Project, http://afamaidshist.org/items/show/135; David Fair, interview with the author, April 13, 2012,

Philadelphia, African American AIDS History Project, http://afamaidshist.org/items/show/136; Wesley Anderson, interview with the author, November 13, 2015.

25. Smith interview. The Philadelphia Main Line is a wealthy neighborhood outside of the city's downtown.

26. David Fair, interview with Dan Daniels on *Gaydreams*, air date March 3, 1985, WXPN-FM, Philadelphia, PA, Scott Wilds Papers, "AIDS in Phila 1984–87" folder, Temple University Manuscripts and Special Collections.

27. Sign-in sheets dated April 6, 1986, and June 8, 1986, held by the Black LGBT Archivists Society of Philadelphia, in the possession of Kevin Trimell Jones. The sheets are not marked as such but according to Jones are from BEBASHI meetings. Center City is again here defined as bounded by I-676, South Street, and the Schuylkill and Delaware Rivers. "Bebashi Moves into 1199C Office Space," *Au Courant*, June 23, 1986; Abdul-Khabeer interview; Curtis Wadlington, interview with the author, May 9, 2012, Philadelphia.

28. Bell, "Racism Charges at Phila. AIDS Task Force Unfounded." According to Bell, *Philadelphia Gay News* editors altered the original headline, "Racism Charges at Phila. AIDS Task Force Unsubstantiated," due to space concerns. Although this did subtly change the meaning of the headline, she takes care to point out, "This wasn't an attempt on PGN's part to change the meaning of my article." Cei Bell, e-mail message to author, February 27, 2018. Bell was also among those who attended the BEBASHI meetings mentioned above.

29. Bell, "Racism Charges at Phila. AIDS Task Force Unfounded"; Abdul-Khabeer interview.

30. Bell, "Racism Charges Unfounded."

31. Although the 1964 Civil Rights Act predated the widespread use of federal block grants to fund local and state programs, the Department of Justice's Office of Legal Counsel determined in a 1982 legal opinion that federal block grants fell within the "literal terms" of the 1964 law. "Applicability of Certain Cross-Cutting Statutes to Block Grants Under the Omnibus Budget Reconciliation Act of 1981" quoted in Bill Lann Lee, "Block Grant Memo," U.S. Department of Justice, January 28, 1999, http://www.justice.gov/crt/about/cor/Pubs/blkgrnt.php; Cei Bell, "Task Force Committed to Black Outreach, Says Ifft," *Philadelphia Gay News*, April 11, 1986.

32. David Wentroble, "PATF Is Attuned to Black Gays with AIDS," *Au Courant*, April 28, 1986.

33. Tommi Avicolli, "Over 2000 Participate in AIDS Walk & Rally," *Philadelphia Gay News*, October 3, 1986; Abdul-Khabeer interview.

34. AIDS vigil video recording, VHS, Rashidah Abdul-Khabeer personal collection, African American AIDS History Project, http://afamaidshist.org/items/show/38; Abdul-Khabeer interview.

35. AIDS vigil video recording.

36. Abdul-Khabeer interview; AIDS vigil video recording.

37. Abdul-Khabeer interview.

38. Bill Whiting, "Divisive Events Hurt Everyone," *Philadelphia Gay News*, October 3–10, 1986; Ryan Hall, "AIDS Candlelight March to City Hall Planned," *Au Courant*, July 28, 1986. Whiting's influence in the Philadelphia gay community is hard to discern, but perhaps tellingly, the *Philadelphia Gay News* paired his letter not with a defense of Hassan but instead with another editorial criticizing the vigil's "heavily religious program." Michael J. LoFurno, "Should Religion Be the Focus?," *Philadelphia Gay News*, October 3–10, 1986, 9. In a letter to the editor

printed before the walk and vigil, Charlie O'Donnell, a resident of Lehighton, Pennsylvania, also criticized the march route for not going down Spruce Street and questioned the commitment of women to the fight against AIDS. Charlie O'Donnell, "Divisiveness Is a Real Shame," *Au Courant*, September 22, 1986, William Way Community Center.

39. Whiting, "Divisive Events Hurt Everyone."

40. Ibid.

41. Ibid.

42. BEBASHI, "AIDS and Minorities: A Crisis Ignored," 1986, Scott Wilds Papers, "AIDS in Phila 1984–87," Temple University Manuscripts and Special Collections.

43. Chris Bull, "Black and White Men Together to Launch AIDS Education Program," *Gay Community News*, October 2, 1988, National Task Force on AIDS Prevention Records, box 4, folder 7, University of California San Francisco Special Collections; "Editorial Viewpoints: Business as Usual," *Philadelphia Gay News*, August 19–25, 1988; Huntly Collins, "AIDS Agency Making Comeback Three Years After Going Bankrupt," *Philadelphia Inquirer*, May 2, 1996; Bebashi: Transition to Hope, https://www.bebashi.org/; "2018 Annual Report," Mazzoni Center, https://www.mazzonicenter.org/sites/default/files/attachments/mazzoni_center_annual_report_2018_digital.pdf.

44. Victoria A. Brownworth, "AIDS Consortium Stirs Controversy Among Activists," *Philadelphia Gay News*, February 15, 1991.

45. Ernest Owens, "Video Surfaces of ICandy Owner Darryl DePiano Saying the N-Word," Philadelphia Magazine (blog), September 29, 2016, http://www.phillymag.com/g-philly/2016/09/29/video-icandy-darryl-depiano-n-word/; Ernest Owens, "Patrons See 'Covert Racism' in Recent Enforcement of Woody's Dress Code," Philadelphia Magazine (blog), September 22, 2016, http://www.phillymag.com/g-philly/2016/09/22/racism-woodys-dress-code/; "Crowd Jams Hearing Full of Allegations About Racism in Philadelphia's LGBT Community," *PhillyVoice*, October 26, 2016, http://www.phillyvoice.com/allegations-racism-erupt-lgbt-community/; Jeremy Rodriguez, "City Releases Gayborhood Racism Findings, Recommends Training," *Philadelphia Gay News*, January 23, 2017, http://www.epgn.com/news/local/11568-city-releases-findings-on-gayborhood-racism-allegations.

46. Ernest Owens, "Michael Weiss Must Step Down from His Public Roles in the Gayborhood," Philadelphia Magazine (blog), March 23, 2017, http://www.phillymag.com/g-philly/2017/03/23/michael-weiss-seth-williams-indictment/; Timaree Schmit, "Whistle Blown: Mazzoni Employees Stage Walkout Calling for Resignation of CEO," *Philadelphia Weekly*, April 20, 2017, http://www.philadelphiaweekly.com/news/whistle-blown-mazzoni-employees-stage-walkout-calling-for-resignation-of/article_9895b994-25ed-11e7-8aa8-afbbcb26dc0e.html; "Mazzoni Center CEO, Board President Resign amid Controversy," *PhillyVoice*, April 24, 2017, http://www.phillyvoice.com/mazzini-center-ceo-board-president-resign-amid-controversy/.

47. Tanner Nassau, Melissa Miller, Chrysanthus Nnumolu, and Kathleen A. Brady, "AIDS Activities Coordinating Office (AACO) Surveillance Report 2017: HIV/AIDS in Philadelphia," City of Philadelphia, October 2018, http://www.phila.gov/media/20190130165248/HIVSurveillanceReport_2017_Web_Version.pdf; "QuickFacts: Philadelphia County, Pennsylvania," United States Census Bureau, http://www.census.gov/quickfacts/philadelphiacountypennsylvania, accessed March 31, 2019; Sunnivie Brydum, "Why Transgender Women Have the Country's Highest HIV Rates," *HIV Plus*, March 2013, http://www.hivplusmag.com/case-studies/2013/04/08/invisible-women-why-transgender-women-are-hit-so-hard-hiv.

Chapter 6

1. On civil rights historiography and homosexuality, see Michael G. Long, *Martin Luther King, Jr., Homosexuality, and the Early Gay Rights Movement: Keeping the Dream Straight?* (New York: Palgrave Macmillan, 2012); Pat Roediger, *Great African Americans in Civil Rights* (New York: Crabtree Publishing, 1996).

2. Kevin J. Mumford, *Not Straight, Not White: Black Gay Men from the March on Washington to the AIDS Crisis* (Chapel Hill: University of North Carolina Press, 2016), 79–98; Horace Griffin, ed., *Their Own Receive Them Not: African American Lesbians and Gays in Black Churches* (Eugene: Wipf and Stock Publishers, 2006); Devon W. Carbado, ed., *Black Men on Race, Gender, and Sexuality: A Critical Reader* (New York: New York University Press, 1999); Delroy Constantine-Simms, *The Greatest Taboo: Homosexuality in Black Communities* (Los Angeles: Alyson Books, 2001); Essex Hemphill, ed., *Brother to Brother: New Writings by Black Gay Men* (Boston: Alyson Publications, 1991); Kai Wright, *Drifting Toward Love: Black, Brown, Gay, and Coming of Age on the Streets of New York* (Boston: Beacon, 2008); *Voices Rising: Celebrating 20 Years of Black, Lesbian, Gay, Bisexual, and Transgender Writing* (Washington, DC: Redbone, 2007); Jeffrey Q. McCune, *Sexual Discretion: Black Masculinity and the Politics of Passing* (Chicago: University of Chicago Press, 2014); Keith Boykin, ed., *For Colored Boys Who Have Suicide When the Rainbow Is Still Not Enough: Coming of Age, Coming Out, and Coming Home* (New York: Magnus Books, 2012).

3. "An Illustrated Guide for the Older Generation," *Ebony*, August 1978, 46, https://archive.org/details/bub_gb_Sc0DAAAAMBAJ/page/n45.

4. "Letters," *Ebony*, January 1979, 17; "The Ebony Adviser," *Ebony*, February 1985, 58.

5. "An Illustrated Guide for the Older Generation," 46.

6. Anita Bryant, *The Anita Bryant Story: The Survival of Our Nation's Families and the Threat of Militant Homosexuality* (Old Tappan, NJ: F. H. Revell, 1977) ; Anita Bryant and Bob Green, *Raising God's Children* (Old Tappan, NJ: Revell, 1977); Martin Bauml Duberman, *Left Out: The Politics of Exclusion, Essays, 1964–1999* (New York: Basic Books, 1999).

7. *Brother Outsider: The Life of Bayard Rustin*, dir. Nancy Kates and Bennett Singer (KQED Films, 2002); John D'Emilio, *Lost Prophet: The Life and Times of Bayard Rustin* (New York: Basic Books, 2003); *I Must Resist: Bayard Rustin's Life in Letters*, ed. Michael G. Long (San Francisco: City Lights Books, 2012).

8. "Gay Point of View," *Ebony*, February 1978, 20; "An Illustrated Guide for the Older Generation," *Ebony*, August 1978, 44–46; Cathy J. Cohen, "Punks, Bulldaggers, and Welfare Queens: The Radical Potential of Queer Politics?," *GLQ: A Journal of Lesbian and Gay Studies* 3 (May 1997): 437–65; Cathy J. Cohen, *The Boundaries of Blackness: AIDS and the Breakdown of Black Politics* (Chicago: University of Chicago Press, 1999).

9. "BWMT Anniversary Banquet," *Chicago's BWMT Newsletter*, August 1981, 1–3.

10. Philadelphia, Pennsylvania Population 2019, World Population Review, http://worldpopulationreview.com/us-cities/philadelphia-population/.

11. C. Brownlee, "A Unified Rainbow of Strength," *Chicago's BWMT Newsletter*, January 1982, 5.

12. "The Discrimination Documentation Project of BWMT," *Chicago's BWMT Newsletter*, January 1982, 5.

13. "BWMT Updates," *Chicago's BWMT Newsletter*, January 1982, 4.

14. "BWMT Updates," *Chicago's BWMT Newsletter*, September 1982, 7.

15. "Have You Heard," *Chicago's BWMT Newsletter*, April 1986, 1.

16. "Co-Chair to NYC," *Chicago's BWMT Newsletter*, August 1986, 2.

17. "Word of Thanks from Simon Nkoli," *Chicago's BWMT Newsletter*, December 1989, 6.

18. C. Offutt, "Rap Groups to Resume," *Chicago's BWMT Newsletter*, October 1981, 1.

19. David Klein, "Brother on Briar," *Chicago's BWMT Newsletter*, March 1982, 2–3.

20. David Klein, "International Association of BWMT Convention '83," *Chicago's BWMT Newsletter*, September 1983, 2–3.

21. "BWMT Updates," *Chicago's BWMT Newsletter*, April 1982, 5.

22. "Dear BWMT/Chicago," *Chicago's BWMT Newsletter*, March 1982, 4–5.

23. Ibid., 5.

24. "Black and White Men," *Chicago's BWMT Newsletter*, July 1982, 5.

25. Joseph Beam, "A New Magazine, a New Movement," *Black/Out* (Summer 1986): 2.

26. Cary Alan Johnson, "Inside Gay Africa," *Black/Out* (Fall 1986): 18.

27. Ibid., 21.

28. Martin Duberman, *Hold Tight Gently: Michael Callen, Essex Hemphill, and the Battlefield of AIDS* (New York: New Press, 2014).

29. Essex Hemphill, "Say, Brother," *Essence*, November 1983, 15.

30. Tamar Carroll, *Mobilizing New York: AIDS, Antipoverty, and Feminist Activism* (Chapel Hill: University of North Carolina Press, 2015); "HIV/AIDS and U.S. History," *Journal of American History* 104 (September 2017): 431–60.

31. Michael A. Oatis, "A Voice in Our Wilderness," *Black/Out* (Summer 1987): 36.

32. Dagmawi Woubshet, *The Calendar of Loss: Race, Sexuality, and Mourning in the Early Era of AIDS* (Baltimore: Johns Hopkins University Press, 2015).

33. Sidney Brinkley, "Checkbook Politics: Glenn Thompson, Badlands, BWMT, and the Selling of the Black Gay Conference," *Blacklight* 5, no. 1 (1984): 23–25.

34. Maulana Karenga, "The Million Man March/Day of Absence Mission Statement," *Black Scholar* 25 (September 1, 1995): 1–11; Michael O. West, "Like a River: The Million Man March and the Black Nationalist Tradition in the United States," *Journal of Historical Sociology* 12 (March 1999): 81–93; Herb Boyd, "Million Man March," *Black Scholar* 25 (September 1, 1995): 12–24; Manning Marable, "Black Fundamentalism: Farrakhan and Conservative Black Nationalism," *Race & Class* 39 (April–June, 1998): 22; Joseph P. McCormick II, "The Messages and the Messengers: Opinions from the Million Who Marched," *National Political Science Review* 6 (July 1997): 142–64.

35. "No Black Humour Please," *London Evening Observer*, October 14, 1982, 5b.

36. "This Sunday's Central Meeting," *County Express*, July 1, 1983.

37. "Eastern Eye 'Tokenism,'" *West Indian World*, March 21, 1984, 2.

38. "Letters, White Decadence," *The Voice*, February 25, 1984.

39. "Dear Editor, Prejudiced Comments," *The Root*, December 1985; "Dear Editor, Feels Manipulated," *The Root*, December 1985.

40. "Black Gays Come Out," *The Root*, October 1985, 12–13.

41. "Dear Editor, Gay Issue," *The Voice*, January 28, 1984; "True Feelings," *The Voice*, February 4, 1984.

42. "Gay Lessons Are a White Plot," *The Journal*, November 21, 1986.

43. Ibid.

44. "Disappointed," *The Voice*, March 3, 1987.

45. Martin Williams, "Walk-out at Garvey Remarks," *The Gleaner*, August 25, 1987.

46. "Calling Lesbians and Gays," *The Voice*, August 16, 1988; "Let's Embrace Homosexuals," *Pope Fiction*, February 27, 2006.

47. "Calling Lesbians and Gays," *The Voice*, August 16, 1988; "Let's Embrace Homosexuals," *Pope Fiction*, February 27, 2006; Mumford, *Not Straight, Not White*, 78–95.

48. "Gay Racism," *Eastern Eye*, October 18, 1994.

49. "Network," *Spare Rib*, May 1989; "Letter to the Editor," *Birmingham Evening Mail*, July 6, 1989; Nirpal Dhaliwal, "Does Anyone Know Any Gay Asians?," *London Evening Standard*, September 20, 2006.

50. "Asian Gay Ball Sparks Outcry," *Eastern Eye*, August 20, 1999.

51. Yasmir Alibhai-Brown, "Some of the Worst Prejudice Can Be Found Among the Ethnic Minorities," *The Independent*, February 10, 2000.

52. "Asians Attack Gay Festival," *The Times*, February 18, 2000; "Asian Gays Celebrate Sexuality Underground," *The Asian*, February 3–9, 2000.

53. "Silent Pride," *The Guardian*, November 8, 2000.

54. Kamila F. Majied, "'Beauty Shop': Date with Guffaws," *New York Amsterdam News*, March 1990, 28.

55. William Hamilton, "'Fortune' Picture Is Brutal, Frank," *New York Amsterdam News*, August 14, 1971, B10.

56. Lionel Mitchell, "'Trade': Stark Presentation of Homosexual Lifestyle," *New York Amsterdam News*, November 19, 1983, 32.

57. Vivian Robinson, "'Staircase,' Tender, Funny Play," *New York Amsterdam News*, February 17, 1968, 20.

58. "Dear Gerri," *New York Amsterdam News*, March 21, 1981, 48.

59. Carlton Barrett, "A Look at What Black Family Therapists Do," *New York Amsterdam News*, November 2, 1985, 15.

60. "AIDS Outbreak Alarms Prison Officials," *New York Amsterdam News*, June 4, 1983, 25.

61. "An Appeal to African-American Professional: Show Outrage over AIDS," *New York Amsterdam News*, November 16, 1991, 3.

Chapter 7

1. Anthony Duignan-Cabrera, "Gay GOPs: The Enemy Within," *Newsweek*, 24 August 1992; Moss Jennings, "The Outsiders," *The Advocate*, 29 October 1997; Nathan Cobb, "The Party's Uninvited Guests," *Chicago Tribune*, 7 October 1992; David Brooks, "Right Out of the Closet" (book review), *New York Times*, 27 June 1999.

2. Robert Bailey, *Out and Voting II: The Gay, Lesbian, and Bisexual Vote in Congressional Elections, 1990–1998* (Washington, DC: New York National Gay and Lesbian Task Force Policy Institute, 2000); "A Survey of LGBT Americans: Partisanship, Policy Views, Values," Pew Research Center, 13 June 2013, http://www.pewsocialtrends.org/2013/06/13/chapter -7-partisanship-policy-views-values/#a-democratic-constituency; Jocelyn Kiley and Shiva Maniam, "Lesbian, Gay, and Bisexual Voters Remain a Solidly Democratic Bloc," Pew Research Center, 25 October 2016, http://www.pewresearch.org/fact-tank/2016/10/25/lesbian-gay-and -bisexual-voters-remain-a-solidly-democratic-bloc/.

3. Sam Frizell, "Caitlyn Jenner Tells GOP Gathering Why She's a Republican," *Time*, 20 July 2016, http://time.com/4414836/republican-convention-caitlyn-jenner/.

4. Log Cabin Republicans, "1996 Spirit of Lincoln Resolution," Queer Resources Directory, 8 July 1996, http://www.qrd.org/qrd/orgs/LCC/1996/spirit.of.lincoln.resolution-07.96.

5. For works on conservatism, see Lisa McGirr, *Suburban Warriors: The Origins of the New American Right* (Princeton, NJ: Princeton University Press, 2001); Donald Critchlow, *Phyllis Schlafly and Grassroots Conservatism: A Woman's Crusade* (Princeton, NJ: Princeton University Press, 2005); Kim Phillips-Fein, "Conservatism: A State of the Field," *Journal of American History* 98, no. 3 (December 2011): 723–43; Michelle Nickerson, *Mothers of Conservatism: Women and the Postwar Right* (Princeton, NJ: Princeton University, 2012). For works on LGBT history, see Martin Duberman, *Stonewall* (New York: Plume, 1994); John D'Emilio, "Placing Gay in the Sixties," in *The World Turned: Essays on Gay History Politics, and Culture*, 23–44 (Durham, NC: Duke University Press, 2002); Lillian Faderman, *Gay Revolution: The Story of the Struggle* (New York: Simon and Schuster, 2015). Several scholars have written histories that focus on LGBT rights and conservatism in roughly equal proportion, but they too speak little about gay conservatives. See Robert Self, *All in the Family: The Realignment of American Democracy Since the 1960s* (New York: Hill and Wang, 2013); Clayton Howard, *The Closet and the Cul-de-Sac: Northern California and the Right to Sexual Privacy* (Philadelphia: University of Pennsylvania Press, 2019). The only historian to detail the history of the Log Cabin Republicans is Angela Dillard, *Guess Who's Coming to Dinner Now? Multicultural Conservatism in America* (New York: New York University Press, 2001), 137–70. For a sociological study of the group, see Mary Rogers and Phillip Lott, "Backlash, the Matrix of Domination, and the Log Cabin Republicans," *Sociological Quarterly* 38, no. 3 (Summer 1997): 497–512.

6. Christina Hanhardt, *Safe Space: Gay Neighborhood History and the Politics of Violence* (Durham, NC: Duke University Press, 2013). Timothy Stewart-Winter, "Queer Law and Order: Sex, Criminality, and Policing in the Late Twentieth Century United States," *Journal of American History* 102, no. 1 (June 2015): 61–72.

7. D'Emilio, "Placing Gay in the Sixties"; Faderman, *Gay Revolution*.

8. Tim Drake, interview with Tracy Baim, Chicago Gay History, 16 August 2007, http://www.chicagogayhistory.com.

9. Mary Brennan, *Turning Right in the Sixties: The Conservative Capture of the GOP* (Chapel Hill: University of North Carolina Press, 1995); John Andrew, *The Other Side of the Sixties: Young Americans for Freedom and the Rise of Conservative Politics* (New Brunswick, NJ: Rutgers University Press, 1997); Rebecca Klatch, *A Generation Divided: The New Left, the New Right, and the 1960s* (Berkeley: University of California Press, 1999); McGirr, *Suburban Warriors*; Nickerson, *Mothers of Conservatism*; Phillips-Fein, "Conservatism."

10. Bruce Schulman and Julian Zelizer, *Rightward Bound: Making America Conservative in the 1970s* (Cambridge, MA: Harvard University Press, 2008); Robert Mason and Iwan Morgan, eds., *Seeking a New Majority: The Republican Party and American Politics, 1960–1980* (Nashville: Vanderbilt University Press, 2013).

11. Marvin Liebman, *Coming Out Conservative: An Autobiography* (San Francisco: Chronicle Books, 1992), 145–46.

12. Ricchiazzi, interview with the author, 7 December 2015.

13. Craig Rimmerman, *From Identity to Politics: The Lesbian and Gay Movements in the United States* (Philadelphia: Temple University Press, 2002).

14. Elizabeth Armstrong, *Forging Gay Identities: Organizing Sexuality in San Francisco, 1950–1994* (Chicago: University of Chicago Press, 2002), 21. For more on Gay Liberation, see Self, *All in the Family*; Faderman, *Gay Revolution*.

15. Stan Aten, interview with the author, 5 January 2016.

16. Christopher Bowman, interview with the author, 14 December 2015.

17. Ricchiazzi interview.

18. Nicole Murray-Ramirez, oral history with Ellen Holzman, Trans Narratives, 7 August 2015, http://www.transnarratives.org/nicole-murray-ramirez.html; Bowman interview, 14 December 2015.

19. Bowman interview, 14 December 2015.

20. Douglas Edwards, "Report: Los Angeles/The Gay Business Community," *The Advocate*, 8 February 1979; Lance Clem, "The Queen City Gives 'Em the Business," *The Advocate*, 19 November 1981; Susan Orlean, "Portland: A Business Boom in Cascade Country," *The Advocate*, 13 May 1982.

21. Douglas Edwards, "Battling Big Government for Small Business," *The Advocate*, 22 February 1979.

22. Lanie Jones, "Gay GOP Club Bucks Prejudice in Bid to Join County's Political Mainstream," *Los Angeles Times*, 2 March 1986; Bowman interview, 14 December 2015.

23. Ricchiazzi interview.

24. Randy Shilts, *The Mayor of Castro Street: The Life and Times of Harvey Milk* (New York: St. Martin's, 1982); John D'Emilio and Estelle Freedman, *Intimate Matters: A History of Sexuality in America* (New York: Harper and Row, 1988); Gillian Frank, "The Civil Rights of Parents: Race and Conservative Politics in Anita Bryant's Campaign Against Gay Rights in 1970s Florida," *Journal of the History of Sexuality* 22, no. 1 (January 2013): 126–60.

25. Drake interview with Tracy Baim.

26. For more on gay suburbanites, see Tim Retzloff, "The Association of (Gay) Suburban People," in *New Histories of Everyday America*, ed. John Archer et al. (Minneapolis: University of Minnesota Press, 2015).

27. Los Angeles estimate from "Gays in the GOP," *The Advocate*, 19 August 1982; San Francisco estimate from Bowman interview, 14 December 2015.

28. Thomas Sugrue, *The Origins of the Urban Crisis: Race and Inequality in Postwar Detroit* (Princeton, NJ: Princeton University Press, 1996); Thomas Byrne Edsall and Mary Edsall, *Chain Reaction: The Impact of Race, Rights, and Taxes on American Politics* (New York: Norton, 1992).

29. Kevin Mumford, "The Trouble with Gay Rights: Race and the Politics of Sexual Orientation in Philadelphia, 1969–1982," *Journal of American History* 98, no. 1 (June 2011): 49–72.

30. Ted Hoerl, interview with Tracy Baim, Chicago Gay History.

31. Bowman, interview with the author, 30 December 2015. Bowman recalled that at the height of the club's growth, there were 6 lesbians out of 118 members. When the group lost members in later years, even fewer women came to meetings.

32. Greg Scott, "The Gayocratic Means of Leonard Greene," *The Advocate*, 14 January 1992.

33. Most of the coverage of the early clubs failed to mention race, but the racial demographics of the clubs surfaced in moments such as the off-the-cuff declaration of one member that he was a "gay WASP Republican." See James Rainey, "'Dyed-in-Wool' Conservative Tells GOP Club He's Gay Activist," *Los Angeles Times*, 13 May 1984.

34. Len Olds and Hugh Rouse, interview with Lisa Vecoli, 19 October 2014, Log Cabin Republican Records, Tretter Collection, University of Minnesota, Minneapolis.

35. Richard Tafel, *Party Crasher: A Gay Republican Challenges Politics as Usual* (New York: Simon and Schuster, 1999), 94–95.

36. Carlye Murphy, "Republican Homosexuals Form Gay Rights Movement," *Washington Post*, 19 May 1984.

37. Michael Abrams, "Prop. A Fights Higher Political Odds," *San Diego Union-Tribune*, 21 October 1985.

38. Bruce Mulraney, "Challenge and Opportunity: Gay Men and Lesbians in the Military," *United Log Cabin Clubs of California Newsletter*, Spring 1990, Log Cabin Republican Club Records, Tretter Collection.

39. Jere Real, "Minority Report: Mad About the Boys," *National Review*, 17 March 1978.

40. Cover, *Time*, 8 September 1975.

41. Real, "Minority Report."

42. Charlotte Low Allen, "Gay Conservatism Is Horse of a Different Color" *Insight on the News*, 17 September 1990. For more on Liebman's battles with other conservatives, see Dillard, *Guess Who's Coming to Dinner Now?*, 139–40.

43. Olds and Rouse interview with Vecoli.

44. Ibid.

45. Bowman interview, 30 December 2015.

46. See, e.g., "Of Local Interest," *This Week in Texas*, 15–21 May 1992.

47. "A Midsummer's Afternoon Roast. . . . A 'Two Party' Party," *Orange County Log Cabin Republican Club Newsletter*, June 1989, Log Cabin Republican Records, Tretter Collection.

48. Aten, interview with the author, 5 January 2016; Paul Rodgers, interview with the author, 16 January 2016.

49. John Locke, "Gays Need to Rethink Political Philosophy," *Windy City Times*, 17 December 1987.

50. United Republicans for Equality and Privacy, "Addendum to Minutes of the 'October Conference,'" n.d. [1988], Log Cabin Republican Records, Tretter Collection.

51. Locke, "Gays Need to Rethink Political Philosophy."

52. Rich Tafel, "Why a One Party Strategy Fails," *Harvard Gay and Lesbian Review* (Summer 1996). African American conservatives pursued a similar strategy. See Leah Wright-Rigeur, *The Loneliness of the Black Republican: Pragmatic Politics and the Pursuit of Power* (Princeton, NJ: Princeton University Press, 2015).

53. "Anderson for Gay Rights Bill," *Chicago Tribune*, 22 April 1980.

54. Bowman interview, 14 December 2015.

55. Ricchiazzi interview; T. W. McGarry, "Ed Davis Warns of GOP's Theocrats," *Los Angeles Times*, 19 July 1984.

56. Mark Pinsky, "Wilson Tells Gay County Republicans Club He Welcomes Their Support," *Los Angeles Times*, 21 August 1988.

57. Ricchiazzi interview; Drake interview with Tracy Baim; Marcia Slacum Greene, "D.C. Council's Lone Republican In a 4-Way Race," *Washington Post*, 20 August 1984.

58. Drake interview with Tracy Baim.

59. Phil Gailey, "G.O.P. Aides Organize on Homosexual Issues," *Boston Globe*, 16 May 1984.

60. Jeffrey Schmalz, "Gay Politics Goes Mainstream," *New York Times Magazine*, 11 October 1992.

61. Kay Longhope, "Gay Vote for Weld was Heavy," *Boston Globe*, 13 November 1990.

62. Nathan Cobb, "The Party's Uninvited Guests," *Chicago Tribune*, 7 October 1992.

63. William Endicott, "Deukemajian's Veto of Gay Jobs Bill a Move to Protect His Right Flank," *Los Angeles Times*, 18 March 1984.

64. Bowman interview, 30 December 2015; "Gay-Bashing and the GOP," editorial, *Los Angeles Times*, 17 March 1990.

65. Marc Lifsher, "Wilson Vetoes Gay Rights Bill, Says It's Unfair to Business," *Orange Country Register*, 30 September 1991.

66. Frontline, *The Age of AIDS, Part One*, 30 May 2006.

67. Alex Wetzel, "President's Corner," Orange County Log Cabin Republican newsletter, April 1987, Log Cabin Republican Records, Tretter Collection. Not all Log Cabin Republicans expressed this kind of frustration, however. Michael Aronowitz remembered that "When I was growing up, Ronald Reagan made me proud to be an American. . . . I'll never forget how Reagan stuck to his guns on SDI and outspent the Russians. The greatest issue in my lifetime is the end of the Cold War." Cited in Tafel, *Party Crasher*, 121.

68. Frontline, *The Age of AIDS, Part One*; Jennifer Brier, *Infectious Ideas: U.S. Political Responses to the AIDS Crisis* (Chapel Hill, NC: University of North Carolina Press, 2006); Tamar Carroll, *Mobilizing New York: AIDS, Poverty, and Feminist Activism* (Chapel Hill: University of North Carolina Press, 2015).

69. Schmalz, "Gay Politics Goes Mainstream."

70. Faderman, *Gay Revolution*, 496.

71. Ricchiazzi interview.

72. Craig Hines, "Convention '92—Republican Gays Weigh a Divisive Conflict over Values," *Houston Chronicle*, 13 August 1992.

73. R. A. Dyer and Ron Nissimov, "Zeroing In on the Republicans—Gay Republicans Fight for Change Within Party," *Houston Chronicle*, 22 June 1992.

74. Bowman interview, 30 December 2015.

75. Rodgers interview.

76. Bowman interview, 30 December 2015.

77. Larry Peterson, "Gay Republicans Fight Resistance of Party," *Orange County Register*, 9 March 1990.

78. Brian Weber, "Homosexual Republicans Pursue in State Party Functions," *Colorado Springs Gazette-Telegraph*, 3 October 1988; John Hammond, "A Gay Republican Speaks Out," *New York Native*, 2 July 1990.

79. Marty Keller, confidential memo to ULCCC Board Members, 22 March 1990, Tretter Collection.

80. Drew Barras, et al. letter, 7 January 1991, Frank Ricchiazzi Papers, Tretter Collection.

81. Tafel, *Party Crasher*, 117.

82. One poll in 1991 found that 13.1 percent of gay men and 6.8 percent of lesbians identified as Republicans. See Nathan Cobb, "The Party's Uninvited Guests," *Chicago Tribune*, 7 October 1992. A second poll in 1998 found that 20 percent of gay voters identified as Republicans. The poll did not distinguish between men and women. See Richard Berke, "The 2000 Campaign: Political Memo; Stakes for Both in Bush-Gays Meeting," *New York Times*, 13 April 2000.

83. "How Groups Voted in 1992," Cornell University, Roper Center, http://ropercenter .cornell.edu/polls/us-elections/how-groups-voted/how-groups-voted-1992/.

84. "The Vote '96: Presidential Exit Poll, Part 1," CNN, 6 November 1996, http://www.cnn .com/ALLPOLITICS/1996/elections/natl.exit.poll/index2.html.

85. Patrick Egan, "The Gay Vote and Gay Issues in U.S. Politics," paper presented at the Annual Meeting of the Midwest Political Science Association, 13–15 April 2004.

86. Scott Giordana, "Trying to Shift the Direction of the Gay Rights Movement," *Bay Windows*, 17 June 1999.

87. Log Cabin Republican Federation, "NJ Governor Whitman Meets with Gay Leaders; Pledges Support for Gay Rights," press release, 9 May 1994, Log Cabin Republican Records, Tretter Collection.

88. Thomas Lueck, "Giuliani Gets Warm Reception from Gay Republicans' Group," *New York Times*, 29 August 1999.

89. According to one report, the church had 15,000 members that year. See Francine Parnes, "Religion Journal: Dressing Down (or Not) for Summer," *New York Times*, 24 August 2002.

90. Michael Cooper, "Giuliani on Homosexuality," *New York Times*, 11 December 2007.

91. Josh Benson, "Belatedly Whitman Comes Out Swinging: Saving Moderates—or a Career?" *New York Times*, 9 January 2005.

92. No author, "Addendum to Minutes of the 'October Conference,'" n.d. [1988], Log Cabin Republican Records, Tretter Collection.

93. "What Issues Confront Log Cabin that Call for Strategies?," memo, Log Cabin Republican Conference, San Luis Obispo, CA, 25–26 March 1995, included with Wayne Peterson, letter to Brian Perry, 6 April 1995, Frank Ricchiazzi Papers, Tretter Collection.

94. Rich Tafel, memo to Andrew Poat, 19 April 1995, Ricchiazzi Papers, Tretter Collection.

95. Richard Tafel, "Club Survey Analysis," n.d., Log Cabin Republican Records, Tretter Collection.

96. Evelyn Kotch and Andy Eddy, "Women Make Their Mark in Log Cabin," *Log Cabin Federation Newsletter*, September 1994, Log Cabin Republican Records, Tretter Collection.

97. Frank Trejo. "Gay Republican Group Celebrates Past, Looks to Brighter Future," *Dallas Morning News*, 7 February 1994.

98. Carolyn Lochhead, "Gay Republicans Venture Deep into Enemy Territory—Log Cabin Holds Convention in Dallas," *San Francisco Chronicle*, 13 August 1998.

99. Daniel HoSang, *Racial Propositions: Ballot Initiatives and the Making of Postwar California* (Berkeley: University of California Press, 2010).

100. See, for example, "Protesters Assail Rising Use of Police Cameras," *New York Times*, 2 February 1998. While the Log Cabin Republicans deserve criticism for supporting candidates such as Wilson and Giuliani, it is important to note that many of these laws had bipartisan support. Bill Clinton, for example, was a strong supporter of federal "three strikes" legislation. For another criticism of gay Republicans' racial, gender, and class homogeneity, see Rogers and Lott, "Backlash, the Matrix of Domination, and Log Cabin Republicans," 501–3.

101. Martha Maire O'Connell, "Woman's Room," *Log Cabin Republican Clubs of California Newsletter*, April 1991, Log Cabin Republican Records, Tretter Collection.

102. Nate Cobb, "The Party's Uninvited Guests," *Chicago Tribune*, 7 October 1992.

103. "Who Are We?," *Cabin Talk*, Volume 2, Number 4, July 1996, Log Cabin Republican Records, Tretter Collection.

104. Alex Wentzel, "Individual Rights for Me, Not for You," *Log Cabin Federation Newsletter*, May/June 1992, Log Cabin Republican Records, Tretter Collection.

105. "Who Are We?," *Cabin Talk*, Tretter Collection.

106. Scott Minos, "Another Rebuttal on Choice," *Log Cabin Federation Newsletter*, May/June 1992, Log Cabin Republican Records, Tretter Collection.

107. Cobb, "The Party's Uninvited Guests."

108. Tafel, *Party Crasher*, 123.

109. Log Cabin Republican Federation, national board meeting minutes, June 1995, Log Cabin Republican Records, Tretter Collection.

110. "Gay Republican Group Backs Dole," *New York Times*, 5 September 1996; "Republicans and the Gay Vote," *New York Times*, 12 August 1999; Robin Toner, "Public Lives: Gay Republican Cleaves to Party Despite Bush Snub," *New York Times*, 29 November 1999.

111. David Kirkpatrick, "Gay Activists in GOP Withhold Endorsement," *New York Times*, 8 September 2004.

112. Andrew Lavallee, "Log Cabin Republicans Fault Platform," *Gay City News*, 2–4 September 2004.

113. Kate Folmar, "Governor Has Expanded Gay Rights, But Won't Sign a Same-Sex Marriage Bill," *San Jose Mercury-News*, 8 March 2007.

114. Patrick Healy, "Gay Republicans Soldier On, One Skirmish at a Time," *New York Times*, 17 April 2005. Some of these new chapters later shut down. See Peter Delvecchio, "The Log Cabin Republicans' Uncertain Future," *The Advocate*, 31 August 2015, http://www.advocate.com /print-issue/current-issue/2015/08/31/log-cabin-republicans-uncertain-future.

115. Michael Mooney, "Why Dallas' Gay Republicans Just Can't Win," *D Magazine*, July 2012, http://www.dmagazine.com/publications/d-magazine/2012/july/why-dallas-gay -republicans-just-cant-win.

116. Lizette Alvarez, "Unexpected Turns for Suit Over 'Don't Ask, Don't Tell' Rule," *New York Times*, 13 October 2013.

117. Tafel, *Party Crasher*, 98.

118. Brooks, "Right Out of the Closet."

Chapter 8

1. Patrick J. Buchanan, Republican National Convention Address, August 17, 1992.

2. Republican National Committee, "The Vision Shared: The Republican Party Platform, Uniting Our Family, Our Country, Our World," adopted August 17, 1992, at the Republican National Convention, Houston, Texas.

3. Jacquelyn Dowd Hall, "The Long Civil Rights Movement and the Political Uses of the Past," *Journal of American History* 91, no. 4 (2005): 1233–63.

4. On the uses of racial analogies in legal arguments about rights based in sex or sexual orientation, see Serena Mayeri, *Reasoning from Race: Feminism, Law, and the Civil Rights Revolution* (Cambridge, MA: Harvard University Press, 2011); Serena Mayeri, "A Common Fate of Discrimination," *Yale Law Journal* 110, no. 6 (2011): 1045–87. Nancy MacLean discusses the ways in which social movements of Latinos, women, and others used the institutional mechanisms put in place by the African American freedom struggle and its legal victories to advance their own civil rights agendas in *Freedom Is Not Enough: The Opening of the American Workplace* (Cambridge, MA: Harvard University Press, 2006). For more on the "minority rights revolution" and the determinative value of being "like black," see John David Skrentny, *The Minority Rights Revolution* (Cambridge, MA: Belknap Press of Harvard University Press, 2002).

5. Bruce J. Schulman, *The Seventies: The Great Shift in American Culture, Society, and Politics* (Cambridge, MA: Da Capo, 2002); Matthew D. Lassiter, *The Silent Majority: Suburban Politics in the Sunbelt South* (Princeton, NJ: Princeton University Press, 2006); Matthew D. Lassiter, "Political History Beyond the Red Blue Divide," *Journal of American History* 98, no. 3 (2011): 760–64; N. D. B. Connolly, "Property Rights and the Black Political Imagination," paper presented at Fractures: Defining and Redefining the Twentieth-Century United States, a Trans-Atlantic Conference, University of Pennsylvania, Philadelphia, May 7, 2012.

6. Barry Koltnow, "Show-Like Aura Pervades Sexual Preference Hearings," *Daily Camera*, February 20, 1974.

7. Barry Koltnow, "Sexual Preference Bill Sparks Controversy: The Opponents' Position," *Daily Camera*, 1974.

8. Koltnow, "Show-Like Aura."

9. Robert O. Self, *All the in the Family: The Realignment of American Democracy Since the 1960s* (New York: Hill and Wang, 2012), 243; "No protected status based on sexual orientation, review and comment," Colorado Legislative Council and the Office of Legislative Legal Services, August 9, 1991, box 5, folder "Legislative Process—1992," Evans v. Romer Records, Western History & Genealogy Division, Denver Public Library (hereafter WHG Division, DPL); "Not in Colorado!," EPOColorado, box 7, folder 1, Equality Colorado Records, WHG Division, DPL.

10. "Discrimination Spreads AIDS," Equal Protection Coalition, November 2, 1987, box 6, folder 20, Equality Colorado Records, WHG Division, DPL.

11. Koltnow, "Show-Like Aura." Boulder experienced a significant economic transformation between the early 1970s, when the first ordinance was proposed, and the late 1980s, when a new ordinance eventually was enacted.

12. "On Nov. 3 Vote 'YES' on #1," Equal Protection Coalition, box 6, folder 20, Equality Colorado Records, WHG Division, DPL.

13. Here again, I am referencing the work of Mayeri, Skrentny, and MacLean. Both Timothy Stewart-Winter and Kevin Mumford write about black-gay coalition politics in this period. Significantly, Mumford in particular describes a shift from organized black opposition to gay rights initiatives in the 1970s to later support for gay rights measures. In Colorado, alliances between gay and black community organizations and leaders were already strong in the 1970s, perhaps because the small size of the state's black population foreclosed the possibilities for significant black political power early on and necessitated a broader political coalition. Kevin Mumford, "The Trouble with Gay Rights: Race and the Politics of Sexual Orientation in Philadelphia, 1969–1982," *Journal of American History* 98, no. 1 (2011): 49–72. See also Timothy Stewart-Winter, *Queer Clout: Chicago and the Rise of Gay Politics* (Philadelphia: University of Pennsylvania Press, 2016).

14. Gillian Frank, "'The Civil Rights of Parents': Race and Conservative Politics in Anita Bryant's Campaign Against Gay Rights in 1970s Florida," *Journal of the History of Sexuality* 22 (2013): 126–60.

15. "Shall an Ordinance of the City and County of Denver Be Adopted to Permit Discrimination Based on Sexual Orientation—Could This Really Happen???," box 6, folder 26, Equality Colorado Records, WHG Division, DPL. I use the term "Hispanic" in this essay because it is the term used throughout the period by members of the group in question. Although "Chicano/a" was also commonly used in certain communities, particularly in Denver and near Colorado's border with New Mexico, it signified a particular political affiliation and was used more narrowly.

16. Steve Lipsher, "Election Loss Won't End Battle over Gay Rights," *Denver Post*, May 23, 1991.

17. Citizens for Sensible Rights, "Action Alert," box 6, folder 24, Equality Colorado Records, WHG Division, DPL.

18. "Shall an Ordinance of the City and County of Denver Be Adopted to Permit Discrimination Based on Sexual Orientation—Could This Really Happen???" and EPOC letter to supporters, March 21, 1991, box 6, folder 26, Equality Colorado Records, WHG Division, DPL.

19. Citizens for Sensible Rights, "Action Alert," box 6, folder 24, Equality Colorado Records, WHG Division, DPL.

20. EPOC letter to committee members, April 27, 1991, box 6, folder 24, Equality Colorado Records, WHG Division, DPL.

21. Citizens for Sensible Rights, "Return Sensible Rights to Denver, May 21," box 6, folder 24, Equality Colorado Records, WHG Division, DPL.

22. Ibid.

23. Ibid.

24. Steve Lipsher, "Election Loss Won't End Battle over Gay Rights," *Denver Post*, May 23, 1991.

25. Lauren Berlant and Michael Warner, "Sex in Public," *Critical Inquiry* 24, no. 2 (1998): 547–66.

26. "Historical Timeline: Our 40th Anniversary; Focus on the Family," Focus on the Family, http://www.focusonthefamily.com/about_us/news_room/history.aspx.

27. "Our Mission," National Legal Foundation, https://nationallegalfoundation.org/about/.

28. Steve Campbell, "Clash of Values: Evangelist Newcomers Challenge Colorado Springs' Live-and-Let-Live Tradition," *Rocky Mountain News*, September 26, 1993.

29. Mary Ann Glendon, *Rights Talk: The Impoverishment of Political Discourse* (New York: Free Press, 1991).

30. "Amendment #2—Enmienda #2—Is *Not* About Special Rights. It's About *Discrimination*," box 7, folder 1, Equality Colorado Records, WHG Division, DPL.

31. Polly Baca, Statement to Colorado Institute for Hispanic Education and Economic Development, April 14, 1992, box 7, folder 6; "There's no place for bigotry in Denver," box 7, folder 13; "Don't Legalize Discrimination" and "Racism. Anti-Semitism. Homophobia," box 7, folder 16; "Amendment #2—Enmienda #2—Is *Not* About Special Rights. It's About *Discrimination*," box 7, folder 1, Equality Colorado Records, WHG Division, DPL.

32. *Colorado Labor Advocate*, box 7, folder 1, Equality Colorado Records, WHG Division, DPL.

33. For in-depth discussions of black-gay coalition politics in this period, Mumford, "The Trouble with Gay Rights"; Stewart-Winter, *Queer Clout*.

34. "Colorado Could Wake Up One Day and Be *Surprised*," box 7, folder 1; "Voting No on Constitutional Amendment #2," box 7, folder 1, Equality Colorado, WHG Division, DPL.

35. "Employment discrimination wastes vitally needed talent," box 7, folder 1, Equality Colorado Records, WHG Division, DPL.

36. "Greater Denver Chamber of Commerce approved responses regarding inquiries about Amendment #2," box 109, folder 31, Denver Chamber of Commerce Records, WHG Division, DPL.

37. As Berlant and Warner remind us in "Sex in Public," "Hegemonies are nothing if not elastic alliances, involving dispersed and contradictory strategies for self-maintenance and reproduction" (553). For the analytic framework of homonationalism, see Jasbir Puar, *Terrorist Assemblages: Homonationalism in Queer Times*, (Durham, NC: Duke University Press, 2007). For an account of the historical instantiation of homonormativity and homonationalism in the United States, see Lisa Duggan, *The Twilight of Democracy: Neoliberalism, Cultural Politics, and the Attack on Democracy* (Boston: Beacon, 2003).

38. Bruce Loeffler to Concerned Lesbian and Gay Groups re: Proposed "Compromise" Amendment to Replace Amendment 2, January 31, 1993, and "Walta's 'Amendment 2 Compromise' Much Worse Than a Repeal," box 5, folder "Repeal Amendment 2," Evans v. Romer Records, WHG Division, DPL.

39. Wes Simmons to Rocky Mountain News, November 8, 1992, box 1, folder 6, Amendment 2 Collection, History Colorado.

40. Miller Research Group, Pre-election focus groups, box 5, folder "Correspondence, Memos Pre-Dating Case," Evans v. Romer, WHG Division, DPL.

41. Talmey-Drake Report, box 7, folder "Election Press," Evans v. Romer, WHG Division, DPL.

42. Colorado for Family Values, "Equal Rights—Not Special Rights. STOP special class status for homosexuality," box 7, folder 1, Equality Colorado Records, WHG Division, DPL.

43. Floyd Ceruli, "Ten Years After Amendment 2: Colorado Voter Attitudes on Gay Rights, 1992–2002," Powerpoint slide #15, presentation to the American Association of Public Opinion Research, Phoenix, Arizona, May 2004.

44. Brian M. McCormick to Tony Marco, re: Analysis of Language in Amendment Initiative, June 13, 1991, box 1, folder 16, Colorado for Family Values Records, History Colorado.

45. "Vote 'YES!' On 2!," Colorado for Family Values, box 1, folder 16, History Colorado.

46. Colorado State Legislative Council, Ballot History, "Amendment 2 Ballot Title," 1992.

47. Karen L. Vigil, "Springs Man Argues Against Homosexuals' Effort," *Pueblo Chieftan*, n.d.

48. "Vote 'YES!' On 2!," Colorado for Family Values, box 1, folder 16, History Colorado.

49. "What's wrong with special 'gay rights'? *YOU* be the judge!" box 1, folder 16, Colorado for Family Values Records, History Colorado.

50. Ibid.

51. Colorado Secretary of State, *State of Colorado Abstract of Votes Cast, 1992*, available from the Secretary of State's office, Denver, Colorado.

52. *Newsweek's* postelection special issue, "How He Won: The Untold Story of Bill Clinton's Triumph" (November/December 1992), included an extensive breakdown of polling data on this question. For more on the uses of family values rhetoric and its political efficacy outside the Mountain West, see Matthew D. Lassiter, "Big Government and Family Values: Political Culture in the Metropolitan Sunbelt," in *Sunbelt Rising: The Politics of Space, Place, and Region*, ed. Michelle Nickerson and Darren Dochuk (Philadelphia: University of Pennsylvania Press, 2011): 82–109.

53. Bob Teeter to Fred Steeper and Daron Shaw, "Second Choice of Perot Voters," 11/10/1992, box 76, Post-Election Analyses—1992 (1), Robert Teeter Papers, Gerald R. Ford Presidential Library.

Chapter 9

The author would like to thank Ana Raquel Minian, Rachel Guberman, Jonathan Bell, and two anonymous reviewers for their thoughtful feedback on several manifestations of this essay, which no doubt made this a stronger work.

1. Testimony of Rachel Jeantel before the prosecution, June 26, 2013, in *The State of Florida v. George Zimmerman* (Sanford, Florida).

2. George Yancy and Janine Jones, eds., *Pursuing Trayvon Martin: Historical Contexts and Contemporary Manifestations of Racial Dynamics* (Lanham, MD: Lexington Books, 2013).

3. Lizette Alvarez and Cara Buckley, "Zimmerman Is Acquitted in Trayvon Martin Killing," *New York Times*, July 13, 2013.

4. Jasbir K. Puar, *Terrorist Assemblages: Homonationalism in Queer Times* (Durham, NC: Duke University Press, 2007); Sarah Schulman, *Israel/Palestine and the Queer International* (Durham, NC: Duke University Press, 2012).

5. Theda Skocpol and Vanessa Williamson, *The Tea Party and the Remaking of Republican Conservatism* (New York: Oxford University Press, 2012), 37–40.

6. Emily K. Hobson, *Lavender and Red: Liberation and Solidarity in the Gay and Lesbian Left* (Oakland: University of California Press, 2016), 11.

7. Brittney Cooper, "Dark-Skinned and Plus-Sized: The Real Rachel Jeantel Story," Salon, June 28, 2013, http://www.salon.com/2013/06/28/did_anyone_really_hear_rachel_jeantel/.

8. John R. Rickford and Sharese King, "Language and Linguistics on Trial: Hearing Rachel Jeantel (and Other Vernacular Speakers) in the Courtroom and Beyond," *Language* 92, no. 4 (2016): 948–88.

9. Testimony of Rachel Jeantel before the prosecution, June 26, 2013, in *The State of Florida v. George Zimmerman* (Sanford, Florida).

10. Prosecution closing arguments, July 11, 2013, in *The State of Florida v. George Zimmerman*.

11. Evelyn Brooks Higginbotham, "African-American Women's History and the Metalanguage of Race," *Signs* 17, no. 2 (Winter 1992): 251–74.

12. Audre Lorde, "Age, Race, Class, and Sex: Women Redefining Difference," in *Sister Outsider: Essays and Speeches*, rev. ed. (Berkeley, CA: Crossing, 2007), 114.

13. Testimony of Rachel Jeantel before the defense, June 27, 2013, in *The State of Florida v. George Zimmerman*.

14. "'Star Witness' Rachel Jeantel: 'Creepy-Ass Cracker' Means 'Pervert' in My Culture," Twitchy Online, June 27, 2013, http://twitchy.com/2013/06/27/star-witness-rachel-jeantel -creepy-ass-cracker-means-pervert-in-my-culture/.

15. "Rachel Jeantel Interview," *Piers Morgan Live*, CNN, July 15, 2013.

16. Ibid.

17. Cheryl Clarke, "The Failure to Transform: Homophobia in the Black Community," in *Home Girls: A Black Feminist Anthology*, ed. Barbara Smith (New Brunswick: Rutgers University Press, 1983).

18. Lisa McGirr, *Suburban Warriors: The Origins of the New American Right*, 2nd ed. (Princeton, NJ: Princeton University Press, 2015), xx, xxi.

19. Joe Concha, "Fox News Most-Watched Cable Network in Early 2018," The Hill, April 3, 2018, http://thehill.com/homenews/media/381473-fox-news-most-watched-cable-network-in -early-2018-msnbc-growth-surges. See also Kathleen Hall Jamieson and Joseph N. Cappella, *Echo Chamber: Rush Limbaugh and the Conservative Media Establishment* (New York: Oxford University Press, 2008).

20. "CNN: The Embodiment of Low Information," *Rush Limbaugh Show*, July 16, 2013.

21. Joseph Cotto, "Robert Zimmerman on George, Coming Out as Gay, and Brotherhood," *Washington Times Communities*, July 5, 2013, http://communities.washingtontimes.com /neighborhood/conscience-realist/2013/jul/7/robert-zimmerman-george-coming-out-gay-and -brother/.

22. Tracy Connor, James Novogrod, and Tom Winter, "Judge Denies Delays, Bars Evidence in George Zimmerman Trial—for Now," NBC News, June 2, 2013, http://usnews.nbcnews.com /_news/2013/05/28/18556018-judge-denies-delay-bars-evidence-in-george-zimmerman-trial -for-now?lite.

23. bell hooks, *We Real Cool: Black Men and Masculinity* (New York: Routledge, 2004).

24. Elijah G. Ward, "Homophobia, Hypermasculinity and the US Black Church," *Culture, Health & Sexuality* 7, no. 5 (October 2005): 493–504.

25. "Rachel Jeantel Interview."

26. August Løvenskiolds, "Zimmerman Case: Don't Be That Bigot," A Voice for Men, July 18, 2013, http://www.avoiceformen.com/mens-rights/false-rape-culture/gender-issues-in-the -george-zimmerman-debacle/.

27. For example, see the online poll in "Message Board Thread: Am I the Only One That Thinks Rachel Jeantel Is Responsible for Trayvon's Death," Godlike Productions, July 19, 2013, http://www.godlikeproductions.com/forum1/message2297551/pg1.

28. "CNN: The Embodiment of Low Information."

29. Sworn statement with Witness 9 conducted by the Sanford Police Department, March 20, 2012.

30. Frances Robles, "'Witness 9' Accused Zimmerman of Sexually Molesting Her," *Miami Herald*, July 17, 2013, http://www.miamiherald.com/2012/07/16/2897557/zimmerman-defense-attorney-will.html.

31. "CNN: The Embodiment of Low Information."

32. "Rachel Jeantel: Trayvon Thought Zimmerman Was a Gay Rapist and Trayvon Wasn't 'That Kind of Way,'" *Rush Limbaugh Show*, July 16, 2013.

33. Jack E. Kemp, "Jeantel and Trayvon—Gay Bashers?," Tea Party Nation, July 17, 2013, http://www.teapartynation.com/profiles/blogs/jeantel-and-trayvon-gay-bashers?xg_source=activity.

34. Jeffrey Lord, "Trayvon, Sharpton, and Homophobia," American Spectator, July 18, 2013, http://spectator.org/articles/55212/trayvon-sharpton-and-homophobia.

35. Bryan Llenas, "George Zimmerman's Family Deliberately Downplayed His Latino Roots," Fox News Latino, July 12, 2013, http://latino.foxnews.com/latino/news/2013/07/12/george-zimmerman-family-deliberately-downplayed-his-latino-roots/#ixzz2ZPYFhjdP.

36. "Statement of Robert Zimmerman," *Orlando Sentinel*, March 15, 2012, http://articles.orlandosentinel.com/2012-03-15/news/os-trayvon-martin-shooting-zimmerman-letter-20120315_1_robert-zimmerman-letter-unarmed-black-teenager/2.

37. Lizette Alvarez, "City Criticizes Police Chief After Shooting," *New York Times*, March 22, 2012; Faith Karimi, "'Raise Your Voice, Not Your Hands,' Cops Urge as Zimmerman Verdict Looms," CNN, July 10, 2013, http://edition.cnn.com/2013/07/10/justice/florida-zimmerman-backlash/index.html?hpt=hp_t2.

38. Larry O'Connor, "Desperate for Racial Narrative, CNN Labels Zimmerman 'White Hispanic,'" Breitbart, July 11, 2013, http://www.breitbart.com/big-journalism/2013/07/11/desperate-for-racial-narrative-cnn-calls-zimmerman-white-hispanic/.

39. *Fox & Friends*, July 15, 2013.

40. Neil Foley, "Straddling the Color Line: The Legal Construction of Hispanic Identity in Texas," in *Not Just Black and White: Historical and Contemporary Perspectives on Immigration, Race, and Ethnicity in the United States*, ed. Nancy Foner and George M. Fredrickson (New York: Russell Sage Foundation, 2004), 341.

41. "Alicia Garza," in *How We Get Free: Black Feminism and the Combahee River Collective*, ed. Keeanga-Yamahtta Taylor (Chicago: Haymarket Books, 2017), 161–63.

42. Eduardo Bonilla-Silva, *Racism Without Racists: Color-Blind Racism and the Persistence of Racial Inequality in the United States*, 3rd ed. (Lanham, MD: Rowman & Littlefield, 2010).

43. Eduardo Bonilla-Silva and Austin Ashe, "The End of Racism? Colorblind Racism and Popular Media," in *The Colorblind Screen: Television in Post-Racial America*, ed. Sarah Nilsen and Sarah E. Turner (New York: New York University Press, 2014), 66.

44. Ibid., 70–71.

45. Keeanga-Yamahtta Taylor, *From #BlackLivesMatter to Black Liberation* (Chicago: Haymarket Books, 2016), 60.

46. Ibid., 52–53.

47. Craig T. Palmer, David N. DiBari, and Scott A. Wright, "Is It Sex Yet? Theoretical and Practical Implications of the Debate over Rapists' Motives," *Jurimetrics* 39, no. 3 (Spring 1999): 271–82.

48. George Chauncey, "The Postwar Sex Crime Panic," in *True Stories from the American Past*, ed. William Graebner (New York: McGraw-Hill, 1993), 178.

49. Estelle B. Freedman, "'Uncontrolled Desires': The Response to the Sexual Psychopath, 1920–1960," *Journal of American History* 74, no. 1 (1987): 98.

50. Roger N. Lancaster, *Sex Panic and the Punitive State* (Berkeley: University of California Press, 2011), 36, 91.

51. Anita Bryant, *The Anita Bryant Story: The Survival of Our Nation's Families and the Threat of Militant Homosexuality* (Old Tappan, NJ: Fleming H. Revell, 1977).

52. Gregory M. Herek, "Gender Gaps in Public Opinion About Lesbians and Gay Men," *Public Opinion Quarterly* 66, no. 1 (Spring 2002): 40–66.

53. See, for example, Ted Byfield and Virginia Byfield, "The Catholic Problem Isn't Pedophiles But Gays, and Cleaning It Up May Mean Breaking the Law," *The Report*, June 24, 2002, 58; Molly Hennessy-Fiske, "Boy Scouts of America Lifts Ban on Gay Youth," *Los Angeles Times*, May 23, 2013.

54. John D'Emilio, *Sexual Politics, Sexual Communities: The Making of a Homosexual Minority in the United States, 1940–1970* (Chicago: University of Chicago Press, 1983), 3.

55. Ibid.; Marc Stein, *City of Sisterly and Brotherly Loves: Lesbian and Gay Philadelphia, 1945–1972* (Chicago: University of Chicago Press, 2000).

56. Ian Lekus, "Queer Harvests: Homosexuality, the U.S. New Left, and the Venceremos Brigades to Cuba," *Radical History Review* 89, no. 1 (Spring 2004): 57–91.

57. Terence Kissack, "Freaking Fag Revolutionaries: New York's Gay Liberation Front, 1969–1971," *Radical History Review* 62 (1995): 104–34.

58. Qtd. in Arthur Irving Bell, *Dancing the Gay Lib Blues: A Year in the Homosexual Liberation Movement* (New York: Simon and Schuster, 1971), 23.

59. Marc Stein, *Rethinking the Gay and Lesbian Movement* (New York: Routledge, 2012), 100–101.

60. Elizabeth A. Armstrong, *Forging Gay Identities: Organizing Sexuality in San Francisco, 1950–1994* (Chicago: University of Chicago Press, 2002), 23.

61. Alexandra Chasin, *Selling Out: The Gay and Lesbian Movement Goes to Market* (New York: St. Martin's, 2000); Jennifer Brier, *Infectious Ideas: U.S. Political Responses to the AIDS Crisis* (Chapel Hill: University of North Carolina Press, 2009), chap. 2.

62. See A. Finn Enke, *Finding the Movement: Sexuality, Contested Space, and Feminist Activism* (Durham, NC: Duke University Press, 2007); Bette S. Tallen, "Lesbian Separatism: A Historical and Comparative Perspective," in *For Lesbians Only: A Separatist Anthology* (London: Onlywomen, 1988), 132–44.

63. Susan Stryker, *Transgender History* (Berkeley, CA: Seal, 2008), 85–89.

64. See bell hooks, *Ain't I a Woman: Black Women and Feminism* (Boston: South End, 1981); Audre Lorde, *Zami, a New Spelling of My Name* (Trumansburg, NY: Crossing, 1982); Gloria Anzaldúa, *Borderlands = La Frontera: The New Mestiza* (San Francisco: Aunt Lute Books, 1987); José Esteban Muñoz, *Disidentifications: Queers of Color and the Performance of Politics* (Minneapolis: University of Minnesota Press, 1999); Carlos U. Decena, *Tacit Subjects: Belonging and Same-Sex Desire Among Dominican Immigrant Men* (Durham, NC: Duke University Press, 2011).

65. "The Combahee River Collective Statement (1977)," in *How We Get Free: Black Feminism and the Combahee River Collective*, ed. Keeanga-Yamahtta Taylor (Chicago: Haymarket Books, 2017), 15.

66. Hobson, *Lavender and Red*.

67. John D'Emilio, *Making Trouble: Essays on Gay History, Politics, and the University* (New York: Routledge, 1992), 244–46; Stein, *Rethinking the Gay and Lesbian Movement*, chap. 4.

68. Brier, *Infectious Ideas*, chap. 1.

69. Ibid., chap. 5; Paul Robinson, *Queer Wars: The New Gay Right and Its Critics* (Chicago: Chicago University Press, 2005), 4–7.

70. Gillian Frank, "'The Civil Rights of Parents': Race and Conservative Politics in Anita Bryant's Campaign Against Gay Rights in 1970s Florida," *Journal of the History of Sexuality* 22, no. 1 (January 2013): 126–60; Matthew D. Lassiter, *The Silent Majority: Suburban Politics in the Sunbelt South* (Princeton, NJ: Princeton University Press, 2006).

71. Daniel Stedman Jones, *Masters of the Universe: Hayek, Friedman, and the Birth of Neoliberal Politics* (Princeton, NJ: Princeton University Press, 2012); Michael Schaller, *Right Turn: American Life in the Reagan-Bush Era, 1980–1992* (New York: Oxford University Press, 2007).

72. Hobson, *Lavender and Red*, chap. 3.

73. Lisa Duggan, *The Twilight of Equality? Neoliberalism, Cultural Politics and the Attack on Democracy* (Boston: Beacon, 2003); Robert McRuer, "Cripping Queer Politics, or the Dangers of Neoliberalism," *Scholar & Feminist Online* 10, no. 1/2 (Fall 2011/Spring 2012): 9.

74. Michael Warner, *The Trouble with Normal: Sex, Politics, and the Ethics of Queer Life* (New York: Free Press, 1999).

75. Jaye Cee Whitehead, *The Nuptial Deal: Same-Sex Marriage and Neo-Liberal Governance* (Chicago: University of Chicago Press, 2011); Laura Briggs, *How All Politics Became Reproductive Politics: From Welfare Reform to Foreclosure to Trump* (Oakland: University of California Press, 2017).

76. Katy Holloway, Trevor Bennett, and David P. Farrington, *Crime Prevention Research Review No. 3: Does Neighborhood Watch Reduce Crime?* (Washington, DC: U.S. Department of Justice Office of Community Oriented Policing Services, 2008); Titus Richard, "Residential Burglary and the Community Response," in *Coping with Burglary*, ed. R. V. G. Clarke and T. Hope (Boston: Kluwer-Nijhoff, 1984), 97–130.

77. National Sheriffs' Association, *Neighborhood Watch Manual*, Bureau of Justice Assistance, https://www.bja.gov/publications/nsa_nw_manual.pdf.

78. National Neighborhood Watch: A Division of the National Sheriffs' Association, http://www.nnw.org/usaonwatch.

79. Mike Sante, "State May Shoot Down Gun Laws," *Miami Herald*, March 24, 1986, 1A.

80. Corrected Opinion, *In re Forfeiture of 1969 Piper Navajo*, No. 77,076, 570 So.2d 1357, Supreme Court of Florida, January 2, 1982, 4.

81. "Critics: Act Helps Draw Class Lines in Communities," *Gainesville Sun*, March 20, 1989, 3B.

82. Stephan McCrea, "Florida's Safe Neighborhood Act of 1987: Politics of Implementation and Citizen Participation," master's thesis, Florida Atlantic University, 1990, ii, 27.

83. Jamie Peck, "Neoliberal Suburbanism: Frontier Space," *Urban Geography* 32, no. 6 (2011): 892.

84. Clayton Howard, "Building a 'Family-Friendly' Metropolis: Sexuality, the State, and Postwar Housing Policy," *Journal of Urban History* 39, no. 5 (September 2013): 939; Tim Retzloff, "Suburb, City, and the Changing Bounds of Lesbian and Gay Life in Metropolitan Detroit, 1945–1985," PhD diss., Yale University, 2014.

85. Tim Retzloff, "The Association of (Gay) Suburban People," *Places Journal*, April 2015, https://placesjournal.org/article/the-association-of-gay-suburban-people/.

86. Hanhardt, *Safe Space*.

87. Regina Kunzel, "Lessons in Being Gay: Queer Encounters in Gay and Lesbian Prison Activism," *Radical History Review*, no. 100 (Winter 2008): 29.

88. Michelle Alexander, *The New Jim Crow: Mass Incarceration in the Age of Colorblindness* (New York: New Press, 2010), 58.

89. Duggan, *The Twilight of Equality*, 44.

90. Urvashi Vaid, *Virtual Equality: The Mainstreaming of Gay and Lesbian Liberation* (New York: Anchor Books, 1995), 245; Duggan, *The Twilight of Equality*, 46.

91. Pat Dollard, "Did Widespread Homophobia in the Black Community Lead Trayvon Martin to Attack George Zimmerman?," PatDollard.com, July 16, 2013, http://patdollard .com/2013/07/trayvon-gay-bash-flashback-gay-protesters-yell-nger-as-they-attack-blacks-for -community-prop-8-support-homophobia/.

92. "Trayvon the Gay Basher?," GayPatriot, July 16, 2013, http://www.gaypatriot.net/2013 /07/16/trayvon-the-gay-basher/.

93. Jack Cashill, "Did Trayvon Martin 'Gay Bash' Zimmerman?," WND Commentary, July 24, 2013, http://www.wnd.com/2013/07/did-trayvon-gay-bash-zimmerman/.

94. House of Representatives, U.S. Congress, National Defense Authorization Act for Fiscal Year 2010, 111th Cong., 1st sess., 2009, H.R. 2647.

95. Michael Sherry, "Dead or Alive: American Vengeance Goes Global," *Review of International Studies* 31 (December 2005): 245–63.

96. Morgan Bassichis, Alexander Lee, and Dean Spade, "Building an Abolitionist Trans and Queer Movement with Everything We've Got," in *Captive Genders: Trans Embodiment and the Prison Industrial Complex*, ed. Eric A. Stanley and Nat Smith (Oakland, CA: AK Press, 2011), 34.

97. Andrew Sullivan, "The First Gay President," *Newsweek*, May 21, 2012.

98. Jane Ward, *Respectably Queer: Diversity Culture in LGBT Activist Organizations* (Nashville: Vanderbilt University Press, 2008).

99. "An Open Letter: Standing Alongside Trayvon Martin's Family and Friends," GLAAD .org, April 2, 2012, http://www.glaad.org/blog/open-letter-standing-alongside-trayvon-martins -family-and-friends.

100. Kevin Naff, "All Aboard the Trayvon Bandwagon," *Washington Blade*, April 9, 2012, http://www.washingtonblade.com/2012/04/09/all-aboard-the-trayvon-bandwagon/.

101. Maya Rupert, "Trayvon's Death Should Concern All Who Seek Justice," *Washington Blade*, April 12, 2012, http://www.washingtonblade.com/2012/04/12/trayvons-death-should -concern-all-who-seek-justice/.

102. Michelle Garcia, "Where Trayvon Martin and Matthew Shepard Collide," *The Advocate*, July 16, 2013, http://www.advocate.com/commentary/2013/07/16/op-ed-where-trayvon -martin-and-matthew-shepard-collide.

103. Tracy Baim, "The Content of Our Character: Trayvon and Us," *Windy City Times*, July 17, 2013, 12.

104. Luke Brinker, "Why Are Right-Wing Media Portraying Trayvon Martin as a Gay Basher?," Equality Matters Blog, July 25, 2013, http://equalitymatters.org/blog/201307250003.

105. "35 LGBT Organizations Call for Justice for Trayvon Martin," Queerty, July 17, 2013, http://www.queerty.com/35-lgbt-organizations-call-for-justice-for-trayvon-martin-20130717/.

106. Darnell L. Moore and Charles Stephens, "An Open Letter to Mainstream LGBT Organizations That Have Remained Silent on Black Lives Mattering," Huffington Post, December 16, 2014, http://www.huffingtonpost.com/darnell-l-moore/an-open-letter-to-mainstream-lgbt -organizations-that-have-remained-silent-on-black-lives-mattering_b_6329048.html.

107. Patrisse Khan-Cullors and asha bandele, *When They Call You a Terrorist: A Black Lives Matter Memoir* (New York: St. Martin's, 2017), 196.

108. Alicia Garza, "A HerStory of the #BlackLivesMatter Movement," BlackLivesMatter, n.d., http://blacklivesmatter.com/herstory/.

109. Jelani Cobb, "The Matter of Black Lives," *New Yorker*, March 14, 2016, http://www.newyorker.com/magazine/2016/03/14/where-is-black-lives-matter-headed; Jeffrey Q. McCune Jr., "The Queerness of Blackness," *QED: A Journal in GLBTQ Worldmaking* 2, no. 2 (Summer 2015): 173–76; Reuben Riggs, "Meeting Queerness and Blackness in Ferguson," *QED: A Journal in GLBTQ Worldmaking* 2, no. 2 (Summer 2015): 184–92.

110. Khan-Cullors and bandele, *When They Call You a Terrorist*, 202–3.

111. Garza, "A HerStory of the #BlackLivesMatter Movement."

112. "Alicia Garza," 159.

113. Khan-Cullors and bandele, *When They Call You a Terrorist*, 214–16.

114. Cherríe Moraga and Gloria Anzaldúa, *This Bridge Called My Back: Writings by Radical Women of Color* (New York: Kitchen Table, Women of Color Press, 1983).

115. "Queers Come Out for #BlackLivesMatter," Facebook, December 24, 2014, https://www.facebook.com/events/376932415802140/.

116. "#BlackLivesMatter Protestors March to the Castro," Hoodline, December 24, 2014, http://hoodline.com/2014/12/blacklivesmatter-protestors-march-to-the-castro.

117. Brier, *Infectious Ideas*, chap. 5.

118. "UndocuQueer Movement," Equality Archive, n.d., http://equalityarchive.com/issues/undocuqueer-movement/; Julia Preston and John H. Cushman Jr., "Obama to Permit Young Migrants to Remain in U.S.," *New York Times*, June 15, 2012.

119. Cathy J. Cohen, "Punks, Bulldaggers, and Welfare Queens: The Radical Potential of Queer Politics?," *GLQ: A Journal of Lesbian and Gay Studies* 3 (1997): 440.

120. "Alicia Garza," 168–69.

LIST OF CONTRIBUTORS

Ian M. Baldwin received his PhD in history from the University of Nevada, Las Vegas. He is currently an instructor of history and the director of honors at Alvin Community College.

Katie Batza is an assistant professor in women, gender, and sexuality studies at the University of Kansas. Her research explores the intersection of sexuality, health, and politics in the final decades of the twentieth-century United States. Having completed her first book, *Before AIDS: Gay Health Politics in the 1970s* (University of Pennsylvania Press, 2018), Batza is currently working on a number of public history projects as well as a second monograph titled *AIDS in the Heartland.*

Jonathan Bell is a professor of U.S. history at the Institute of the Americas, University College London. He is the author of *The Liberal State on Trial: The Cold War and American Politics in the Truman Years* (Columbia University Press, 2004) and *California Crucible: The Forging of Modern American Liberalism* (University of Pennsylvania Press, 2012) and coeditor (with Timothy Stanley) of *Making Sense of Modern American Liberalism* (University of Illinois Press, 2012). Bell is currently working on a book dealing with the relationship between LGBT activism and the health and welfare systems in the United States.

Julio Capó Jr. is an associate professor in the Department of History and the Commonwealth Honors College at the University of Massachusetts, Amherst, where he researches inter-American histories with a focus on queer, Latinx, race, (im)migration, and empire studies. Capo's book *Welcome to Fairyland: Queer Miami Before 1940* (University of North Carolina Press, 2017) has received six honors, including the Southern Historical Association's Charles S. Sydnor Award for the best book on the U.S. South.

Rachel Guberman is the digital humanist at the Schlesinger Library, Radcliffe Institute, Harvard University, where she leads a project on gender, voting rights, and citizenship. Previously, she taught at Indiana University and was a book editor at the *Journal of American History*. Guberman holds a PhD in history from the University of Pennsylvania.

Clayton Howard is an assistant professor of history at Ohio State University. He is the author of *The Closet and the Cul-de-Sac: The Politics of Sexual Privacy in Northern California* (University of Pennsylvania Press, 2019). Howard is currently working on a new book project on the history of gun control activism in the late twentieth-century United States.

Kevin Mumford is a professor of history at the University of Illinois at Urbana–Champaign. He is the author of *Interzones: Black/White Sex Districts in New York and Chicago in the Early Twentieth Century* (1997); *Newark: A History of Race, Rights, and Riots in America* (2007); and *Not Straight, Not White: Black Gay Men from the March on Washington to the AIDS Crisis* (2016). Mumford is the recipient of awards for his scholarship from the Organization of American Historians, the American Historical Association, the American Library Association, and the Society for the Study of Sex, among others.

Dan Royles is an assistant professor in the Department of History at Florida International University and is a historian of the United States, African American life and culture, public health, sexuality, social movements, and the human body. His current book project, *To Make the Wounded Whole: African-American Responses to HIV/AIDS*, examines grassroots responses to the disproportionate impact of HIV and AIDS on black communities.

Timothy Stewart-Winter is an associate professor of history at Rutgers University–Newark and the author of *Queer Clout: Chicago and the Rise of Gay Politics* (University of Pennsylvania Press, 2016).

INDEX